W9-ASJ-039

WRITING
TELEVISION
SITCOMS

WRITING TELEVISION SITCOMS

Revised and Expanded

Evan S. Smith

A Perigee Book

A PERIGEE BOOK
Published by the Penguin Group
Penguin Group (USA) Inc.
375 Hudson Street, New York, New York 10014, USA
Penguin Group (Canada), 90 Eglinton Avenue East, Suite 700, Toronto, Ontario M4P 2Y3, Canada
(a division of Pearson Penguin Canada Inc.)
Penguin Books Ltd., 80 Strand, London WC2R 0RL, England
Penguin Group Ireland, 25 St. Stephen's Green, Dublin 2, Ireland (a division of Penguin Books Ltd.)
Penguin Group (Australia), 250 Camberwell Road, Camberwell, Victoria 3124, Australia
(a division of Pearson Australia Group Pty. Ltd.)
Penguin Books India Pvt. Ltd., 11 Community Centre, Panchsheel Park, New Delhi—110 017, India
Penguin Group (NZ), 67 Apollo Drive, Rosedale, North Shore 0632, New Zealand
(a division of Pearson New Zealand Ltd.)
Penguin Books (South Africa) (Pty.) Ltd., 24 Sturdee Avenue, Rosebank, Johannesburg 2196,
South Africa

Penguin Books Ltd., Registered Offices: 80 Strand, London WC2R 0RL, England

While the author has made every effort to provide accurate telephone numbers and Internet addresses at the time of publication, neither the publisher nor the author assumes any responsibility for errors, or for changes that occur after publication. Further, the publisher does not have any control over and does not assume any responsibility for author or third-party websites or their content.

Copyright © 2009 by Evan S. Smith
Cover design by Edwin Tse

All rights reserved.
No part of this book may be reproduced, scanned, or distributed in any printed or electronic form without permission. Please do not participate in or encourage piracy of copyrighted materials in violation of the author's rights. Purchase only authorized editions.
PERIGEE is a registered trademark of Penguin Group (USA) Inc.
The "P" design is a trademark belonging to Penguin Group (USA) Inc.

PRINTING HISTORY
First Perigee trade paperback edition / September 1999
Revised Perigee trade paperback edition / December 2009

Revised Perigee trade paperback ISBN: 978-0-399-53537-6

The Library of Congress has cataloged the first Perigee edition as follows:

Smith, Evan S. (Evan Scott), 1956–
    Writing television sitcoms / Evan S. Smith.—1st ed.
        p.   cm.
    Includes bibiliographical references and index.
    ISBN: 978-0-399-52533-9
    1. Television authorship.   2. Television comedies.   3. Television plays—Technique.   I. Title.
    PN1992.7.S64   1999
    808.2'25—dc21   99-23459 CIP

PRINTED IN THE UNITED STATES OF AMERICA

10   9   8   7   6   5   4   3   2   1

Most Perigee books are available at special quantity discounts for bulk purchases for sales promotions, premiums, fund-raising, or educational use. Special books, or book excerpts, can also be created to fit specific needs. For details, write: Special Markets, Penguin Group (USA) Inc., 375 Hudson Street, New York, New York 10014.

For Christine, Ryan, and Connor
Alison and Dan

ACKNOWLEDGMENTS

Many terrific people helped to make this book happen. First, I thank all of the talented writers, producers, and executives quoted herein. With combined credits that read like a Top 20 list of TV's best comedies, from *The Simpsons* and *Everybody Loves Raymond* to *Late Night with David Letterman* and *All in the Family*, they include Sandy Frank, Ian Gurvitz, Lawrence Konner, Maxine Lapiduss, Michael Reiss, Ellen Sandler, Matt Williams, and screenwriting pioneer Irma Kalish.

I also thank . . .

My editor, the wise and insightful Meg Leder, for her many contributions to this edition.

Professors Carla Lloyd and Michael Schoonmaker, two colleagues at Syracuse University's Newhouse School who provided invaluable logistical support for this project.

Anthony Mattero and Melissa Ryan, two industry professionals who, no matter how busy, always cheerfully make time to help me find hard-to-locate scripts.

And I thank Anne and Erick Taft, mother and brother of Alex Taft, a most promising Newhouse graduate who was recently lost in a car accident. As a small tribute to Alex, a talented writer and extremely likeable person, we've included several excerpts of his work in this book.

Lastly—I can't say it better than I did in the first edition—I thank the many writers, performers, teachers, students, friends, and family members who have made me laugh, and who have taught me a thing or two about comedy writing.

CONTENTS

Part 2. Writing a Professional Script

Part 3. A Battle Plan for Launching Your Career

INTRODUCTION

First, I want to offer one more thank-you. By word of mouth, those who read the first edition of *Writing Television Sitcoms* made it a trade-book bestseller by the fourth week of its release; it hit number one in Amazon.com's and (Barnes & Noble) bn.com's "comedy writing" and "television writing" categories and stayed there, or close to, for years.[1] Even now, a decade later, the first edition outsells most of the new books in the field. *WTS* has garnered glowing reviews from different countries; praise from working screenwriters who teach at top film schools like USC, Columbia, and UCLA; and numerous thank-you notes from readers declaring that they became better writers or even landed jobs as a result of the book's teachings.

But that's yesterday's news. In prepping this new edition, my goal was to create a version that even readers of the original book would want to have on their shelves. Certainly, much has changed in recent years:

- Sitcom story structure is evolving and audience expectations have changed.

- New career opportunities have surfaced in cable TV and the digital world.

- TV networks are producing series based on homegrown pilots.

- Job-hunting strategies have shifted as technology has changed the industry.

- Amazing new resources have become available to help writers improve their craft and find work.

This new edition explores all of these recent developments, and updates the essential elements that made the first book such a success, including . . .

A Proven Comedy Method

Writing Television Sitcoms provides a complete description of premise-driven comedy, a proven comedy writing method that focuses on developing a story's humor from the ground up. I have taught this approach to numerous screenwriters and students, with terrific results, and now offer a fresh take in this edition, complete with examples from recent shows.

Depth of Material

This book is designed to help both beginning and established writers. It is divided into three comprehensive sections:

- Part One of the book focuses on comedy writing theory. This section draws insights from existing schools of thought and describes my method for creating premise-driven comedy.

- Part Two of the book explains the craft of writing a professional script by putting comedy theory into practice. This section follows the same steps that a professional writer takes as he generates ideas, beats out a story, and creates drafts of a script. Along the way, it also describes the real-world dynamics that come into play when you are working on an actual script assignment, facing impossible deadlines and surly producers.

- Part Three offers up a no-nonsense battle plan for getting work. Figuring that most writers would rather spend their time writing than groveling for a job, this book presents an aggressive, step-by-step strategy designed to get you back at the keyboard as quickly as possible. This plan covers everything from broad goals to subtle tactics, and provides numerous insider tips.

While this book was written primarily for comedy writers, the subjects that it covers—from drama theory to the scriptwriting process, to pitching techniques, to job-hunting strategies—are of interest to all screenwriters.

Advice from Industry Experts

To supplement my own knowledge base, I have solicited input from a number of leading writers, producers, and executives. Some are quoted in different sections of the book and several reviewed the manuscript.

How to Create Your Own Series

In the last edition of this book, I cautioned new writers that attempts to create an original series were a waste of their valuable time. Development executives and producers were only interested in buying shows from established writer-producers, and spec pilot scripts made for poor writing samples. But, great news, times have changed. Now those same execs and producers are actively seeking new ideas from untested writers, so I've added a section that explains how to develop an original series premise and how to pitch your concepts using traditional and new-media approaches.

Examples Drawn from All Types of Sitcoms

This edition offers numerous story and script examples from a wide variety of sitcoms. I've chosen shows that should be familiar to most people, from current hits like *The Office*, *Two and a Half Men*, and *Family Guy*, to push-the-envelope series like *South Park*, *Californication*, and *Entourage*, to everybody's-seen-them classics like *Seinfeld*, *Frasier*, and *Dick Van Dyke*.

Ease of Use

For quick and easy reference, this book is divided into the three distinct sections mentioned above, and each chapter includes numerous subheadings. Important definitions, names, titles, and addresses are presented within the text, where they will be of most use, rather than in lists buried at the back of the book. To supplement these references, additional material is presented in Appendix B.

Author's Credentials

There aren't a lot of people who have worked on three different sides of the sitcom writing desk. During my thirty years in the business, I have served as a screenwriter (for companies such as Paramount, MTM, CBS, NBC, and FOX), as a vice president of programming (developing both comedy and drama projects for network television), and as a lecturer and script consultant (teaching comedy writing theory and techniques). Been there, done that, and that, and that, which gives me three perspectives on this highly competitive field.

Enough said, let's get to it. You now hold in your hands the official, bestselling, "if I could only buy one" insider's guide to sitcom writing. Welcome to *Writing Television Sitcoms*—revised edition, new and improved.

Part 1

Writing Premise-Driven Comedy

1

THE GAME PLAN

You want to write? You feel a need to write? You'd love to see your work produced, your name up on the screen? Maybe make a little money?

Okay, lots of money. Tons. And you want a Porsche and a beach house, in Malibu, right next to Brad Pitt's. Yeah, yeah, sounds good.

Well, sorry, no guarantees on the money or that house thing. Try selling computers, become a lawyer. (Sell Brad a computer, become his lawyer.)

But if you enjoy writing for writing's sake, and if you tend to express yourself with humor, then I have good news: You can actually earn a living by writing sitcoms. Sometimes a very good living.

But aren't sitcoms a dead form? Killed off by reality programs and downloads? Evolving, yes, but dead, no. Networks are still actively developing sitcoms and audiences are happily watching them—on TVs, computers, cell phones, handheld gaming devices, you name it. (Other than porn, comedy is the primary format driving the digital revolution!) The folks writing today's shows are making as much as $23,000 in up-front fees per episode, plus residual fees, plus money if they work on a show's staff, plus money from development deals. . . . But let's talk about that later.

Sure, some writers are paid even larger fees to write feature films, but look at the numbers. Only about 750 mainstream films were produced in the United States last year,[1] and only a quarter to a third of those were comedies, and many of those were written *on spec*. (Meaning, you starve for the three months to ten years it takes to write the thing, and just pray that you—or your ex, after she divorces you for neglecting her—can sell it after it is finished.)

In television, most of your compensation is paid up front as you write the script. And the odds of your work actually being produced are much greater, which can further increase your income. And you have a better shot at protecting the integrity of your work, since television is dominated by writers while film is a director's medium.

So if you want to work as a comedy writer and keep eating too, sitcoms are not a bad way to go. Sure, it's a competitive field, extremely so. And it's hard, hard work. But so is a job at McDonald's, UPS, or a doctor's office, if that is not where you really want to be. Right?

The question is, how does one become a sitcom writer?

Career Paths

We will get into the nitty-gritty details of the sitcom business—the politics, players, jobs—later in the book. But before you invest energy in this career path, it might help to have a general sense of what lies ahead. Think sunny Los Angeles. Picture a manicured estate off Sunset Boulevard. There's a pool, a pool boy, lunch by the chaise lounge. . . . No, you don't live here, some producer does. But you might, someday—how do you think that producer got there?

For right now, you're new in town. Maybe you're unemployed, without an agent or a promise of work. But you have a little talent and the sense to realize that life is short. If you don't take your shot, you will always regret it. Always.

So you get a job to pay the rent and you start networking. And you write. And write. You write sample scripts, called *spec scripts*—meaning, episodes of existing television series and maybe a pilot script for a new show you've dreamed up. These spec scripts are the calling cards that you will use to, hopefully, land some form of representation, either an agent or manager, or both. (Sorry, but the odds are a thousand-to-one against anyone actually buying a TV spec script you've written, as I will explain later; their primary purpose is to get you work writing new material.)

To land that agent or manager, you submit your samples to every industry person you can, trying to get someone who knows someone who knows someone to read your scripts. Eventually, if the work is good, someone will take you on. Then, you and he, or she, will circulate your samples to sitcom producers and executives until someone deems them good enough to hire you.

Getting hired can happen in one of three ways. First, you might be invited in to pitch for a freelance assignment.

A what? A freelance assignment is an assignment given by a show's producers to an outside writer, to write one episode of an existing series. You pitch ideas and the producers pick one, or they might assign you an idea of their own. Then you write an outline, and maybe the first and second drafts of the script. In and out, you're done in three to five weeks. And you pocket enough change to cover twelve months of rent or maybe a dinner at L.A.'s newest bistro.

Then, you keep writing spec scripts and circulating your material as you try to scare up your next job. (The episode credit that you have already earned should make this easier.) If you are talented and tenacious, you might land a job *on staff*. Meaning, you are given a contract for a set amount of time—weeks, maybe months—that pays you a large amount of money to work full-time on a series. Typically, you work in an office at the studio lot where the series is produced. And you put in sixty, seventy, or more hours a week, writing alone and in groups, attending production meetings, watching rehearsals, and eating lots of take-out food.

Working on staff is crazy, exhausting, fun, and challenging—and it pays very, very well.

If you are good, if you are well liked, and if the show and your producers survive long enough, your contract is renewed. You work your way up through the ranks, trying to become a producer. You move on to different shows, get promotions, earn more money. And maybe, someday, you even get a chance to produce a series that you have created, or run a production company that produces several different sitcoms. Or you might parlay your success into directing assignments or jobs in feature films. Or, like Conan O'Brien and Tina Fey, your writing skills might propel you into a career in front of the camera.

If you are talented, tenacious, and lucky, this can all happen very quickly. A surprising number of sitcoms are run by thirty- to thirty-five-year-old producers.

Of course, circumstances are different for everyone. I said earlier that your first writing job can happen in one of three ways. The traditional path described above, starting out with a freelance assignment, has recently become less common. Nowadays, more and more new writers start their careers by landing a staff gig *as their very first job*. They're given a short but renewable contract and a couple of months to prove themselves. Whether they survive or not, they've got a great first credit and can move on from there.

The third way is even less common but it does happen—you, an untested writer, write a pilot script or produce a homegrown pilot that a network loves, and you're hired as one of the writer-producers on the new show. Not the head writer or producer probably, but you're on the team and now have an impressive first credit. Again, this happens very rarely, but it has happened, so we'll discuss this new approach later in the book.

Where do sitcom writers come from? Everywhere. Some are recent college grads who hopped a plane to Hollywood the day after commencement. Some writers start out as an executive's assistant or a producer's secretary; they write spec scripts and schmooze their boss until he tosses them a freelance assignment, and they're on their way.

Other writers come from completely different professional careers, having already established themselves as successful lawyers, artists, doctors, cabdrivers, or executives. Bored with their jobs, they finally find the courage to try their luck at writing. These people tend to have some money in the bank, which helps them to weather the financial ups and downs that a new writer usually faces. (Of course, money in the bank does not guarantee a successful writing career.)

Some people back into the business through pure coincidence, utter dumb luck. They are in the right place at the right time, and suddenly someone hands them a writing job. Maybe they are related to someone, they are someone's drinking buddy, they impress a producer at a cocktail party, whatever. They land the job and off they go.

NOTE: In this highly competitive field, it is important to look before leaping. Before you move from Wisconsin or resign from that cushy corpo-

rate job, please consider the advice presented in this book regarding ways to prepare for your assault on Hollywood. After all, it is a lot easier to crank out winning sample scripts or reel in an agent if you don't have the added pressure of a landlord screaming about overdue rent.

So those are some typical career paths for a sitcom writer. What should your game plan be?

Getting Started

The first step to launching your career is to write a couple of dynamite spec scripts—the samples that will, hopefully, get you that agent or manager, and lead to your first job. (No, do not start out by hounding producers and executives for work. How can anyone hire you if you don't have any writing samples to show them?) These spec scripts have to be fantastic, better than the produced episode you watched last night on TV. Otherwise, why should anyone be impressed? ("Gee, this *Office* spec is worse than the episodes I see every week—let's hire this guy!")

To get started, I suggest the following game plan: First, before you write anything, read Part One of this book, *Writing Premise-Driven Comedy*. It will give you a better understanding of comedy writing theory, and it will arm you with a powerful method for weaving seamless, premise-driven comedy into your script. (Why not just dive in and start writing something? Because it is too easy to become married to scenes and jokes that, in the long run, might hurt your script.)

Then, begin writing your script as you read Part Two, *Writing a Professional Script*. The steps described in that section mirror the steps followed by professional sitcom writers.

Finally, once you have written at least one polished spec script, a sample good enough to show to professional contacts, you can use the strategy presented in Part Three, *A Battle Plan for Launching Your Career*, to attack the job market.

Of course, you have the option of skipping directly to Part Two of the book if you want to start a script right away. Or, if you have at least one script that represents your best writing, you can begin the job search outlined in Part Three. However, I advise that you not rush into things. You usually get only one shot at impressing a contact. If you submit anything less than your best writing, that producer or exec will probably inform her assistant that she does not need to see any more of your work in the future. Ouch—there goes one potential employer. Forever.

Instead, why not start at the beginning? Let's explore some comedy writing theory.

2

FIRST, SOME THEORY

What a fuss. For over two thousand years, scholars have argued about what causes laughter and about how comedy works. The funny thing is, most of these theorists—dramatists, philosophers, physiologists, psychoanalysts, evolutionists—seem to have drawn very similar conclusions, but were too busy sniping at each other to notice the fact.

Why should you care?

Well, several of the widely shared, yet universally contested, concepts espoused in their theories have evolved into important tools of the professional comedy writer. So, while we wait for scholars of the field to develop and embrace a single unified theory of comedy, let's look at a few of these ideas.

The Mechanics of Laughter

First, we should consider the basic mechanics of humor-related laughter (as opposed to laughter triggered by mental illness, physical disorders, or other less-than-humorous causes). Sigmund Freud declared, in his book *Jokes and Their Relation to the Unconscious*, that laughter is a "discharge of psychical energy."[1] Meaning, we invest energy in suppressing our feelings about a subject, but laughter can serve to release (or discharge) those inhibitions, giving us pleasurable relief. A number of other theorists before and after Freud have offered similar emotion-based, laughter-as-release theories; note Dana Sutton's declaration, in his more recent book *The Catharsis of Comedy*, that laughter is a "purgative" that relieves an audience of bad feelings.[2]

Of course, physiologists who hear such blatantly intuitive theories (based solely on observations of human behavior) get a little upset. They object because Freud and other "philosophical types" usually fail to address the tangible roles that chemical, nervous, and muscular functions play in making laughter happen. Physiologists like to describe laughter in terms of contracting muscles, the expulsion of air, and an interruption of one's respiratory cycle. But as for what causes these actions? That's harder to explain. Famed theorist Herbert Spencer tried, in an article titled "The Physiology of Laughter," by suggesting that "nervous excitation always tends to beget muscular motion."[3] Funny, but "nervous excitation" sounds a lot like "psychical energy," and "muscular motion" might well describe a "discharge" via laughter.

If physiologists appear perturbed by the emotion-based models that Freud and his friends preach, evolutionists seem downright offended. In Robert Storey's article "Comedy, Its Theorists, and the Evolutionary Perspective," he declares that Freud and other "philosophers of comedy" must be given a wide berth. After all, he states, smiles and laughter are clearly "evolved responses" that developed because they strengthened the human gene pool, thereby promoting man's survival.

To explain laughter's function, evolutionists refer to formal studies of primate behavior and the actions of human infants (who have yet to be influenced by social conventions). Their findings suggest that the human smile evolved from our early ancestors' bared-teeth display which, in certain circumstances, was used to express hierarchical submission or reassurance within the troop; today, modern man uses his smile to indicate submission, reassurance, friendliness, and low-key amusement. Similarly, evolutionists theorize that laughter originated (in our ancestors) as a bared-teeth, loudly vocalized response to a hostile threat; today, man laughs in response to a humorous incongruity rather than a life-threatening predator.

On another front, physiologists and evolutionists jointly criticize the emotion-based, laughter-as-release theories by pointing out a simple fact of biology: Laughter does not directly cause physical relaxation, as claimed, but instead accelerates respiration, increases circulation, and raises blood pressure.

So who is right? And when sitting at the keyboard, puzzling over a punchline for *South Park*, do we really care?

First, all are right, to some extent. And second, yes, we care. For, as much as the above scholars disagree about emphasis, justification, and labels, all keep alluding to one vital element of laughter—*tension*. Call it "psychical energy" or "nervous excitation," proclaim it biological rather than emotional in nature, the bottom line is that some form of tension is necessary to laughter, and therefore to comedy.

Just as dramatic tension is released through the resolution of story conflict, comedic tension is paid off through a punchline. Extrapolating from the above theories, it seems reasonable to speculate that, many times, comedic tension is not supplied by a simple joke setup or mere wordplay alone. As we will explore in the coming chapters, other factors—the stress in our lives, universally shared gripes, even dramatic tension—can contribute to the comedic tension that makes a joke work.

Confused? No problem. Just remember the concept—tension, then a release. For a better understanding of how it applies to writing that joke for *South Park*, let's discuss some common characteristics of comedy.

Characteristics of Comedy

Though theorists are still struggling to explain the mechanics of laughter, they have known for centuries that certain kinds of stimuli can cause us to laugh. Here is a brief list of characteristics that can be found in most jokes or funny situations:

1. Incongruity

Wit lies in the likeness of things that are different,
and in the difference of things that are like.
—MADAME DE STAEL (1766–1817)

When a thought or action is incongruous with the situation at hand, we often find that funny. Picture *Seinfeld*'s Kramer being hired as a Calvin

Klein model, or Michael Scott attempting to provide diversity training at *The Office*. Simply join two dissimilar notions together and the incongruity generates a—you guessed it—*tension* just begging for release.

Freud describes a related process as the "displacement" of an audience's train of thought; as in, the setup for a joke causes an audience to have certain expectations, but the punchline yanks the rug out by providing a very different, incongruous payoff. The result? Tension is discharged and the audience laughs.

Some modern evolutionists prefer to view humorous incongruity in terms of an audience's "mastery" of a joke. Meaning that, through the course of hearing the joke, from setup to payoff, the audience moves from confusion to understanding. The audience hears the punchline, instantaneously deciphers and masters the incongruity, and laughs in triumph at its accomplishment. (An amusing note: Freud and the other "philosophers of comedy" so often belittled by modern evolutionists came up with their own "bewilderment and illumination" theory over a hundred years ago.[4])

Whatever the explanation, what matters to us—practicing comedy writers—is the concept of using an incongruous twist as a comedic payoff. We can accomplish this by exploiting similarities and differences to turn a simple situation into a funny predicament, or a boring character into a comic figure, or a normal response into a funny punchline. (On *30 Rock*, Tracy Jordan's menacing bodyguards, Grizz and Dot Com, turn out to be two of the most sensitive and insightful members of the cast; when Satan visits *South Park* to wreak havoc on humanity, he's sometimes sidetracked by relationship issues he's having with his lover, Saddam Hussein.)

How do we come up with these incongruities? By using free association. By opening our minds to unique, unexpected connections. By looking at situations from different angles. By asking the question that all comedy (and drama) writers regularly chant, "What if . . . ?"

2. Surprise

A no-brainer, right? Everyone knows that once you have heard the punchline of a joke, it just is not as funny the second time around. (Unless you are the one telling the joke, in which case the audience must be at fault.) The reason is that once we know the outcome, the incongruity is resolved, the tension dissipated. There is nothing left to "master," so the joke is no longer funny.

On another level, all humor incorporates some element of surprise within its structure. When we create a funny scene or joke, we try to reel the audience in with a realistic setup, then hit them with a surprise twist at the end. Why delay the punchline? Because otherwise, "Take my wife ... please!" becomes "Please take my wife!" The surprise twist is lost and the joke falls flat. (We will discuss setups and punchlines in Chapter 6 of this book.)

So use surprise to get laughs—save the punchlines and payoffs for last.

3. Truth

When a thing is funny, search it for a hidden truth.
—GEORGE BERNARD SHAW, *Back to Methuselah*

Tell a joke that carries a thread of truth, that strikes a chord with the audience, and that joke will seem doubly funny. You win extra laughs for being not only amusing, but also clever and insightful.

Look at *Seinfeld*. Entire storylines were based on things like having a bad hair day or arguing with a Soup Nazi—the little things in life that we can all relate to. (We have been there, Seinfeld is us!) The subjects explored in that show's stories were small and seemingly unimportant, but they rang true. By capitalizing on the tensions in our everyday lives, the setups for *Seinfeld*'s jokes reeled us all the way in, producing bigger laughs (release of tension) when we heard the punchlines.

Obviously, truth means different things to different people, particularly when one is dealing in insult humor. Bigots find truth in prejudice expressed as a punchline, while many people are greatly offended by the same joke. Writers should consider both their audience's point of view and their own standards of taste when developing material.

And, of course, not all jokes or funny bits incorporate a shared truth. Some jokes consist solely of a playful incongruity or wording, or some amusing physical comedy. The joke is the joke, that is all you get. An example from *My Name Is Earl*:

> NOTE: *The script excerpts that follow are* not *printed in correct script format. That subject is covered in Appendix A.*

```
    EARL
    But Jessie eventually tracked me
    down. Which wasn't hard. There
    were two places I liked to drink.
    And since I wasn't in my El Camino,
    she found me.⁵
```

How can truth help our writing? Well, first, we should pause to consider our audience's perspective and see what funny truths become apparent. (After all, the audience for an eight o'clock show is different from that for a ten o'clock show; the fans of *South Park* are different from those of *Two and a Half Men*.) And second, we should explore our own truths, the big and little experiences that we share with, oh, probably about a billion other people on the planet. Both efforts will turn up lots of funny material and also help to keep us in tune with our audience.

4. Aggression

> *There's no trick to being a humorist when you have*
> *the whole government working for you.*
> —WILL ROGERS (1879–1935)

Telling jokes is a great way to vent. Humor provides us with an outlet for our anger and frustrations by allowing us to disguise a verbal attack as entertainment. That way, we don't get punched by the attack-ee.

Whom are we attacking? The people and things that create stress in our lives—authority figures, oppressive institutions, personal antagonists. The boss, the post office, the brother Mom always loved best.

Freud said that such "tendentious" or "purposeful" humor not only provides an outlet for anger but also allows us to vent other repressed inhibitions.[6] He put sex at the top of the list (big surprise, coming from Freud), noting that obscene humor provides a way of exposing that most delicate of subjects to an audience. The goal of an obscene joke can range from a flirtatious testing of the waters (when addressing a potential sex partner), to an act of malicious aggression (when forcing smut on an unwilling audience).

Whatever the intent, aggressive jokes can pack an extra punch for the same reasons that truthful jokes do—an empathetic audience laughs even harder because it identifies with the *content* of the joke, in addition to appreciating its comedic strengths. We enjoy the Will Rogers quote above for two reasons: because it provides a clever twist, and because we too are frequently annoyed by government blunders.

Of course, it is not always necessary (or even wise) to actually name the object of our joking aggression. More often than not, a writer alludes to the object by targeting a symptom or characteristic of the thing. Or, by going after someone who exhibits certain bothersome traits or represents a particular category of people. Consider this line from novelist P. G. Wodehouse (1881–1975):

> It was one of those parties where you cough twice before you speak, and then decide not to say it after all.

While, on the surface, this observation seems to be directed at a type of party, the true target is that elitist class of society that revels in holding social functions solely to exclude and impress.

What role does aggression play in modern sitcom writing? It is everywhere! Aggressive humor is a standard component in sitcom stories, dialogue, and—most notably—in caustic characters like *South Park*'s Cartman, *Earl*'s Joy, *The Office*'s Dwight, and at least half the cast in *Everybody Hates Chris*. Why? Because aggression, like truth, promotes audience identification, which yields big laughs.

5. Brevity

Every book, article, or thesis ever written about comedy includes that tired quote from Shakespeare's *Hamlet*, "Brevity is the soul of wit." Why? Brevity, mainly.

That line, better than any other, defines an immutable law of comedy. There is no mystery here, no theoretical construct to decipher. Centuries of practical experience have demonstrated that humor must be lean and mean, completely uncluttered. Otherwise, the incongruity gets lost, the surprise muddled, the truth diluted.

When in doubt, remember that less is more.

And in some cases, less might still be too much. A hundred years ago, professor Theodor Lipps wrote that "A joke says what it has to say, not always in few words, but in *too* few words.... It may even actually say what it has to say by not saying it."[7]

Remember "Take my wife . . . please!"? It says it all, without saying it.

Enough said.

One last note about the characteristics of comedy. Scholars and writers identified these and other traits long ago, but have not always agreed on their relative importance. For additional perspectives, see Sol Saks's book *The Craft of Comedy Writing* and Melvin Helitzer's book *Comedy Writing Secrets*. (Or buy lunch for a successful comedy writer.)

The Importance of Tension

By now, the reasoning behind my earlier speculation is probably clear. All theories of laughter, and all laughter stimuli, seem to depend on an underlying process of establishing, building, and releasing tension. An IN-CONGRUITY creates comedic tension. A SURPRISE twist releases tension. TRUTH and AGGRESSION increase tension. BREVITY brings tension into high relief.

Often, much of the tension in a funny situation or an individual joke comes not from comedic structure, but from shared stress in our lives. And the more tension in a joke, the bigger the release (or laugh).

It is helpful to keep these dynamics in mind when developing stories and sculpting jokes. Not that we should get hung up on labels and theories when trying to create—that's a surefire recipe for bland (but technically correct?) comedy. Instead, our goal is to explore these concepts so that they can float around in our subconscious, occasionally stepping forward to suggest or shape a bit of humor. That, and we can apply this knowledge in a more deliberate fashion during rewrites, when a couple of rules and tools can sometimes fix material that inspiration has left broken.

Moving On

It is one thing to analyze humor theory, another to apply it when writing comedy. Let's take a closer look at how sitcom writers work.

3

PUTTING THEORY INTO PRACTICE

Different writers have different strengths. Some are good with story structure, some with dialogue; some are related to the producer.

And all comedy writers have good days, funny days, and bad, sad, can't-make-it-happen days. Sometimes a script will practically write itself, it just spills over with grade-A humor. Other times, it just lies there, limp and dull, fodder for someone's eulogy. (Yours, once the producer sees it.)

Hey, comedy writing only looks easy. If there is one constant in the process, it's that all comedy writers share certain creative goals. These include:

Seamless Humor

Producer MATT WILLIAMS: We have a phrase called "writer's hand." "That's funny, but it's writer's hand." It refers to self-conscious writing. It sounds like a sitcom writer. You can feel their hand writing the line and [hear them] chuckling, as opposed to the line coming organically out of the moment, out of that character's mouth.

Good comedy writing is seamless rather than forced. Meaning, humorous situations should flow naturally from a story; they should not feel like a detour taken because the writer was desperate to cram in a few jokes. Likewise, funny dialogue should sound like something the characters would actually say; it should not sound like ill-fitting one-liners lifted from someone's stand-up routine.

A joke can be hilarious, the funniest thing that you will ever write, but if it does not belong in your script it will break the audience's suspension of disbelief. It will distract viewers, leaving them with the impression that they have just been subjected to a joke. Not good.

Even the broadest of comedies can boast of seamless humor, as long as the show's jokes remain true to its overall premise. Consider wacky classics like *I Love Lucy* and *Gilligan's Island*, and more recent shows like *My Name Is Earl* and *South Park*. As outrageous as these shows can be, the comedy that they offer seems completely organic and natural. The payoff? Their viewers find it easy to relax and go along for the ride.

Consistency

Good writers, either deliberately or instinctively, try to maintain consistent levels of humor in their scripts. Meaning, they provide an amount and type of humor that is appropriate for the story they are writing, and they maintain those levels from beginning to end. Weak scripts, inconsistent scripts, tend to bounce back and forth. A funny sequence might be followed by a serious scene, followed by a stretch of dry humor, followed by loads of physical shtick, etc. At the story's beginning, the audience is cued to enjoy a certain amount and type of comedy, but then those expectations aren't met due to inconsistency, and the audience loses interest.

In sitcoms, the style of humor is dictated by the creators of the series premise. The challenge is to identify and consistently reflect that style in the episodes that you write.

Comedy Output

I have never heard a producer say "Too much humor in this script—make it less funny."

Sitcom writers are always looking for ways to increase their comedy output. After all, the average half-hour script eats up two to four solid jokes *per page*. Of course, comedy writing is not just about the amount of humor in a script. You are always trying to improve the quality too, always looking for that next joke that is just a bit better than the one already sitting on the page.

The challenge is to come up with enough terrific humor to satisfy your audience and yourself, *without* forcing the jokes. Because, as much as your producers will always clamor for more comedy, the last thing you want to hear anyone say is "This script is too jokey." (Meaning that your script is thick with obvious setups and punchlines—so much for seamless humor.)

NOTE: Audience responses seem to come in three forms: a smile, a grunt or chuckle, and a full-fledged laugh. Broad, wacky, physical comedy—comedy that incorporates lots of outrageous situations and big surprises—usually generates a healthy number of laughs. Sophisticated, subtle, adult humor— comedy distinguished by wit and clever repartee—is more likely to garner quiet smiles. Picture Curb Your Enthusiasm's *Larry battling a handicapped man over a parking space for the first, and* 30 Rock's *Liz Lemon trading barbs with Jack Donaghy for the second.*

The Traditional Approach to Sitcom Writing

How do sitcom writers achieve these goals? How do they create seamless humor, consistent humor, more humor?

In the industry today, much of this work is left to the rewriting process. The average writer starts work on a spec script, his next writing sample, by dreaming up an episode premise and cranking out a first draft. Too often, he does not bother to create a story outline first—a bad idea unless you are one of those obnoxious types who can completely map out a story in their head. Prior to circulating the script, the writer and his trusty readers (friends, wife, the mailman) examine the first draft to identify weak spots. The writer makes his revisions and sends the thing off.

Sometimes this system works just fine. The writer correctly identifies script problems and turns out a dynamite spec. However, there can be a tendency to address all script problems, some of which have nothing to do with a lack of humor, by cramming additional jokes into the dialogue. This can result in forced humor—the writer ends up with one very funny but very bad script. And no job.

Freelance writers who have been hired to write an episode and writers on the staff of a show operate in a similar fashion, but they almost always work from a written story outline. (This outline has either been supplied by the show's producers or created under their supervision.) The standard approach is to have the writer or writing team do an outline and a first draft, which is then subjected to a seemingly endless cycle of rewriting. Much of this rewriting takes the form of *roundtable writing*, a process in which five, ten, or more writers jointly go through a script, rewriting line after line, hunting for opportunities to wedge just one more joke into the material. Efforts to repair and improve the script usually last all the way through the shooting process, with revisions being tossed to actors even as the scenes are being filmed. (As anyone in Hollywood will tell you, it seems that three-quarters of all writing is rewriting—you rewriting you, you rewriting others, others rewriting you.)

Most of the time, roundtable writing is a great way to increase a script's joke count and remedy story problems—no doubt that's why it became a tradition in the first place. And, no question, last-minute rewriting is an invaluable tool for fine-tuning a script. It allows the producers to adjust for a performer's timing, account for staging problems, or capitalize on someone's brilliant last-minute inspiration.

But when you're working alone on a spec script, you don't have ten professional writers to back you up. If you leave too much of the creative burden to the rewriting phase, it's easy to end up with some of that forced humor or to overlook story problems and opportunities. You won't know what's wrong—you just won't get any work. What can you do?

Perhaps a slight shift in effort would help. If you want to keep your script on track and create rich, seamless comedy, I suggest an approach that's all about building humor from the ground up. . . .

4

LEVEL ONE:
PREMISE-DRIVEN
COMEDY

Our favorite drama writers explore all opportunities to build conflict into their stories, be it "man against nature," "man against man," "man against self," or what have you. These writers start with an interesting story premise, and then compound dramatic tension when they create story sequences and again when they create individual scenes. The result is a strong narrative that is both organic and rich.

Similarly, the best sitcom writers instinctively integrate *comedic* tension into all levels of their work—from episode premise, to sequence, to scene. By the time they get down to writing dialogue, the comedy that they have planted at the first levels of the script automatically produces more laughs, bigger laughs, and more seamless laughs than are otherwise possible.

And that's the key. Start by building comedic tension into your episode premise. Then, add to that tension and draw from that tension as you create sequences, scenes, and dialogue. It is a simple, intuitive approach, no tricks. While it is certainly not intended to replace rewriting, this method enables a writer to draw as much comedy as possible from the stories he creates.

Exactly how do you create this Premise-Driven Comedy? It's all starts with . . .

A Different Approach: Comedy in the Story Premise

Just picture: There you are, sitting down to start work on that new script for *Family Guy*. And you think to yourself, "Time to go for some of that premise-driven comedy. But how, dammit, how?"

Simple. You start by weaving funny elements into the premise of the episode. (Do not worry about scenes and dialogue yet; focus on the overall story.) The comedy that you plant at this, the first level of your script, will automatically generate funny situations and jokes throughout the material. Plus, the resulting humor will seem natural and seamless, because it grew out of the story rather than having been crammed into it.

To illustrate, imagine this storyline: A housewife gets a chance to be on a game show. She answers the questions, wins a big prize, goes home happy. End of episode. An interesting story? No. Funny? Don't think so. But, if we play with the premise a bit . . .

That housewife gets her chance on the game show. She answers the questions just fine, until . . . she is tricked into admitting, on national TV, that her husband's famous boss is secretly bald! The boss is celebrity Alan Brady, her husband is Rob Petrie, and suddenly you have a terrific storyline for the classic sitcom *The Dick Van Dyke Show*. Laura must confess to Rob, Laura tries to save Rob's job, Rob tries to save Rob's job. It is a great episode, hilarious throughout, and all because of comedy that grew out of the story premise.

Consider another example, this one from a feature film: Two guys, buddies, witness a mass murder—eight or ten people are machine-gunned to death before their eyes. The two pals are spotted by the killers but they manage to escape. The pals run off to another city, trying to disappear, but run smack into the killers!

Interesting story? Sure. But funny? Maybe to psychos. Most people, hearing this description, would expect to see a tense thriller full of jeopardy, suspense, and violent death. But, tinker with that premise and you might get . . .

The two guys witness the massacre, they need to escape . . . so they don disguises. Dresses! They pretend to be women and join an all-female band that is leaving town for a gig . To complicate matters, both guys fall for the same gorgeous woman, another band member. One of the guys—dressed as a woman—inadvertently ends up sharing a bed with the goddess, and must struggle to maintain his disguise in the face of great temptation. The other takes on a second disguise, posing as a playboy, so that he can court the woman. But at the same time, he is forced to play female best-friend-and-confidante when the woman needs to discuss her new beau (him!). Then, the gangsters show up, there is mix-up after mix-up—

The movie? *Some Like It Hot*, a popular classic that stars Jack Lemmon, Tony Curtis, and Marilyn Monroe. What might have been a tense thriller, a bloody gangster flick, was transformed into a hilarious G-rated comedy—all because of funny elements woven into the film's premise.

Okay, so how do you accomplish this in your writing? How do you lace comedy into a story premise? I will list four ways and then we will explore each in detail:

Predicaments

Build an escalating series of predicaments into your story. The incongruity inherent in each situation will generate comedic tension, and that tension will be compounded by each subsequent, larger predicament.

Character Mix

Think character *relationships* rather than just "Plumbers are funny, I'll make this guy a plumber." For example, the Pam and Jim characters on *The Office* aren't that amusing by themselves; they're low-key, pleasant under-achievers just muddling along through life. But when storylines subject them to Michael Scott's obnoxious behavior or other office-mates' antics, their roles in the character mix (as foils and commentators) contribute much to the show's comedy.

Style of Comedy

This, as we will discuss, is determined by a show's genre, type of humor, amount of humor, and consistency of humor. The producers of a sitcom make these decisions when they create a series. The writer's job is to identify and exploit these decisions in the episodes that she writes.

Casting

In most instances, writers have little say in casting decisions. But consider the impact that these decisions can have on humor at the story level. Imagine how differently you would tailor a role for *Two and a Half Men's* Charlie Sheen versus one that you would write for his co-star, Jon Cryer.

Very talented writers instinctively apply all of these concepts when creating a story. Less talented writers do so occasionally. Unfortunately, occasionally doesn't get you work.

So let's look more closely at each of these techniques for maximizing comedy in your story's premise.

Predicaments

Webster's defines a predicament as "an unpleasantly difficult, perplexing, or dangerous situation." Gee, sounds like a laugh riot.

Yet, predicaments can generate humor. How? By creating tension. As long as the viewer perceives that characters facing a predicament will not come to any real harm, that tension can be used to produce comedy. (It can be shaped into a humorous incongruity that calls out for a funny payoff.) Of course, we must first cue the audience that our story is meant to be funny, or jokes based on a character's unfortunate predicament might seem offensive and fall flat.

A funny predicament confined to one scene will pump up the humor for those few pages. But a sustained predicament built into the story premise can generate humor in scene after scene, from "Fade In:" to "End of Episode." (Think of Jack Lemmon and Tony Curtis in those dresses.) Create a funny predicament at the first level of your script and it can become a joke-producing machine for the duration of your story, or at least until said predicament is resolved.

NOTE: Permanent predicaments are often built into the overall premise of a sitcom. Remember those seven people stranded on Gilligan's Island? *When trying to think of funny storylines for an individual episode, a writer should start by exploring any permanent predicaments that already exist within the series premise. "No phone, no lights, no motorcar" might suggest the perfect story predicament for your episode.*

And there is another benefit (to creating escalating predicaments). A continuing, unresolved predicament in your story leaves your viewer hanging. It creates a sustained expectation, an underlying suspense, as she waits for the final payoff. The great thing about this? Situations and jokes that are *not even related* to the predicament seem funnier because the viewer is operating with a heightened sense of anticipation.

Cool.

Want some examples? Here are some classic predicaments that have been featured in sitcom episodes. They should look familiar—we have seen them used time after time, in show after show. Some of them have even been listed in screenwriting books as examples of stories to write. Am I suggesting that you should rehash old storylines? No. These models are presented here for only one reason: They provide great examples of how you might build funny predicaments into an *original* story premise.

The Big Lie

A lead character tells a lie during a weak moment. Either he wants to impress someone or hurt someone, or he gets caught in a compromising situation, or he wants something that he cannot have. The first lie often leads to another lie and then another, each bigger than the last. (Tension, tension, tension.) The situation gets out of hand, eventually backfires, and laughter ensues.

Example? In one *South Park* episode, Cartman hears a kid with Tourette's syndrome blurting out obscenities, and decides that this is his golden ticket to saying anything he wants to anyone. Cartman has a ball faking the affliction so he can torment others, and is even asked to guest on a *Dateline* TV segment devoted to Tourette's. But suddenly he starts blurting out embarrassing truths at the worst times—he can't stop himself. He tries to get out of his *Dateline* appearance, but host Chris Hansen won't let him; Cartman is doomed to humiliate himself on national TV. But at story's end, Kyle, while trying to expose Cartman's lie, inadvertently causes a diversion that disrupts the TV broadcast, and evil Cartman is saved from disaster!

Technically speaking, the funny incongruity created by the first lie in this story grows larger and larger with each new lie, but is finally resolved when the truth is revealed at story's end. In episodes featuring a "big lie," the guilty character sometimes gets carried away by the good fortune generated by his lies. (As when Bart Simpson claims that he has performed some heroic deed, then starts to believe his own press.) Sometimes the character finds himself faced with a moral dilemma, in which he must choose between his interests and those of a more deserving character. Usually, a big lie is eventually exposed and order is restored. However, some episodes, like this *South Park* example, end with a clever twist that allows the character to escape with his dignity and "the prize" intact.

The Big Secret

In these stories, a lead character discovers a secret about another character but is somehow prohibited from sharing that information. Things usually start off simply enough, and then turn into a huge, dying-to-tell burden. A loose-lipped lead might blab the secret to assorted friends, and have several close calls in which he almost blabs to the person involved. Eventually, of course, he does blab to that person at the worst possible time. An example: In an episode of *The Office* titled "The Secret," Michael agrees to keep Jim's crush on Pam a secret, then accidentally blabs it to the whole office. Jim recovers nicely, telling Pam that the crush was an old one, but then Michael blabs again, revealing that Jim still has feelings for Pam.

Sometimes a secret is passed on but misinterpreted, leading to funny complications. Other times, those who learn the secret finally become so incensed that they take desperate action; they confront the two-timing husband or expose the corporate scam, only to discover that they have misread the situation and caused a humiliating scene.

The Misunderstanding
(I Got Tired of Calling Everything "The Big...")

One character misinterprets something that he is told or that he overhears, and gets into trouble when he acts on the misinformation. Comedic tension is created the second that we, the viewers, realize that the character has misunderstood. It builds each time the character does something that makes the predicament worse.

Example: *30 Rock*'s Liz becomes suspicious of her brusque new neighbor, Raheem, when she spies maps covering his apartment walls. Observing more odd behavior, she wonders if he might be a terrorist and contacts Homeland Security, which promptly nabs the guy. She's a hero—until Raheem is released because it's determined that he was just compiling an audition tape for *The Amazing Race*. What's worse, he informs Liz that he is now so angry from having been tortured that he plans to "create something spectacular."

A Rock and a Hard Place

These predicaments feature a lead character of the series having to choose between two very good things or two very bad things. Examples include many episodes of *My Name Is Earl*, in which Earl locates the person on his karma list that he wronged in the past, but discovers that if he wants to right his wrong he must meet some very difficult challenge—such as apologize to a stripper he injured, by donning tassels and dancing on a runway, or sleep with an ex-con's elderly mother to avoid being murdered for making her unhappy.

These stories often involve growing levels of deceit and sometimes take the form of a moral dilemma. In the old days, the lead character could be counted on to eventually choose the high ground, sacrificing her interests for another character's. Now, just as often, the lead will shamelessly pursue the more selfish goal, but end up losing everything by the story's conclusion. (Or not; the days of selfish deeds always being punished are long gone.)

The Surefire Scheme

The second a lead character says the words "Trust me, what could go wrong?" we all know what lies ahead. Be it Bart or Homer Simpson, *Entourage*'s Johnny, or one of the *Two and a Half Men*, that character is about to unleash a surefire plan to get rich, get even, or get laid, or all three. Of course, he and his cohorts immediately encounter an escalating series of unexpected problems, bad decisions, and foolish risks, all of which land them in hot water. Usually, by story's end, their surefire scheme completely backfires. The characters are worse off than before, and we enjoy a pleasing release of tension as order is restored.

Example: In a *South Park* episode, Kyle, Stan, and Kenny decide to punish Cartman for the way he treats "ginger kids"—kids who have red hair, freckles, and "no soul." The boys sneak into his bedroom and dye his features to give him "gingervitus," and Cartman learns what it's like to be treated like an outcast. But the boys' scheme backfires when Cartman rallies other ginger kids in a campaign to end the discrimination, by convincing them that they should kill everyone who's not a redhead—starting with Kyle, Stan, and Kenny!

Something That Rocks the Boat

In these stories, all is normal in sitcomland until some event rocks the boat. Sometimes this event takes the form of a past acquaintance or a relative coming to visit, or a new business rival or troublesome neighbor moving in. For example, in several episodes of *30 Rock*, Jack Donaghy suddenly finds his career in jeopardy when his arch nemesis, Devon Banks, pops up with a new scheme to grab the promotion that Jack covets. On *Everybody Hates Chris*, when Greg's father leaves on a trip and Chris invites his friend to stay for the week, the gesture backfires when suddenly the family starts doting on Greg and forgets that Chris even exists.

These stories create tension by threatening the status quo. They often build up to some sort of showdown, an emotional confrontation during which misunderstandings are revealed. Then they usually end with the boat-rocker returning to wherever it is that he came from.

Time Bomb

These stories feature a race against time. The characters get themselves into a predicament in which they must accomplish an impossible goal by a fast-approaching deadline. Of course, the harder they try, the worse matters get. How often have we seen the story in which a teenager throws a big party while the folks are out of town? The place gets trashed, a treasured vase is broken, then—uh-oh!—the folks call to say they will be home early!

Right, too often. Other variations include rival characters competing on a dare, a character boasting himself into an impossible deadline at work, or characters hurrying to exploit a big opportunity before others beat them to the punch.

Trapped in a Space

This is such an old one, I'm reluctant to even mention it. But surely we'll see it used again, and again, so here goes.

The lead characters get themselves trapped in a small space, usually accompanied by a pregnant woman or a closet claustrophobic, and must keep from killing each other as they wait to be rescued. Inevitably, one or more characters are overdue at some important event—a speech, a wedding, maybe *their* wedding. And sometimes their lives are actually in danger, with a clock ticking.

Why does this worn premise work? It's a pressure cooker. The small space forces opposing characters to remain in close proximity, which gets sparks flying. Plus, the concept of being trapped creates tension in all of us at some primal level, since that predicament usually leads to getting beaten, eaten, or sent to jail. Plus, missed appointments add even more tension, and they open up lots of story possibilities.

A related predicament that can be just as funny? *Locked outside, naked.* These predicaments, however, are usually resolved in one scene or a brief sequence rather than used as the spine of a fully developed story. Think episodes of *Family Guy*, *The Simpsons*, even the dramatic series *Desperate Housewives*—locked out or trapped in, these situations produce tension galore, and naked is always funny.

Sex

These predicaments often involve an aggressive romantic or lust-driven pursuit, featuring a lead character as either the pursuer or pursu-ee. Sometimes a character suddenly finds himself in a compromising situation with an unwanted suitor. Other times, there is temptation on both sides—should they or shouldn't they? And often, there are small complications, like a wife and twelve kids waiting at home.

Or maybe both parties work at the same place. Or a boss or best friend is already involved with the acquaintance. Whatever the complication, by injecting romantic tension into the story, with maybe some naked people thrown in, sex can serve as a great source of funny predicaments.

The Dead Body

Talk about tension—stick one of your characters with a dead body and the possibilities are endless. Does she have to hide the corpse? Will she be blamed for the death, even accused of murder? Must she assume the stiff's identity to avoid a disaster or close a big deal? Or break the news to the new widow? Or get stuck with the stiff's nasty little dog?

For some dead-body stories, you don't even need a corpse. One of the best-remembered, Emmy-winning episodes of *The Mary Tyler Moore Show* ("Chuckles Bites the Dust") revolved around people laughing and suppressing laughter after finding out that a colleague dressed in a peanut costume was crushed to death by a parade elephant.

Again, these are just some of the predicaments that you might use to launch a funny story. I am not suggesting that you should rehash plot lines like the examples provided above. (We will discuss techniques for creating *original* stories in Chapter 8.) I have listed these classic predicaments only because they illustrate how to build comedy into an episode premise.

And oh—don't smirk too much. If you become a working sitcom writer, you will someday take a second glance at a wonderful story that you have developed, only to realize that . . . yikes! you have just recycled that old *Big Lie* premise. Well, do not despair. Those old predicaments keep popping up for two reasons: They reflect human behavior and they are funny. As long as you apply them in a fresh manner, true to your characters, it's okay to use (reuse) them.

Character Mix

Place Dwight Schrute (*The Office*) in almost any situation—in a crowded elevator, at the post office, in a company meeting—and funny bits just pour out onto the page. But put his office-mate Jim Halpert in the same situations and what happens? Do jokes automatically materialize?

Some characters are inherently funny, anywhere, anytime, because of their design. (And because of the actors who play them.) Other characters—more normal characters?—are less funny out of context. They get most of their laughs through involvement in story predicaments and interactions with surrounding characters. Most of Jim Halpert's humor comes from him playing a normal person who serves as a foil or contrast to the nuts around him; sometimes he goads, other times he comments, and still other times he just reacts as we would, topping off the funny bits delivered by his colleagues.

Why is this important? When creating original characters for a sitcom (a subject that we will discuss in Part Two of this book), pay attention to the *mix* of characters. To maximize opportunities for generating humor, characters should complement rather than duplicate each other—each should actively contribute something fresh. Perhaps a character provides a conflicting point of view, as Jim does when sparring with Dwight; characters who have different opinions usually end up in conflict, which creates tension, which can be turned into comedy.

Or perhaps a character might have a tendency to get himself and others into trouble, as *Family Guy*'s Peter Griffin does. The result? Conflict and comedy.

Or the character might behave in a strange manner or live a bizarre lifestyle, as *Seinfeld*'s Kramer did. The reactions from other characters, and contrasts with other characters, can be funny. And the strange character's behavior often results in other characters being roped into unusual predicaments.

Whether you are creating a cast of series regulars for a new series or a one-shot visiting character for a single episode, the concept remains the same. Want some examples? Here are a few more of those classic sitcom models, these based on character relationships rather than story predicaments.

Role Reversal

This dynamic occurs when a character is forced to assume a role that is contrary to his nature. He is then confronted with numerous obligations, expectations, and obstacles that he is ill equipped to meet. Picture a young dad who suddenly finds himself a single parent to three toddlers. How many times have we seen that concept? Of course, sometimes there are two dads or six kids, or even three men and a baby.

There also are the episodes in which one character assumes another's job responsibilities (role) on a dare, with disastrous but funny results. And episodes in which one character gets roped into pretending that he is another character's lover or spouse, even though both characters actually hate each other. Tension? Comedy? You bet.

Two of the most successful examples of role reversal, at the series premise level, surfaced in the late eighties. America was gaga over upbeat family sitcoms like the original *Cosby Show*. But then came the FOX network and two new shows, *Married with Children* and *The Simpsons*. Role reversal? Instead of featuring the nice, friendly families that audiences were used to, these two series featured *anti families*. Irresponsible mother Peggy, loser dad Al, slut sister Kelly, childlike parent Homer . . . In both shows, a classic premise was turned upside down, roles were reversed, and the result was fresh comedy. Audiences tuned in and the new network took off, and today the concept of an anti-family character mix is a sitcom staple (e.g., *Family Guy*).

Fish Out of Water

Write characters into a world where they don't belong, and you will end up with a mix of individuals who have dissimilar social skills, cultural traditions, educational backgrounds, religious points of view, intelligence levels, and even eating habits. Differences that are bound to spawn conflict and humor. Remember *The Beverly Hillbillies*? Think of all the funny episodes that were based entirely on some small, simple contrast between the Clampetts and their neighbors. As when Dr. Granny treats Mrs. Drysdale to a hit of her hundred-proof tonic. Or when Jethro decides to become a sophisticated Beverly Hills playboy. Or when the family mutt impregnates the neighbor's thoroughbred poodle.

Or consider *Entourage*, a series which took four average guys from Queens and plunked them down in Hollywood to enjoy all of the perks and excesses that come with celebrity. Or *Weeds*, in which many episodes grow from soccer mom Nancy's stepping into the unfamiliar world of drug dealing in order to support her family.

Odd Coupling

Create a character mix in which you force two complete opposites to exist in the same space, and funny things will happen. The best example of a series (and a play, and a film) that featured a pairing such as this? *The Odd Couple*, of course. In that series, Felix and Oscar differed in countless respects—clean freak vs. slob, cultural snob vs. blue-collar guy, sensitive man vs. crass lug. The two men argued about everything from personal hygiene to politics, and this resulted in a wealth of funny stories, funny scenes, and funny lines. Other examples of odd coupling in a show's permanent character mix include brothers Charlie and Alan in *Two and a Half Men*, and nerdy Liz and slick Jack in *30 Rock*. At the single-episode level, one might create a temporary odd-couple situation by importing a visiting relative, romantic interest, business associate, etc., whose contrasting personality completely disrupts the life of a lead character.

Sex

Yes, we already named sex as a means of generating story predicaments, but it can also be useful when creating a character mix. (And can one really talk too much about sex?)

In terms of relationships between characters, it is sometimes wise to create or exploit an ongoing sexual tension between two leads. Meaning, you might create two characters that urgently need to consummate their relationship and become full-fledged lovers, but are somehow prevented from doing so. Consider the on-again, off-again Dwight–Angela and Pam–Jim connections in *The Office*—how many storylines have those relationships spawned?

Occasionally, in a show's fourth or fifth season, the producers might weaken and allow flirting characters to consummate a sexual tension. Sometimes the decision works and other times it damages the character mix. Consider the effect on the classic series *Cheers* when Sam and Diane finally got together: The change weakened the show, but the producers realized their mistake and broke the pair apart again, and even duplicated the original sexual tension when designing Diane's replacement, Rebecca.

Another type of character mix exploits sex by featuring two lovers or spouses who enjoy a healthy, normal, or even in-your-face sex life, as in *The King of Queens*. Comedy in these shows frequently comes out of disruptions to the physical relationship—such as kids interfering with planned date nights, a passing criticism blown out of proportion, or a fear that the healthy relationship is growing stale.

In recent years, it seemed that networks and producers were growing increasingly bold about incorporating homosexuality into a sitcom's character mix. *Will and Grace* proved that America was happy to embrace the concept if the series was well written and dealt with issues all can relate to. However, little new has occurred on this front since that show's demise, other than gay supporting or visiting characters occasionally popping up here and there (such as Lloyd on *Entourage*, Devon on *30 Rock*, and Oscar on *The Office*). While that's unfortunate news in terms of social progress, it could mean an opportunity for you when developing characters and storylines, since this subject obviously carries a lot of useful tension with it.

Pretense

This is a big one. As sitcoms have become more sophisticated (thank you, HBO!), more and more stories have sprung from this trait because it flows so naturally from a character's personality. Pretense can lead to small, embarrassing moments or huge, crazy misadventures, and all viewers can relate to the sin of putting on airs now and then.

In TV terms, when a comedic character pretends to be something that he is not, he is usually doomed to exposure and humiliation. As Freud describes it, the character has "seized dignity and authority by a deception," and needs to be taken down.[1] Recent examples include Michael Scott of *The Office*, Johnny "Drama" Chase of *Entourage*, and Larry David of *Curb Your Enthusiasm*. Each regularly puts on airs or feigns knowledge of some topic, making himself a prime target for a comeuppance.

At the episode level, a writer can either exploit pretense that has been built into a show's character mix (if any), or lure a normally unpretentious character into putting up a pretense. Either way, the bluff will usually backfire by story's end. Bart Simpson cheats on a test to gain special treatment—then finds himself overwhelmed by life in the gifted-student lane. Michael Scott boasts of his amazing talent for comedy improv—then is shown to be a talentless pariah in the acting class he attends.

Lastly, any discussion of character pretense has to include that old standby, the tired storyline that screams "this show's producers are burned out"—the *class reunion* episode. As when a lead character is anxious to impress her former lovers and rivals at her high school reunion, so she pretends to be rich, thin, happily engaged, and/or married. Usually, the charade is uncovered in the final act, and these stories often end with a double twist in which an obnoxious rival turns out to be an even bigger fake than the series lead. Tension is relieved, order is restored, and all ends happily.

> *NOTE: Exceptions always make the rule and sometimes even flip it on its head;* 30 Rock *once featured a very fresh and funny episode that showed Liz attending a reunion to face her bullies, only to discover that she was the one who had bullied everyone else.*

Again, the above archetypes are presented to illustrate how a character mix can be used to generate comedy. You could come up with more classic examples if you tried—which might be a worthwhile exercise, since such traits are used again and again in all forms of comedy.

Style of Comedy

While the last two sections ("Predicaments" and "Character Mix") dealt with comedic elements that might be woven into a story premise, this section will deal with overall stylistic approach. A writer needs to know what type and what amount of humor are appropriate for his story. And his style of humor must be consistent throughout the script.

In a completely original script, such as a pilot for a new series, there are many decisions to make—you are creating the thing from scratch. But if you are writing for an existing series, the producers have already done this job. Your task is to study their series in depth so that you can identify and match the show's style of comedy. This is important. If your script does not look, sound, feel, and smell exactly like the real episodes that are produced every week, you won't get the job. No matter how funny your material is, no matter how exciting the story.

We will discuss, in Chapter 7 of this book, specific steps that you should take to analyze a series. For now, let's focus on how different styles of comedy can affect humor in a story.

Genres, Sort Of

First, let's talk genres. And just to illustrate a point, let's talk feature films rather than sitcoms, because a sitcom can, conceivably, present a different genre every week. (*The Simpsons*'s Homer might be featured in a romantic story one week and a sci-fi tale the next.)

In films, most stories fall into a particular genre or incorporate several different genres. What's a genre? It's a class of stories that share certain attributes. For instance, love stories usually feature two people who start out as strangers or even enemies, but who are inevitably drawn together. The seemingly mismatched couple encounters a series of romantic obstacles but is forced to pair up just long enough for romantic sparks to fly.

In a detective genre, we expect to see murder victims and an investigation. The hero is usually a surly outsider, a man with a past, whose search for clues leads him into great personal danger and, possibly, a romantic entanglement.

Other genres include horror, suspense, action, sci-fi, buddy-cop, coming-of-age, personal redemption, etc.—each of which is distinguished by its own set of attributes. While some films feature only one genre, most combine several. Consider *The Princess Bride* (part romance, part fantasy, part action, part comedy) and *Tropic Thunder* (part action, part parody, part comedy).

Why are genres important? Because audiences expect to see certain story elements when they watch a particular genre. Writers can either play to those expectations or, better yet, cut against them (reversing the norm to surprise viewers). But if writers ignore those conventions altogether, the audience might feel cheated.

Okay, but what do film genres have to do with sitcoms?

While sitcoms do fall into broad categories—domestic, odd couple, out-of-the-closet with a vengeance, etc.—these categories are not synonymous with genres. By themselves, sitcom categories do not clue us in to the set of attributes that define a specific series. Technically, *Two and a Half Men* and *The Simpsons* are both domestic sitcoms, each featuring a family unit in a home environment, but, clearly, that's where the similarities end. Same category, different story attributes.

On another level, as noted above, a television series might feature a different genre every week since each episode features a new story.

The point is that when writing for sitcoms, it might be useful to think of each series as being its own genre. The premise of each series dictates a unique set of attributes that we should see, and that the audience expects to see, in each episode. On a broad level, this might include elements such as delivering moral lessons in the final sequence, or the use (or avoidance) of controversial story themes. In terms of comedy, a show's attributes might range from *South Park*'s running gag that had the Kenny character being killed in (almost) every episode, to *Family Guy*'s frequent use of funny flashbacks.

In short, each series features a distinct *style* of comedy and those attributes must be reflected in your script. To get a feel for a show, it might help to just start asking specific questions, such as these:

Where Does the Humor Come From?

- Does most of the show's humor come from funny predicaments? Specific characters or relationships? The characters' environment?

- Does the show deal in small, human stories or in outlandish, bigger-than-life predicaments? Or in small stories made outlandish?

- Does the lead character usually cause the trouble or is she usually dragged into it by others?

- Is the show's comedy generated by internal events or initiated by visiting characters?

How Broad or Subtle Is the Humor?

- Does the show go for big belly laughs (usually the province of broad, wacky sitcoms) or just smiles-and-nods (typical of more sophisticated shows)?

- Does it indulge in incredible fantasies such as alien encounters and Halloween spooks, or are all of its stories realistic and plausible?

- Is much of the humor in the series visual or does it come from dialogue?

How Does the Humor Affect Story?

- Does humor overpower credibility, sacrificing story logic for the sake of laughs?

- Do episodes climax with an explosive comedy run in the final act, or maintain an even level of humor throughout?

- Are the stories influenced by classic comedy genres, such as farce (mistaken identities and misunderstood actions), parody (campy send-ups), or romances from the thirties and forties (snappy repartee)?

Of course, the best way to get a feel for an existing show's style of comedy is to watch episodes and read produced scripts. Then the trick is to write a script that uses that show's conventions in a fresh, exciting manner.

Even better, write that rare episode that expands (but does not change) a show's premise; create a visiting character worthy of becoming a series regular, open up a new story direction, or reveal a facet of an existing relationship that warrants further exploration.

Be Consistent

One last, very important thought. Once you have studied a show and gotten a feel for its style of comedy, be consistent in your writing. New writers, bad writers, new bad writers, frequently make the following mistakes:

Too Funny to Pass Up

You come up with a fantastic joke or predicament, so funny even your dad laughs, but it just doesn't quite fit the character or the series. ("Jack Donaghy goes on *Survivor* to settle a bet, takes over his tribe, buys the island, and replaces Jeff Probst with demographic darling Ryan Seacrest!")

Sorry. But if that marvelous bit is not consistent with the show's premise and style of comedy, you must dump it. Otherwise, it will damage your story, distract the reader, cost you the job, and ruin your career.

Suddenly, it doesn't seem so funny, huh?

The Genre Shuffle

New writers frequently shift comedic genres mid-story, ruining a script. (Blending genres throughout is not the same as shifting from one to the next.) Typically, they start out by writing in a style of comedy that is appropriate for a show, but then lose focus. ("After the beer-belching contest, Earl visits the kid in the hospital. The boy's on a respirator, in horrible pain; his mom just got killed in a car accident. . . .") Suddenly, the tone of jokes, the number of jokes, and the pacing of jokes change, disrupting the feel of the material. The result? See above, under "cost you the job, ruin your career."

In short, be consistent. Remain true to the show's style of comedy.

Casting

Why is casting listed here? Casting is not a part of sitcom writing, and unless a writer is also a producer, or is sleeping with a producer, he or she has little influence in this area.

True, but casting can have a big effect on comedy in a story, so we should take a quick look.

To illustrate, imagine that your agent just called—you've won a shot at pitching for Jim Carrey's new sitcom! You dive right in, developing a long list of storylines that feature broad, physical comedy: Jim gets stuck in a gorilla cage, Jim studies ballet, Jim accidentally gets shock therapy.

You show up at the pitch meeting, raring to go, but discover that . . . oops, your agent made a tiny mistake. The star isn't Jim Carrey, it's Drew Carey. And Drew doesn't do pratfalls. Drew doesn't have a rubber face. Drew doesn't get shock therapy.

Suddenly, casting's impact on comedy in a story premise is painfully clear. You politely excuse yourself from the pitch meeting and cruise over to your agent's office to share this revelation with him.

How can we make this lesson work for us?

Part of studying an existing series (a subject that we will discuss later) involves looking at the actors' comedic strengths. Play to those, exploit those, and your comedy will flow more naturally from the characters that the actors portray. John Krasinski (Jim of *The Office*) gives marvelous understated reactions, so use this by subjecting him to outrageous events and pairing him with outlandish characters. Alec Baldwin is able to play imperious and pompous while still remaining likeable, so stick him with a pack of goofballs and underachievers. Charlie Sheen has made a career out of playing a guys' guy and ladies' man—who better to write as an affable, unflappable bad boy?

At the same time, there are instances when *casting against type* can bolster an episode's comedy, especially when filling guest roles. (Casting against type means casting an actor who is known for traits that are the opposite of those that define the character.) My favorite example is Christopher Walken. A man famous for playing menacing psychos and villains, he occasionally pops up as a guest on *Saturday Night Live*, where he is always hilarious in sketches that cast him as a meek geek or neighborhood nutcase. (Resulting in humor from role reversal, but through casting.)

Bottom line, casting has a huge effect on comedy and it is important to tune a script to suit an actor's strengths—something to keep in mind when you attain sitcom producer status, or start sleeping with that producer, and can finally influence those decisions.

Moving On

We have explored several ways to weave comedic tension into a story premise. Our next goal is to build on that tension and draw from that tension as we create sequences and scenes.

5

LEVEL TWO: COMEDY IN SEQUENCES AND SCENES

After brainstorming until your ears explode, you finally come up with the perfect idea for a script. And this premise is funny. You have explored all of its comedy potential, it's got primetime Emmy written all over it.

Now it is time to get serious, time to beat out the story. As in all fiction, a sitcom script must have a dramatic structure, a beginning-middle-end that is both logical and compelling. The difference is, your story also has to get laughs.

So you sit down to map out individual *sequences* and *scenes*. (A sequence is a series of consecutive scenes that feature one continuing action, such as a chase sequence. A scene is a segment of story that occurs in one location over one period of time; change either the location or the time and you have started a new scene.) While developing the story's dramatic structure, you should also explore the next level of comedy in your script. How? Well, you already thought up some humorous sequences and scenes in the premise when you created it; they are the hooks that made the story seem funny in the first place. If you conjured up a "Peter goes to the sperm bank" premise for *Family Guy*, perhaps you envisioned a scene that features Peter's happy discovery that one can actually get paid to contribute sperm. Or scenes that show him lying about his credentials to land the job.

But don't stop there. Don't leave the rest of the humor-building to dialogue alone. As you shape your story, you should harvest a few more of the comedic elements that you planted in the premise. Think big, play with bold, funny ideas. As writer-producer Sheldon Bull points out in his book, *Elephant Bucks*:

Humor comes from exaggeration. . . . Most sitcom characters are created without the "self-edit button" that inhibits all the rest of us. Sitcom
characters aren't as good as we are at pretending to be mature and rational. Sitcom characters are therefore more honest with their emotions
and less inhibited about expressing them. Sitcom characters act more
impulsively than real people. Sitcom characters have big reactions to
problems and situations that real people can take in stride.[1]

Here are some ways to find that humor.

Compound Story Predicaments

Peter wants to be a sperm donor? And he lies on the application? Crank
up the comedy by complicating his situation—add more layers of funny
predicaments. When Peter goes to make his first donation, maybe there's
a slight misunderstanding—he thinks that he actually has to sleep with
the prospective mother. Or Peter's friends find out and try to horn in on
his action. Or Lois suddenly suspects that Peter is playing around. Or, or,
or . . . There are a ton of funny options, *all driven by the original premise.*

Compound a predicament at the story level and the comedic tension
doesn't just double, it increases exponentially. And it prolongs the duration of the funny predicament over a larger section of story. More laughs,
bigger laughs. It isn't just Jim (*The Office*) having to ask Michael to keep
quiet about Jim having a crush on Pam—Michael takes Jim's request to
mean that they're now really close friends, so now Jim has to hang out
with Michael.

What is the difference between predicaments created at this level, in
sequences and scenes, and the type used in the overall premise? Not much.
You can compound a story predicament by adding additional layers of the
same type of predicaments. A "Big Lie" can lead to Bigger and Bigger
Lies, until everything backfires in a funny way.

Or you can mix and match. Maybe a "Big Lie" puts a character between a "Rock and a Hard Place." With a "Dead Body." "Trapped in a
Space." (These worn examples are presented only to make a point; obviously, your goal should be to come up with fresh predicaments that compound an original premise.)

The primary difference between predicaments at the first and second levels of your script is that those used in sequences and scenes are usually more finite events that tend to occur in real time. The predicament pops up, is played out, and then resolved, all in one continuous segment of story.

Stir Up the Character Mix

Screenwriting guru John Truby counsels that drama is about "people acting against people, not things." I am sure that he would say the same thing about comedy.

A great way to draw comedy from a sitcom story is to stir up the character mix. The show's producers wove humor into the overall series premise when they created the original mix, an ensemble of amusing characters that are supposed to interact in funny ways. Now, as you map out sequences and scenes, you might decide to extract even more comedy from that mix by *temporarily* shifting character roles or relationships.

Example? The character mix of *Seinfeld* included a neighbor whom Jerry hated—the infamous Newman. In a typical episode, Jerry and Newman found themselves arguing, competing, and even feuding with each other. But some episodes generated a lot of laughs by temporarily changing the character mix. They featured a sequence in which either Jerry or Newman had to approach the other for assistance or advice; the two characters reversed roles and formed an unnatural alliance that ran contrary to the original series premise. Comedic tension doubled because we were waiting for not only the resolution of the episode's story predicament, but also the inevitable collapse of the temporary alliance. The payoff was extra sweet when that collapse occurred and the boys resumed their feud, and order (the character mix) was restored.

Mix and Match

Obviously, you can also generate humor at the sequence and scene level by mixing story predicaments and character shifts together. To illustrate, if your episode premise involves a character that is hunting for the courage to ask a second character out for a date, you might complicate things by having the second character suddenly show up with a new squeeze. Then, the second character makes things worse by asking the first to befriend the new squeeze. Then, the new squeeze asks the first character for advice on how to seduce the second character. In this example, the first character's original predicament is *compounded by a second predicament*, the request from the second character, and then made unbearable by the requirement that the first character *shift character roles* to play confidant to the squeeze. Tension builds throughout the episode, generating comedy that flows naturally from the story.

Three Things to Remember

As you explore comedy at this, the second level of the script, here are three things to remember:

Escalation

Just as a dramatic plotline should become more involving and compelling as it progresses, so should the comedy in a script. Otherwise, its development seems too linear or flat, or even anticlimactic. Yes, the jokes have to be funny from page one. But usually, the predicaments and the comedic tension that they cause should escalate to a sort of comedy climax in the script's final scenes. (In fact, some series always feature a raucous *comedy block* at the end of each episode.)

Look to the Series Premise

It often seems that the best stories are drawn from a main character's foibles, her human weaknesses. While many a sitcom episode has been based on importing some funny situation from the outside world, you can't go wrong by looking back at the original series premise to find ideas. At the least, the material that you come up with will flow naturally from the characters and seem true to the show.

Be Consistent

When mapping out your sequences and scenes, remember the importance of maintaining a consistent style of comedy. Find the right mix—the right tone of humor, the right amount of humor—and make sure that it is reflected in all sections of your script. Otherwise, if some sequences seem hilarious while others read like a funeral announcement, you might have a problem. If you see inconsistencies, take the time now to review and reshape your scenes before writing any dialogue—better to do it now than when your judgment is clouded by funny line jokes.

Moving On

We have demonstrated that if you plant humor in a story premise, it is easier to create funny, natural sequences and scenes. Now that we have developed a story chock-full of comedy, let's discuss the art of writing funny dialogue.

6

LEVEL THREE: COMEDY IN DIALOGUE AND ACTIONS

Now comes what many consider to be the most enjoyable part of script-writing—dialogue. If you have done your job right, you have constructed a story that is not only fresh and exciting, it is also a comedy-generating machine. It is brimming with humorous situations and characters that automatically suggest a number of funny lines. And, since those lines are *drawn from* the story rather than *forced into* it, they should sound completely natural. (If you haven't done your job right, if you haven't explored the comedy potential of your premise, then you must now generate most of your humor through jokes and wordplay alone—not always an easy task.)

How do you take advantage of all of your groundwork? How do you make that premise-driven comedy pay off?

The raw materials are in place, so now it comes down to turning your funny ideas into funny jokes. Setups and punchlines. Only, we're not talking those obvious one-liners that pepper a comedian's monologue. Humor in dialogue should be absolutely seamless. Every funny line should sound just like something a character would say (under the given circumstances of a scene).

How do you create these seamless, just-like-a-character, non-monologue-like jokes? It helps to know a little about basic joke mechanics, so let's start there; after all, the do's and don'ts of building jokes apply whether you are writing topical gags for Conan O'Brien or a clever retort for Dwight Schrute. Along the way, we'll look at excerpts of produced sitcom scripts to illustrate how those clunky joke elements can be magically transformed into smooth, funny dialogue.

> *NOTE: As much as I believe that writers can benefit by studying comedy theory and the creative process, you don't want to get too hung up on joke mechanics. The funniest lines that you create will probably just pour out onto the paper while you are writing away, born of instinct rather than conscious thought. So, yes, arm yourself with technical knowledge, but be aware that its greatest value lies in editing and repairing, not creating.*

Building Jokes

You know the basic model—setup, then punchline. More precisely, a setup, or straight line, introduces the subject of the joke and hints at some complication or incongruity, producing tension. The punchline supplies a twist that resolves the joke in an unexpected fashion, releasing that tension. Laughter and gainful employment follow.

While punchlines always get the big headlines, setups are the true unsung heroes of joke warfare. Here are a few pointers to remember when beginning a joke.

Setups

The Setup Should Be Reasonable

The goal of a joke is to reel the audience in with a reasonable setup, then club it over the head with an unexpected punchline. The key to reeling the audience in is to present a situation that seems completely feasible, logical, even unremarkable. Otherwise, if the setup seems improbable or odd, the audience will know that something is up. All surprise will be lost and the punchline will fall flat.

Consider the setup in the following joke from an episode of *My Name Is Earl*. Earl, Randy, and Catalina are relaxing in a hotel room when Randy gets a surprising letter from Earl's ex-wife, Joy:

RANDY
(OPENS HIS MAIL AND STARTS READING
SLOWLY) You—are—cordially—invited—to
Joy and Darnell's wedding.

EARL
(CONFUSED) Joy's getting married? (LOOKS
OUT THE DOOR) I wonder if Willie dropped
my invitation in the parking lot.

CATALINA
I don't think so. This says "Randy
Hickey plus anybody but Earl."[1]

Anything remarkable about this setup? No. Ex-wives can remarry and an invitation can be dropped in a parking lot, right? So the setup—Earl's invite is missing—seemed like a perfectly normal bit of conversation. But while you probably guessed that Earl wasn't invited, few would guess that "anybody but Earl" was welcome. So the punchline manages to supply an unexpected twist.

Many Shapes and Forms

A setup can consist of one line, several lines, or the same line repeated. Part of a setup might be visual—a character gives a funny reaction, or someone is discovered in a compromising circumstance. Whatever shape a setup takes, it usually contains at least two parts: First, it introduces the basic premise of the joke (the topic about to be covered), and then it provides a beat or two of development (caused by complications or an incongruity). This second part of the setup is *very* important. Without it, there is not enough tension to make the joke pay off—the punchline can't provide a funny twist, it just comes off as additional information.

Consider these lines from the pilot for *30 Rock*. Liz Lemon (named "Lisa" in this draft) has just met her new boss, Jack, a corporate suit who works for GE, and they're sparring about control of her show:

JACK
Are you familiar with the award-winning
GE Tri-vection oven?

LISA
I don't cook very much.

JACK
Sure. I got you. New York third-wave
feminist. College-educated. Single and
pretending to be happy about it. Over-
scheduled, under-sexed. You buy any
magazine that says "healthy body image"
on the cover, but your kitchen's got
nothing but SnackWell's and expired
yogurts. You reject traditional female
roles, but every two years you take up
knitting for a week.

PETE
(IMPRESSED) That's dead on.

LISA
Are you gonna guess my weight now?

JACK
You don't want me to do that.[2]

In the first part of the setup, Liz tries to shut Jack down by deflecting his boasting about the oven, by saying she doesn't "cook very much." In the second part, Jack refuses to be shut down and launches into detailed, intrusive speculation about her life. (Funny stuff that creates tension, and it reveals much about both characters.) Not only does this all serve to set up the big punchline coming up (about him guessing her weight), but the speech itself also includes several mini-jokes along the way, little observations that are funny because they are truthful and we can relate.

However, if the writers had cut back on the second part of the setup, the development, we'd have gotten something like this . . .

> JACK
> Are you familiar with the award-winning
> GE Tri-vection oven?
>
> LISA
> I don't cook very much.
>
> JACK
> Sure. I got you. New York third-wave
> feminist.
>
> LISA
> Are you gonna guess my weight now?
>
> JACK
> You don't want me to do that.

Still funny but not as funny. Plus, it seems much more openly hostile, which isn't true to the characters in this show. Clearly, that second part of the setup, the development of comedic tension, was very important.

Spreading Out the Setup

In good dialogue, the jokes are invisible. The script doesn't read like a bad comedian's stand-up routine, rife with blatant setups and predictable punchlines. Different parts of a setup might even be spaced out within a scene, making them less obvious. Or elements of a setup might occur long before the punchline, even several scenes before it, comfortably laced into earlier dialogue. When the unsuspecting viewer finally does trip over the punchline, the joke not only scores on its own merit, it gets extra points for artful design.

Example? Here's part of a scene from *Two and a Half Men*. The boy, Jake, is about to be suspended for giving his teacher the bird. His uncle, Charlie (Sheen), is urging him to apologize:

> JAKE
> But I'm not sorry.

> CHARLIE
> You're not listening. You don't have to
> be sorry, just say it. Or better still,
> just shut up and look sorry. You've got
> those big cute eyes. Use 'em![3]

By showing a parental figure giving a kid very nonparental advice, the joke creates comedic tension and gets a laugh. But this bit also serves as the setup for a payoff that comes pages later, when the kid is delivering a weak apology to the teacher and gets nudged into giving her a "wide, doe-eyed 'I'm sorry' look." Then, when that doesn't work for the kid, the writers top the second joke by having Uncle Charlie give her the very same look.

If the first bit hadn't set up the concept of going cute-eyes to charm the teacher, creating an initial level of tension, the second and third jokes would have seemed far less funny.

No Hints

A setup should not hint at its punchline or it will ruin its surprise, and the joke. As always, less is more. Consider these lines from an early episode of *The Simpsons*. Homer is hosting a barbecue and Barney shows up carrying a large beer keg:

> BARNEY
> Hey, Homer. Thanks for inviting me to
> your barbecue.

> HOMER
> Wow, Barney! You brought a whole beer
> keg.

> BARNEY
> Yeah. Where can I fill it up?[4]

If the setup had hinted at the punchline, the joke would have been ruined. As in:

> BARNEY
> Hey, Homer. Thanks for inviting me to your barbecue.
>
> HOMER
> Wow, Barney! You brought a whole beer keg. Is that thing full?
>
> BARNEY
> No. Where can I fill it up?[4]

Life Is a Setup

Many times, as discussed earlier in the book, universally shared miseries can serve as half of your setup. Go after someone or something that causes tension in people's lives, and that tension will feed right into your joke. Consider how much the following excerpt from a *Seinfeld* episode depends on our ability to relate to a joke's premise. In this classic bit, Jerry and Elaine are trying to rent a car, but the obnoxious rental agent, Lydia, is refusing to honor Jerry's reservation:

> JERRY
> Well, what was the point to the reservation? Why did I make a reservation?
>
> LYDIA
> I didn't take your reservation. Let me speak to my supervisor.
> (LYDIA CROSSES TO HER SUPERVISOR.)
>
> JERRY
> (TO ELAINE) She's going to talk to her

supervisor. You know what she's saying
over there? "Hey Marge, these people
think I'm talking to you so just pretend
you're talking to me. Okay, now you
start talking."

ELAINE
(PLAYING ALONG) "Oh you mean like this?
So it looks like I'm saying something
back to you even though I'm not saying
anything at all."

JERRY
"Good. Now I'll say something else and
they won't yell at me because they think
I'm checking with you."

ELAINE
"Great. I guess that's enough. I'll see
you later."

JERRY
"Okay. Thanks. I'll go back and talk to
them and tell them I spoke to you."

LYDIA
(RETURNS) I'm sorry, my supervisor says
there's nothing we can do.[5]

Of course, life's contribution to joke setups isn't just limited to comedic-tension-building *shared miseries*. Sometimes quick references to *shared cultural experiences* (e.g., a famous TV show or infamous celebrity, a religious ritual, the president—all things *Star Trek*) can contribute to a setup. When the audience catches the connection, the joke wins extra points for being clever.

Tension Can Supply the Setup and the Punchline

Series like *Entourage* and *Californication* represent a newish trend toward adult shows that push the boundaries of what used to be deemed good taste. They are considered funny shows, but do they feature a lot of jokes? Do they offer up a lot of punchlines or are they more about hip dialogue and snappy comebacks? They're supposed to be comedies, but where does their humor come from?

At least some of it comes from:

- Titillation caused by outrageous actions and language, from casual sex to creative cursing

- Classic comedy archetypes, such as Vince (the naive hero), Ari (the trickster), Karen (the temptress), and Johnny (the fool)

- Very dynamic characters that raise tension by being sexually aggressive, confrontational, and opportunistic (compared to typical, more passive sitcom characters)

- Classic story predicaments built into the series premise, like having four regular guys unleashed in Hollywood (fish out of water in *Entourage*) and forcing an irresponsible rake to deal with domestic issues (role reversal in *Californication*)

These shows generate plenty of comedic tension through their characters and storylines, but don't feature many traditional dialogue jokes. Instead, many times, the setup and even the punchline take the form of story beats rather than dialogue. Sometimes it's a blend of both.

Example: In one episode of *Entourage*, the setup for a funny bit was launched when Johnny boasted that he had just landed a date with a woman he lusted after years ago. He invites Turtle to double-date with him, guaranteeing that Turtle will get laid if he comes along.

The setup is developed/complicated when the boys meet up with the two women, and Turtle's date turns out to be loud and unattractive. The dialogue is mildly amusing, but the funniest moments come more from facial reactions and outrageous behavior than from punchlines. Comedic tension grows because Johnny might lose his golden opportunity if Turtle decides to bail.

> *NOTE: Is this "double-date-disaster" premise new? Hardly. But the show's use of this worn predicament succeeded because of titillation and the characters' bold/shameless actions; they were so open about sex and their intention to have sex that this version of the story seemed just new enough.*

Then we get even more tension: While at a restaurant, Turtle's date is so completely obnoxious that he tells Johnny he can't take any more. Johnny begs him to stay and Turtle reluctantly agrees, and we get a rare sitcom-y punchline involving the restaurant bill when Johnny has the nerve to ask, "We're still going to split this, right?" (An example of a setup coming from story and a punchline delivered via dialogue.)

Then the big payoff: The two couples hit the hot tub and Johnny is finally about to realize his ultimate sex fantasy, but the girls announce that they're switching partners! Johnny's gorgeous date walks off to have sex with Turtle, and scheming Johnny is stuck having sex with the obnoxious friend.

In this example, the setup, comedic tension, and punchline are all supplied by character actions, not dialogue. There is dialogue and some of it is amusing, but the big payoff comes from the final plot twist. In *dramedies* (i.e., shows that are half-drama, half-comedy) like *Entourage* and *Californication*, we tend to see fewer jokes and few punchlines, but the comedic tension is always percolating and unexpected story turns provide much of the humor.

On a related note . . .

Tension Added by Story

A joke within a story has an advantage over a stand-alone joke—the comedic tension of its setup is often boosted by *dramatic* tension in the story. Meaning, if a predicament that has been woven into the story already has us on the edge of our seats, that overall tension contributes to the weight of each individual joke in that story sequence.

Similarly, if tension exists in certain character relationships (e.g., the sexual tension between Pam and Jim at *The Office*), that character baggage might also contribute to the weight of a joke. This synergistic advantage, over individual jokes presented out of context, is subtle, but every little bit helps when writing comedy. Which is why many of our favorite comedians give their stand-up monologues a structure, a beginning-middle-end that develops and exploits dramatic tension.

Punchlines

Writers use different terms to describe a punchline—"switch," "reversal," "surprise," "twist," "a surprise twist," etc. I think of a punchline as a sudden twist that makes both sense and nonsense; it resolves the setup, but from a different direction than the audience was led to expect. In doing so, it utilizes the characteristics of comedy that we discussed earlier—incongruity, surprise, truth, aggression, and brevity.

Here are a few things to remember when writing punchlines:

Last Things Last

In most cases, the punchline (or punch word) comes at the very end of a joke. Otherwise, the surprise is lost. There is no incongruity left to conquer, no tension to release, no amusing payoff. Consider this exchange from a script for *The Office*—Dwight is lecturing Jim on how to be an informed voter:

> JIM
> So what do you read?
>
> DWIGHT
> I read the *Scranton Christian Science Reader* and the *Scranton Daily Worker*.
>
> (JIM TALKING HEAD—RESTAURANT)
>
> JIM
> I'm pretty sure Dwight doesn't realize that the *Daily Worker* is a communist paper. I think that he thinks it's a paper for people who work. Daily.[6]

Which is much funnier than ...

```
JIM
. . . that the Daily Worker is a com-
munist paper. I think that he thinks
it's a daily paper for people who
work.
```

So, simple rule, put the punchline last.

Don't Go Past the Joke

In dialogue, the punchline doesn't just come at the end of the joke; it usually comes at the end of a character's speech. Otherwise, if the character keeps talking after successfully delivering the payoff, he might trample the thing—which is worse than never having joked at all.

If multiple jokes are included in the same speech, they are sometimes separated by scripted pauses (using dialogue cues like "beat" or "pause," or an ellipsis placed between sentences). However, it's best to trust your actors and director to leave the necessary space, a little breathing room, after each joke. True, they will sometimes plow over a subtle punchline, but that's better than clogging up your dialogue with unwanted directions.

> *NOTE: Is it ever okay to break these "rules"? Absolutely. For instance, on some occasions, the rhythms of a character's speech patterns are such that she will deliver a punchline and then add a related phrase or two. Maybe the character is naturally verbose, or rambling because of some story element, or adding humorous embellishment. If you feel that the additional words supply a necessary rhythm to her speech and are true to her character, then go ahead, add the extra dialogue.*

Topping a Joke

Sometimes a joke lends itself to a series of punchlines, one after the other, each funnier than the last. Writers love these jokes because they are so wonderfully economical. You make a joke and get the laugh, then add a second punchline, and maybe a third—all based on one setup!

Here's another example from *The Office*. Michael is trying to think up some prize incentives to get his salespeople fired up, and clueless Dwight is trying to help.

```
MICHAEL
Well, first what we have to do is find
out what motivates people more than
anything else.

DWIGHT (OS)
Sex.
(CAMERA ZOOMS OUT TO REVEAL DWIGHT
STANDING BEHIND MICHAEL.)

MICHAEL
It's illegal, can't do that. Next best
thing.

DWIGHT
Torture.⁷
```

First, we have a reasonable setup—Michael wants to beef up sales and needs to think up some great prize. Then comes the first punchline, set up partly by our familiarity with Dwight's character and his misguided views on managing people. Then, Michael tops the first punchline by suggesting that they can't offer sex, but only because it's not legal. Then, Dwight tops it again with his second suggestion—how about torture!

This last jump from sex to torture is so huge it's completely unexpected and very funny. And it's funny on several levels—it's truthful, because torture does motivate, and it associates sex and relationships with torture, which is somehow truthful and funny (at least to those of us who are married).

Not only does *topping a joke* bump up your joke count, it also increases the chances of getting big laughs. Why? Because the first joke establishes a momentum, gets the audience smiling. Then you hit them again and again—quickly, before they can recover. The audience is caught off balance; they're surprised not once but several times. They laugh more, and louder.

In sitcoms and joke-rich films, toppers are your best friend. (Not usually in dramedies—they can call too much attention to the joke in those stories.) But there are three things to watch for when adding punchline upon punchline: First, you probably shouldn't top a joke more than two times, max. Any more and the audience will notice.

Second, take care to not dilute a healthy joke by plowing over it with additional punchlines. Some jokes are best left alone. Perhaps they deliver an important dramatic moment, or they are critical to a scene's pacing, or they just feel like they say all that needs to be said on a subject. So rather than ruin a good thing, think twice before piling on punchlines.

Third, just to warn you—use the term "topper" in front of other comedy writers and they will line up to make fun of you. The concept hasn't aged but the label is dated, yet nobody has come up with a better word. So, just so you know . . .

Running Gags

Running gags are another great way to earn comedy bonus points. Tell a complete joke in one scene, and then come back to it two or three times later in the story. (When you refer back to the original joke, the new punchline is called a *callback* joke.) You might create a running gag by having the same character restate the original punchline under different circumstances, resulting in a fresh laugh. Or different characters might restate the same punchline under different circumstances. Or different characters might state variations of the same joke, all playing off the original setup.

Sometimes, each time a repeating punchline pops up, it takes on a second meaning, making it both funny and clever. And sometimes, the final installment of a running gag is presented with an ironic twist or reversal, ending the joke series with a big laugh.

Consider this example from *Two and a Half Men*: Young Jake's teacher is threatening to suspend him for giving her the finger, so Uncle Charlie decides to change her mind by turning on the charm. He starts by getting young Jake out of the way. . . .

```
                CHARLIE
           (TO JAKE) Here, go to the vending
           machines and get Miss Pasternak a cup
```

```
of coffee and a bag of Skittles.
(JAKE RUNS OFF.)


CHARLIE
(THEN, SMILING, TO MISS PASTERNAK) I'm
sorry, it is Miss Pasternak, right?⁸
```

The last line is funny because we know Charlie is a womanizer, and it's clear that he is resorting to his one talent, seduction, to manipulate this woman. He succeeds, and scenes later, the gag resurfaces to signal that it's mission accomplished—Charlie has taken control and is relishing his new "hot for teacher" relationship:

```
(SHE TAKES HIM IN HER ARMS AND KISSED
HIM.)


CHARLIE
Oh, Miss Pasternak.


MISS PASTERNAK
Why don't you ever call me by my first
name?


CHARLIE
I don't know. This is so much hotter.⁹
```

But then, scenes later, the tables turn when Charlie tries to dump the teacher (because she's a wacko), and the gag resurfaces to show that he is losing control. He makes his move at a restaurant . . .

```
CHARLIE
. . . Listen, Delores, we need to
talk.


MISS PASTERNAK
Oh, call me Miss Pasternak.
```

```
CHARLIE
Uh . . . not right now. Delores, you're
a terrific woman and I've enjoyed being
with you very much, but I know in my
heart that you can do so much better
than me.

MISS PASTERNAK
Okay, I understand.

CHARLIE
Good. Thank you.

MISS PASTERNAK
You're insecure. But don't worry, I'm
not going to abandon you.[10]
```

Things quickly go from bad to worse: Miss Pasternak reveals that God has told her that Charlie and she belong together. She ignores all of Charlie's objections, and at the end of the scene, the running gag is used to deliver one last bit of irony—Charlie, the great manipulator of women, finds himself trapped and as helpless as a little schoolboy.

```
MISS PASTERNAK
[I'm going] to be God's instrument. To
help you become a better man, to achieve
your potential. Now, sit up straight
and eat your pie.

CHARLIE
All right.

MISS PASTERNAK
"All right" what?

CHARLIE
All right, Miss Pasternak.
```

(CHARLIE GLUMLY EATS HIS PIE AS . . .)[11]

Why do running gags earn extra laughs? They're quick and economical because much of the setup has already been delivered. And perhaps the audience is impressed by how clever you are for retooling one joke so that it can be used several times. And perhaps the audience is pleased with its own cleverness at having caught the subtle joke connection.

Occasionally, a running gag will become a standard element of a show's premise, recurring in many episodes or even every episode of the series. For instance, *Seinfeld* got a laugh every time Jerry encountered his hated neighbor, Newman; each man greeted the other by pronouncing his name with obvious distaste, setting a humorous tone for the exchange that followed.

On a more morbid level, *South Park* helped to make a name for itself by featuring a running gag (during the show's early years) in which a primary character, Kenny, was killed *in almost every episode*. Week after week, the poor kid was subjected to a violent death, only to reappear—without explanation—at the top of the following week's episode. The gag generated comedic suspense with little additional setup, because viewers were just waiting to see how Kenny would be killed in each story.

Finally, running gags are sometimes referred to as *runners*. However, many people also use this term to refer to a very minor subplot of a story, which may or may not be funny.

> *NOTE: Sitcoms eat up a lot of jokes, usually two to four per page. So being able to play several punchlines off the same setup, by topping a joke or using running gags, can come in very handy.*

When You Can't Find the Right Punchline

Here's a tip: When you can't find the right punchline, go back and check the setup. Once, I agonized over a joke through several drafts of a script, spending hours trying to replace a single weak punchline. A producer who was passing by my office tossed off a casual suggestion—"Change the setup?"

Hmm. I went back, tweaked the joke's premise, and suddenly—half a dozen great punchlines popped into my head. Problem solved.

Producer MICHAEL REISS: One thing I learned from *The Simpsons* is, if you're in a hole, if you need a joke somewhere, there's always a joke there no matter how difficult the spot is. It has to be funny, it's got to serve plot, and it can't make the character look bad. And you'll sit there and you might work for two hours, but you'll get it, that joke always exists.

The moral of this tale? Sometimes even producers have a good idea. And if a punchline isn't working, *check the setup*. See if you need to establish a different incongruity or a bigger contrast in the first half of your joke.

Go for Literal

When stuck for a funny punchline, see if you can exploit the literal meaning of the joke's setup. As Melvin Helitzer states in his book *Comedy Writing Secrets*, by playing off of "the literal meaning of a key word, we surprise the audience, who's automatically interpreted the expression with its traditional reference. It makes logic illogical . . . 'Call me a taxi.' [leads to] 'Okay, you're a taxi.'"[12]

Here's a better example, from *My Name Is Earl*. Earl has convinced a senile old woman that he's her long dead husband, and is enjoying a meatloaf dinner with her while Randy hides under the table. Earl sneaks Randy some food—it's awful, Randy chokes, and Earl makes choking sounds to cover up. Once the old lady exits, Randy comes out from under the table . . .

```
           RANDY
           This stinks, Earl.


           EARL
           (RE: MEATLOAF) Hold your nose. It tastes
           better than it smells.


           RANDY
           Not the meatloaf. Having to hide.[13]
```

Earl's interpretation of the word "stinks" is funny because it makes sense but isn't the response we expected after watching this scene. The payoff is both literal and ironic.

An interesting thing about literal jokes? We tend to see them coming from either very dumb or very clever characters—characters who see things in the simplest light, or those who are clever enough to deliver an ironic retort.

Funny Actions

Okay, we have discussed how setups and punchlines can be smoothly woven into dialogue. Now let's get to the "Actions" part of this chapter. Meaning that sitcom writing isn't just about verbal humor. It also features funny actions and sounds. Here are some examples:

Mannerisms

Recognizable actors and the characters that they portray are usually known for certain physical traits. They exhibit funny mannerisms that we have come to expect and adore. Ray Romano can get ten seconds of laughs by milking his deer-caught-in-the-headlights look. Charlie Sheen can shrug his way out of any difficulty. Homer Simpson always greets his mistakes with "D'oh!"

While many mannerisms are developed by actors or are part of an actor's real-life personality, some are created by a show's writers as they attempt to build comedy into a show's premise. Something to keep in mind when you're creating new characters.

Stage Business

Funny actions can take the form of an actor doing *stage business* while performing in a scene. Meaning, an actor might fiddle with something or perform an amusing physical action while talking, both to get a laugh and to help define his character. Sometimes stage business is designed to contrast with ongoing dialogue, to beef up comedic tension. Sometimes stage business can build up to its own punchline; as when a character finally stops fiddling with the fragile knickknack and puts it back on the shelf— then the shelf crashes down! And sometimes a bit of minor business, unrelated to anything else in the story, might be used merely to increase the humorous tone of a scene.

A Take

A character is surprised, he reacts with a funny expression, and we laugh. Called a *take*, a look, or a reaction, the character's simple physical response is frequently the only punchline that is needed to complete a joke. If you feel that someone might miss the payoff, it's okay for a script to indicate when a take should occur, perhaps by providing the brief cue " (REACTS) " or by indicating a pause (or "(BEAT)") before the next line. Better yet, let the actor and the director decide when a take is appropriate.

Slapstick

Falling, dropping, whacking, breaking things. Since Og and Mog first tripped into a tar pit, we've gotten laughs out of cartoonish violence and physical mishaps. Tension, surprise, aggression—these gags have it all. And they often utilize the same structure as a dialogue joke, moving from setup to payoff.

An example of a slapstick setup? One character gives his friend a loving pat; the friend pats back, a little too hard; the first character, irritated, gives a little shove back; soon, the two friends are wrestling like maniacs on the carpet. The incongruity of the setup comes from friends making friendly gestures that suddenly turn hostile. It's surprising and it rings true, because we have all experienced similar (if less violent) misunderstandings.

Physical actions can also serve as the setup or punchline for a dialogue joke, as illustrated in this classic bit from *Seinfeld*: Kramer decides to test the strength of his latest invention, an oil-filled balloon, by dropping it out of a high window. Tension builds when Kramer trespasses in an office building to perform the test and uses the help of a student intern even though the kid's college has canceled his internship (with Kramer). Just as Kramer counts down to the balloon drop, Jerry's new girlfriend appears in the parking lot below, pausing right at ground zero (launching the setup). Jerry yells to her, but she misinterprets the warning (dialogue develops the setup and builds tension). The oil-filled balloon drops and . . . Even though we don't actually see the aftermath, the (physical) payoff gets a huge laugh.

Slapstick humor is considered very broad, even unrefined, but it can be a great way to get big laughs—*if* broad humor is appropriate for your show premise.

Funny Visuals

Some funny visuals don't involve physical injury. Perhaps a character starting a new job is required to wear a humiliating "House of Wieners" uniform. Or a couple of would-be lovers dining in a restaurant are so hungry for each other that they eat in a sexually suggestive manner.

Sometimes sight gags involve someone hiding something, such as an old girlfriend whom the wife doesn't know about, or a thousand pieces of a just-busted vase. As the guilty character lies to cover his tracks, the contrast between what he says and what we see (or know to be true) creates an amusing incongruity. It provides chuckles as we go and builds to a big, satisfying payoff when the truth is finally revealed.

Funny visuals are frequently used to get a laugh out of a character entering a scene. As in, "But who could possibly be so stupid?" followed immediately by Stupid's entrance. This joke has been done to death, but variations will probably be used throughout eternity because they provide a clumsy but convenient way to get Stupid into the story.

As with slapstick humor, a funny visual can serve as a setup or a punchline. However, not all sight gags are part of a fully structured joke. Some bits are just funny to see, or maybe they contribute to the dramatic tension of a scene.

Funny Sounds

Sometimes sound can supply a punchline or boost the humor of a joke. Examples include a scream of surprise from the next room, a car crashing outside (because someone goofed), someone falling down stairs, a toilet flushing at the worst time, a character whispering something that is then repeated loudly enough for all to hear.

On a more subtle level, writers can even get laughs out of a simple phonetic pattern—alliteration. Just begin several words in the same phrase with the same sound and, for some reason, that amuses us. Consider these lines from an episode of *King of the Hill*. Hank has rushed to the doctor after suddenly becoming ill:

```
HANK
How bad is it?


DOCTOR
Your heart's in good shape—considering
you seem like a man who butters his
bacon.14
```

Is this (alliteration) even funny? Change the doctor's line to "... butters his steak," and see if you notice a difference.

Freud suggested that our favorable response to aural rhythms evolves from childhood learning-play, when we discover the pleasurable effects "which arise from a repetition of what is similar, a rediscovery of what is familiar, similarity of sound, etc."[15] Yeah, well, maybe. Whatever the explanation, there are moments when a dose of alliteration adds just the right leavening to an otherwise unfunny speech. By itself, it rarely gets a laugh. But sometimes it earns a smile or, at the least, keeps the material from losing all comedic momentum during a more serious passage.

Foreign Accents

Another (not so subtle) source of funny sounds is the foreign accent. Foreigners are fair game even in today's politically correct environment, though most writers elect to create stories that laugh with, rather than at, those characters. In sitcoms, foreign characters can make goofy mistakes just like everyone else, but they're not often portrayed as fools, crooks, or sleazebags. The boldest comedies, like *South Park* and *The Simpsons*, frequently flip stereotypes on their head by using foreign characters or the mistreatment of foreign characters, like Starvin' Marvin and Apu, to target bigotry against foreigners.

Of course, foreign characters offer more comedic value than just mangled pronunciations and funny phrasings. The biggest laughs can be found by exploring the many differences between a foreign character's native culture and life in America. Talk about fish-out-of-water humor—look beneath that foreign accent and you'll find plenty of amusing contrasts to drive jokes and story turns. (Some differences will be innocent and others not so—a show's premise and your personal tastes will dictate which you should or shouldn't use.)

Miscellaneous Comedy Tips

Now that we have explored some of the basics of joke mechanics, here are a few general tips about creating comedy:

Less Is More . . . Usually

Always remember that less is more, whether you are trimming excess words out of a punchline or dumping an entire scene from a script. As Sol Saks notes in his book *The Craft of Comedy Writing* . . .

> *Clarity* and *simplicity* are, again, desirable in all writing, but necessary in comedy. They are crucial ingredients because in comedy you *must* have your audience's undivided attention. If they puzzle over a word or thought ever so slightly, if they are distracted by an unnecessary word or phrase, you lose their concentration and the temperamental comedy disappears in a huff.

Saks adds that "the best comedy has *precision*, which, put simply, is the exact word in its proper place."[16]

Come on, a word or two can make a difference? Absolutely. Every syllable affects the rhythm of a joke. Every surplus word hurts your chances of keeping the audience focused until you can surprise them with the punchline. A good rule of thumb is that anytime you ask yourself if something should stay in or not, you should probably go with "not."

Any exceptions to the less-is-more rule? Sure. You might create a moment or a character for which *more* is more. Ellen DeGeneres sometimes uses this technique when looking for humor in awkward situations; she babbles and babbles, and then babbles about her babbling, making a bad situation worse by dragging it out. A person's natural inclination would be to say as little as possible and beat a hasty retreat, but Ellen gets laughs by going for more rather than less.

To sum up, keep it lean and clean. Clutter and imbalance can kill a joke. Unless they *are* the joke.

Bigger Really Is Better

Most comedy writers agree that bigger is better. Exaggerate parts of a joke and you are more likely to get a big laugh. Laura Petrie didn't reveal Alan Brady's baldness only to her friend Millie—she broadcast it to the entire nation. Michael Scott doesn't offend just one coworker with a racial joke—he lectures the whole office on diversity issues. Little Kenny of *South Park* didn't just take a ribbing every week—the kid was killed. The lesson? Unless it runs contrary to a character's nature or the show's premise, think big when going for big laughs.

Small Truths, Big Laughs

A reminder: The truth can be funny! If you strike a universal chord with the audience, you will score big points. Consider how much the following joke from *The Office* depends on our ability to relate to its premise. Michael has just urged the troops to hit the phones and make more sales. Dwight, anxious to best his rival, Jim, dives in, all juiced up:

>   DWIGHT
>   (AS HE DIALS) Surf's up, Jim. Watch me
>   ride this wave of inspiration! (GRINS,
>   INTO PHONE) Yes, I'll hold.[17]

The punchline works because it rings true—we can all relate to being really juiced up, and then stalled by someone or something.

Remember the Rule: There Are No Rules

Humorist James Thurber (1894–1961) once said that "the only rules comedy can tolerate are those of taste, and the only limitations those of libel."

Censorship is death to comedy, yet we exist in an era of political correctness. Is modern humor suffering? Not really. In fact, many of today's ethnic comedians have boosted their careers by turning insult humor on its head. Lifting a page from the Woody Allens and Rodney Dangerfields of yesteryear, they have taken non-PC jokes and directed them at themselves. Instead of maligning their own personal shortcomings, these performers have targeted political hot buttons such as (their own) race and culture. They dish out seemingly insensitive putdowns, but it's hard to take offense when they themselves are the ones being insulted. Their approach lessens the pressure to be PC, which enables them to target even the most sensitive of subjects.

Yes, there will always be opinions about what is or isn't acceptable comedy, but a writer's job is to tackle delicate issues, to be fresh and daring. So heed your own tastes, and those of your producers, and just go and be funny in the best way that you know how.

About All of These Labels

The problem with discussing joke mechanics is that you start tossing out a lot of labels and rules. It just seems so . . . mechanical. But I believe that, just as music composers study chord progressions and orchestration, comedy writers should learn the tools of their craft. Some writers disagree, arguing that one cannot learn comedy by studying joke structure and such. Yet when asked why a particular joke doesn't work, they describe the problem in the same terms presented above. (They must have learned the stuff back in the womb.)

No, not everyone is capable of writing comedy. But those who are naturally funny can certainly hone their skills by studying the creative process and learning the craft. So watch shows, examine scripts, take classes, read books, and keep writing. And, if possible, find a professional mentor or two, as famed comedy writer Larry Gelbart (*M*A*S*H*, *Tootsie*, *A Funny Thing Happened on the Way to the Forum*) managed to do early in his career:

When I worked under Bill Manhoff's tutelage on *Duffy's Tavern*, I had just turned 17. Other than having the knack of being funny on demand—of being able to provide jokes that fit a specified situation—I was not familiar with the vocabulary of the trade, the articulation to describe what kind of punchlines those situations might require. If that sounds vague, perhaps it still is to me after all these years. I guess what I learned most from Bill was just punching away until what seemed the right line finally dawned on me or anyone else in the room.[18]

Learn the craft, develop your skills. How you do it doesn't matter.

Finding Your Comedic Voice

Different writers have different strengths and each has her own take on what makes something funny. A benefit of developing a script's humor from the ground (or premise) up is that, whatever your strengths are—story structure, funny dialogue, physical comedy—this approach prompts you to explore all types of humor at all levels of the script. It encourages you to develop all aspects of your comedic voice rather than merely settle for, say, cramming funny jokes into unfunny scenes because funny jokes are what you do best.

Conversely, this from-the-ground-up approach can also help you to identify and compensate for weaknesses in your writing. Are your characters dull? Are your stories too serious? Do your scripts start funny, then fade? It's hard to overlook these problems when your first priority is to draw comedy from the overall premise. When problems do surface, this approach gives you a better shot at identifying where you might be weak, so that you can train yourself to apply more energy in those areas.

Moving On

So ends our discussion of premise-driven comedy. It's just three simple steps:

- Weave funny elements into your story premise

- Exploit and compound those elements at the sequence and scene level

- Draw from your story's built-in humor to create natural, seamless dialogue and actions

It's all about *building* rather than *repairing*. Do your job right and you will get Laura Petrie winning on a game show—and humiliating her husband's boss. Or Jack Lemmon and Tony Curtis running from mobsters—disguised as female musicians. Or Cartman, Homer, Liz, or Dwight posting a little joke on Facebook—and being banned from the Internet.

Now let's look at how comedy writing theory can translate into a professional sitcom script.

Part 2

Writing a Professional Script

7

DOING YOUR HOMEWORK

How do you get work as a television sitcom writer? By flashing a fancy Harvard degree? By submitting that play you wrote for Mom's church group? By showing off those clever articles about breastfeeding?

You get sitcom work by showing people that you can do sitcom work, by submitting sitcom spec scripts and perhaps a sitcom pilot script. (A *spec* is a sample script that consists of an episode of an existing television series, written without pay or the producers' authorization.) Before hitting the job trail, a would-be writer should have *at least* one dynamite sitcom spec under his arm, preferably two. This section of our book will show you how to create those work samples by following the same steps used by working professionals.

Sure, some producers and executives boast that they like to judge writers by reading other types of original work—stage plays, movie scripts, books, etc. But only a bold few actually hire new writers based on such material. Too frequently, the response is "Fantastic, great stuff. And do you have any sitcom specs I can see? Just to show the others, of course."

And, yes, the business has actually gone through cycles when a Harvard degree increased the odds of a person getting work. Some top writer-producers have come from Harvard and prefer to hire its alums. (I was actually confronted with the Harvard question during a pitch meeting once; I responded with "Sorry, I went to Brown. Guess that makes me, what, only 80 percent as funny?" Oddly enough, I didn't get that job.)

And, of course, there are other ways to break in. Exposure as a successful stand-up comedian might do it. Or if your Uncle Morty runs a studio, that could definitely do it. But those clever breastfeeding articles? Don't think so. And even if you are blessed with an Uncle Morty, when he goes to twist some poor producer's arm, he'll still need a writing sample to stick in the guy's other hand.

My point is that many people in Hollywood like to sound encouraging and open-minded; it's flattering to them and it keeps them out of negative, confrontational conversations. But talk is cheap—for them. The truth is that the odds of getting work in a particular creative form are best if you can prove that you can write *in that form*. (Analogy: You might be a great proctologist, but does that make you qualified to perform heart surgery?)

In fact, the distinction goes even further than that. When hiring writers, many producers differentiate between writing samples based on types of sitcoms. You submitted a *Family Guy* spec? "Sorry, we don't do a cartoon show." A *30 Rock* spec? "Loved it, but our show is more edgy." A *30 Rock* spec to a different show? "Sorry, too edgy."

I know—a great script should be enough, shouldn't it? But trust me, producers are extremely discriminating.

If you are serious about writing for television sitcoms, *you should focus all of your creative energy on writing spec scripts* for the type of shows that you like to watch. DO NOT waste time writing a movie script. DO NOT write a one-hour dramatic spec, a book, or a play. Because while you are letting yourself be distracted by some creative whim, more focused writers are cranking out a *Family Guy*, then an *Office*, then another sitcom spec. They are submitting sample after sample after sample to producers, and they are getting the work. Your work. (Remember, even if someone likes one of your specs, what's her first question going

Producer **MICHAEL REISS:** We would read eight hundred spec scripts a year to find the eight scripts that we thought, "Wow, that's great." It's like mining for gold. Make sure that you have the script that jumps out. Know that your script is one of hundreds of scripts read, and the person reading your script is looking for a chance to bail on it at any point. It's got to be inspired in conception, you've got to have those characters dead-on, and it's got to be funny all the way through.

to be? "What else have you written?" If the answer is "Nothing yet," well . . .)

So your new mission in life is to write a killer spec sitcom script. Then another and another, until someone is paying you to write. To get started, here are some issues to sort out before you develop a story.

Which Series to Pick

Decision number one: Which series should you pick for your next, or first, spec script? Jurgen Wolff, in his book *Successful Sitcom Writing*, offers some practical advice: Write for a "show you really like," a "quality show," "a show that has been on the air for at least one season" and is "likely to remain on the air for at least another season."[1] His thinking behind three of these points is obvious, but why is picking a "quality show"—a highly esteemed, critically acclaimed show—helpful?

Two reasons, I believe. First, most producers are television literate and therefore more likely to enjoy scripts written for better shows—the shows that they would be inclined to watch. Second, some producers turn out cheesy shows but are convinced that their turkeys are on par with *Entourage* and *The Office*; send them a script for an equally cheesy show and they will look down their noses at it. So, within the style of writing that you want to do (physical comedies, family-themed shows, young urban series, whatever), select the most esteemed of the bunch for your spec. Choose *30 Rock* instead of *Hollywood Humps*.

And here are some other factors to consider, just to confuse you:

Pick a Show with High Ratings

Even if the show is goofy, high ratings will give it extra cachet. Plus, that means that the show is likely to be around for a few seasons, giving your spec a longer shelf life. Television ratings are posted in trade magazines such as *Hollywood Reporter* and *Variety*, and online at sites like www.zap2it.com; check out the numbers to see which shows seem healthy and to develop a sense of what the country is watching.

Avoid Old Shows

People are tired of watching them. Agents and producers are real tired of reading them. And they tend to get canceled just about the time you're typing "End of Episode" on that new spec.

Ask Around

Check with agents, writer friends, and contacts at shows and the networks to see which scripts are coming in every day. If everyone is writing samples for the same show, it will make it more difficult for your script to stand out. Conversely, you might discover that a new dark horse series is the hip show to spec and decide to jump on that bandwagon.

At this point, you might be asking, "Gee, if my life's dream is to work on *Two and a Half Men*, shouldn't I be writing only *Two and a Half Men* spec scripts?"

Naw, too logical. The script submission process works like this: You write a sample script for SHOW X and submit it to *other* shows in the hope of being hired to write a *new* script. Yes, you can submit your SHOW X sample to the producers of SHOW X, but the odds of them being impressed are slim; writing staffs are notorious for being overly harsh when judging specs written for their own show.

"But, surely, if they saw a great script—my script—they would want to buy and produce it? To save the hassle of developing a different one from scratch?" Sorry. That never, hardly ever, happens. Why? Probably some wasn't-created-here, mama-never-loved-me thing. Whatever the reason, just know that if you want to write for one show, you are usually better off submitting a spec for a different, but similar, show.

Any exceptions? (Aren't there always?) If you have a strong connection to someone important on a show's staff, it sometimes does pay to submit a spec based on that person's show. Your contact will still be as critical when evaluating your script, but that might be outweighed by the flattery factor; jazzed that you like his show enough to crank out an episode, he might extend himself more in an effort to help (hire?) you.

Obviously, in a perfect universe, you could simply pick whichever brand-new show is going to be the hit of the next five seasons and write a spec for that. Of course, if you had that type of crystal ball, you'd be a billionaire by now.

Researching the Series

Years ago, I invited a successful producer, Stephen J. Cannell, to appear as a guest speaker in a workshop that I presented for the American Film Institute. When the discussion turned to writers' pitching strategies, he recounted a unique meeting that he had experienced. A noted film writer deigned to approach Cannell about doing an episode of the producer's detective series. The writer came in, they exchanged pleasantries, and Cannell invited him to unleash. The entire pitch? "Clowns." (PAUSE.) "Clowns?" "Clowns. Intriguing, you know? That whole clown thing. It just works."

And that was it. All he had. He had no idea what Cannell's series was about and he certainly hadn't prepared for the pitch. Bad move. It's an insult to the people who work on the show. You don't get the assignment and you don't get invited back.

What should you do instead? Writing is a business, your business, so take it seriously—do your homework! Before starting a spec script or going in for a pitch, study the show in question. Even if you have been watching it religiously, record, download, or buy copies of three or five recent episodes and analyze them. You can't find any episodes? And you're going in to pitch this Thursday? Ask your friends or another writer; one of them might have stockpiled copies of the shows you need. Or ask your agent or other industry contacts if they have or can get episodes. (Though you should try to avoid using up favors from these folks—it's better to have them helping you by tracking down job leads.)

If you have actually been invited to pitch a show, the production staff is usually happy to lend you episodes and scripts before you come in. Ask for copies of their favorite episodes, so it does not seem that you are not familiar with the show. You should also ask if they have a *series bible* and *story breakdowns* that you could look at. (A series bible usually contains character backstories and a detailed description of the show's overall premise. Story breakdowns provide synopses of episodes that have already aired and perhaps stories that are currently in development, and sometimes include descriptions of ongoing or planned long-term story arcs.) These additional materials can save you from pitching an idea that has already been done on that show, and they often give valuable clues to underlying subtext in the series.

While studying copies of episodes is important, it is even more instructive to read produced scripts from the show. (Especially those penned by the producers who give out the writing assignments.) Things look different on paper than they do on the screen, and your work will be on paper, so get several recent scripts and start reading.

You might be able to obtain these scripts from the sources named above. Or check the scripts-for-free Internet sites listed in Appendix B; nowadays, one can download scripts for many shows at no charge and seemingly without infringing on anyone's copyright. Or check with one of the script "stores" listed in Appendix B to see if they sell scripts for that show.

While you're at it, use an Internet search engine to see if there are any websites dedicated to the show. Such sites often list loglines for episodes that have already aired, which can save you from wasting time developing an idea that's already been produced. Also, perusing these summaries might spark new ideas by providing a quick review of topics and themes that have worked in the past.

Lastly, if these efforts fail, you might be able to find some published scripts from successful TV shows on the shelves of your local bookstore. Or a local college's television-film department might have recent scripts in its library, especially if the school is in or near Los Angeles or New York City. Or, if it is geographically feasible, you can visit the libraries of industry organizations such as the Writers Guild of America or the Academy of Television Arts and Sciences to see if they have copies.

One final note about scripts downloaded from the Internet: Do not rely on those scripts to show you how an episode should look on paper; few web postings are laid out in the correct format. (More on script formats later.)

Studying the Premise

Sounds a bit technical, huh? Researching shows, studying them. The truth is, some very talented, very successful writers scoff at the idea of analyzing a creative work in such a deliberate fashion. At the same time, one of the most frequent complaints that producers have about spec scripts is "Sorry, but our characters would never behave like this." Your script might be funny, dramatic, and touching, but too bad, you just blew it—because you didn't know the show.

Each television series has its own creative format. That format might change and evolve over the years, but the producers are the ones who will make those refinements. Your job is to know and follow the show's current format to a tee.

Scripts first, episodes first, it doesn't matter. Get some paper and start looking for patterns that define the show. If, along the way, you trip over a great story idea or a funny bit that you might use, write it down and *put it aside*; do not get distracted from your current objective!

It is easier to study prerecorded episodes than to watch shows as they are broadcast. Using TIVO, a DVR, a disc player, downloads, or even an old VCR will allow you to zip back and forth, and you can use the playback machine's clock display to note the duration of scenes and the points in a story when events occur. If you're unfamiliar with a series, you might want to view the show once to get a feel for it, and then go back to work through the material at your own pace.

Different writers look for different things when they study an episode. I usually list the following, from left to right: the number of the script page (or minutes into the recorded episode) that the scene starts on; a brief phrase to identify the scene; and, vertical columns labeled "A," "B," "C," etc., in which I note the story beats that occur for each plot or subplot. Finally, I indicate each commercial break by underlining the scene that precedes it.

Then I ask a few questions, usually starting with *story elements*. These might include:

- What types of stories are used? (Small and personal? Wacky? Controversial stories? Stories about nothing?)

- Who is the audience (demographic target) for this show? What do they want to see?

- Is this an eight o'clock show (featuring softer stories designed for kids and teens) or a more adult show (featuring harder-edged, sophisticated material, or more nudity and coarse language)?

- How many storylines does each episode feature? (Just one main "A" story? Or an "A" story with a "B" subplot? Or three to five story threads that are all equally important?)

- Do some or all storylines continue across several episodes? Many episodes?

- Do certain elements seem to be present in almost every episode? (Do "A" stories always feature *Family Guy* Peter while baby Stewie only rates an occasional "B" story? Does each episode express a theme or end with a lesson being learned? Does each have a happy ending?)

- Pacing-wise, how long are most of the scenes? Is each episode composed of short, snappy scenes, or long, talky scenes, or some other identifiable mix?

- Does the show use flashbacks and flash-forwards? Or other stylistic devices? When and how often?

- What are the standard sets? What other types of locations are used, if any?

And, of course, I look at *characters*:

- Does the show feature a single lead, a shared lead, or an ensemble cast?

- Which characters usually drive the stories?

- Does a character always get herself into trouble or is she usually the normal person who has to solve problems caused by others (e.g., Marge in *The Simpsons*)?

- Do characters experience growth in a story (even if it only lasts until next week's episode)? If so, what kind?

- What dramatic functions do the regular characters serve (e.g., ally, rival, confidant, busybody, commentator, etc.)?

- How is each character distinguished by his dialogue and behavior?

- Is there some ongoing subtext that influences the characters' actions (e.g., romantic tension, emotional baggage, feud, etc.)?

- How are visiting characters used?

Along the way, I make note of the show's *broadcast format*, the schedule of commercial breaks that interrupt each episode:

- How many pages do this show's scripts average? Which script format is used (see Appendix A)?

- Does the show start off with a *teaser* scene/sequence (to hook the audience) and then go to titles? Or skip titles and just flash opening credits over the first scenes?

- How many commercial breaks interrupt the body of the show?

- Are the story segments between commercial breaks of roughly the same duration, or is one usually longer than another? (For instance, *The Simpsons* used to feature a long first act, a shorter second act, and an even shorter third.)

- Does the show include a brief *tag* scene at the end, placed after the last commercial interruption but before (or during) closing credits?

And, of course, I look at the show's *style of comedy*. I might ask questions such as those listed under the earlier section dubbed, aptly, "Style of Comedy" (see Chapter 4). In short, who and what make this show funny?

Lastly, as I make my way through the episodes and scripts, I automatically make mental notes of what I did or didn't like. What worked? What failed? What lessons can I apply to my own script?

Do I literally ask all of the above questions when studying a show? Of course not. Most of the answers are readily apparent and writing is not a fill-in-the-blank process. The above lists are offered as a guide, cues to trigger whichever questions will best peg a show's format for you. If you take the time to study a show, subtle elements in its premise will become apparent. If you weave those elements into your script, it will read more like an actual episode of the series—a huge plus in any producer's eyes. As a bonus, your exploration of the show's premise will probably turn up some great story ideas and comedy bits that would not have occurred to you otherwise.

So do your homework unless you are one of those "very talented, very successful writers" who doesn't need to. Once you have picked a series and dissected the beast, good news—you are ready to begin work on your own script.

8

DEVELOPING AN
EPISODE PREMISE

First, you need an idea for a story. Just two or three sentences that describe the basic premise of your episode.

Of course, finding the right idea is easier said than done. Your job is to dream up a long list of possibles, then pick the one gem that can be developed into a fantastic spec script.

Or, if you are creating stories because you have been invited to pitch an existing show (a process that we will discuss later), your mission is to develop ten to fifteen terrific ideas. If all goes well, the producers will pick one and pay you to write a script.

Or, if you already work on the staff of a sitcom, part of your job is to pitch new story ideas to your producers or maybe to the entire writing staff. Eventually, you will be instructed to develop a script based on a particular concept, though it might not be one of the ideas that you created.

And just what types of story ideas are you looking for?

Advice from Our Producers

Here is what some of the producers interviewed for this book look for in a story premise.

MATT WILLIAMS: I think the biggest thing is, what are you going to explore or expose about your lead character's personality? If you would say, "You know what, I want to expose one of [the lead character's] insecurities," then you can build a story around that. I'm intrigued by that, because you're showing me something different about the character.

LAWRENCE KONNER: Like drama, the essence of comedy is conflict. You have to be very clear on what each character wants from the other in every scene. I think jokes will fall flat, comedy will not work, if there isn't a sense of somebody wanting something from the other person. David Mamet talks about that as the central idea of all drama writing. It applies to comedy, as well, and I think that's where the laughs come from.

I don't think an overly complicated story is going to impress anyone. I think a fresh story certainly will but that's hard to come up with. So, [at least try to come up with] a fresh spin on an old story, you know, a little bit of spin that we don't expect.

IAN GURVITZ: One thing that truly annoys me is whenever I see spec scripts based on worn-out clichés, like "the grandmother from hell," "the mother-in-law from hell." Whenever I see scripts like those, it's like a red flag indicating that the writer is not really capable of much original thought.

SANDY FRANK: The story should really make sense in two ways: It should make sense action-wise [meaning that the story should develop logically]. And it should also make sense on an emotional level; you should know exactly what the characters are thinking and feeling and wanting at each moment. Because viewers really do identify with characters emotionally, and also because that's what the executives are going to be bugging you about from day one.

Okay, but how do you come up with ideas for an episode?

Dreaming Up Stories

Get a piece of paper and write down every story idea that comes to mind. Just scribble a few words for each, no more than a phrase or two—details will only bog you down. (Several ideas probably occurred to you when you were studying your chosen series, so begin by listing them.)

Then look at the show's overall premise to see what its built-in humor might suggest. Review our discussion of premise-driven comedy and start thinking about escalating predicaments, character mix, cast strengths—ways to create an episode full of comedic tension.

Look at your main characters, and the emotions and goals that define them, and imagine how those traits might launch an interesting story. George Costanza was virtually unemployable—what if he got the world's neatest job? (Which he at one point did, leading to many funny storylines.) Dwight Schrute and Jim Halpert hate each other—what if they had to share a room at a business conference? In *Everybody Hates Chris*, it seems that everybody does—what if suddenly everybody loved Chris?

You also might ask questions such as these:

- Has your life been affected by an event or discovery that could launch a good story?

- What universal truths strike you as being funny and episode-worthy?

- What controversial subjects would you like to explore?

- What recent news item might be turned into an episode?

- What unique (as in, scary/alluring/needy/vengeful/insane/disaster-prone) visiting character might spark a story?

- How about a parody of some big movie? Or another TV show? Or an overblown celebrity?

- What if your characters got involved in a mystery?

- Is there a unique (and affordable) location that suggests a story?

- What ghost from the past might pay a visit?

- Who or what deserves a really good comeuppance?

- What if a main character's lifelong dream came true? Or his worst nightmare?

Our best stories often come from our own personal experiences, past events—good, bad, happy, sad—that are very important or meaningful to us. Think back to an emotional experience you've had, troublesome flaws that have tripped you up, or relationship moments that have rocked your world, and see if any if those trigger a story idea. Anger, jealousy, betrayal, procrastination, hurt feelings, yearning—a story's circumstances don't have to match your experience, it's the emotions that count. Ask yourself, what similar events might spark the same feelings in your characters, and what (amusing/funny/crazy/foolish) actions might they take in response?

And, of course, there's always the infamous dream-sequence episode. (Just kidding; those stories are usually too gimmicky for spec scripts.)

Still nothing? No ideas? Then take this book back and see about a refund. Time for med school!

More likely, you now have fifty or a hundred ideas in front of you. Some are wrong for this show, some aired on TV last week, and some are just lame. But a few seem almost doable. The next step?

Picking Your Best Ideas

Once you have developed a long list of story ideas, the next step is to winnow it down. Skim through the list, crossing out the obvious losers. Seen it before? Have no idea where the story might go? Just not funny? Gone, dump it.

When you hit a promising idea, if you think of additional elements that might enhance or develop it, scribble them down in the margin so that you don't forget. Then go through the list again. Compare each idea to the others. Which stories seem most interesting? The easiest to make funny? Which stories would you most like to see on TV?

In addition, consider the following:

Lag Time

If you write about current events or a new fad, is your story going to seem dated before you even finish the script? How will it hold up four months from now? A year from now?

Don't Name Celebrity Guest Stars

If you plan to pitch a *Two and a Half Men* story that features Angelina Jolie as a guest star, and you personally can guarantee that Angelina will take the role, then congratulations—you'll probably sell that idea. However, if you can't guarantee a particular celebrity's participation, it is usually best to avoid naming that person in your story pitch or script.

Use Insider Information

If you have been invited to pitch a show and you discover that the producers are anxious to explore a certain type of story, try to meet that need. A few years ago, an executive at a network tipped me that the producers of a show were looking for a chance to bring a previous guest star back for another episode. When I went in to pitch, I tossed out a story featuring exactly that type of guest star. I then (bending the "celebrity" rule just mentioned) casually suggested that the perfect person to play the guest role might be, oh, the very guy that they wanted to have back. By the end of our meeting, not only had I been hired to write that script, but the producer was claiming credit for the casting idea.

Remember Whose Show It Is

They call it *Family Guy*, *(Everybody Hates) Chris*, and *(My Name Is) Earl* for a reason. While TV episodes usually include subplots that feature supporting characters or visiting characters, main stories must be driven by main characters. A secondary character can bring a main-story trigger into an episode, but that problem or opportunity must then become the main character's problem or opportunity. Ellen Sandler gives the following advice in her book *The TV Writer's Workbook*:

1. The story must have an emotional conflict for the Central Character.

2. The Central Character drives the action, that is, his choices make the plot progress.

3. The Central Character resolves the problem.

In other words, the story is told from the Central Character's point of view. It happens to him, and even more important, he makes it happen.[1]

Avoid Holiday Episodes

They seem less appealing out of season and sometimes feel as if their merit is largely due to holiday spin. (An emotional perception that, true or not, can diminish your spec script.)

Don't Rely Heavily on Physical Comedy

Some shows derive a large portion of their laughs from physical comedy. Unfortunately, that plays better on a screen than it reads in a spec script. And some executives and producers are just not very good at visualizing scripted physical gags. (Rumor has it that some even boast that they don't bother to read stage directions, just dialogue—meaning that they skip over much of a script's humor.) So if a show is very physical, write it that way, but make sure that your dialogue is chock-full of verbal humor too because some of your readers will judge your script primarily by that.

As you go through your re-revised list of story ideas, a few more will fall away and others will start to shine. The next step is to develop the more promising concepts into springboards, to see which can be turned into full-fledged stories.

Turning Ideas into Springboards

A *springboard* is a three- to five-sentence description of a story. The first line or two sets up the premise of the story by introducing a hook (the story's inciting incident) that causes the main character to pursue a *new goal* or deal with a *new problem*. The next couple of sentences hint at funny, intriguing complications (plot points that present more problems, bigger hurdles, and unexpected twists) that the main character causes or encounters as he drives the story forward.

Springboards present the beginning and middle of the story to hook the listener, but do not always include a resolution. They are a screenwriter's selling tool, the first pitch that you throw at producers in the hope of getting a script assignment. A good springboard makes the listener want to hear more—it quickly reveals what the main character wants, what his opponent wants, and what is at stake for the main character. (Some writers refer to springboards as *loglines*, a reference to the brief program descriptions one used to see in weekly TV guides, but nowadays that term is most often used to describe a one- or two-sentence premise for a *movie* story.)

Here's an example of a springboard based on an actual *South Park* episode titled "Miss Teacher Bangs a Boy":

> Kyle discovers that his young brother, Ike, has been seduced by his pretty kindergarten teacher. When Kyle alerts the police that his brother is being molested by, not a man, but a hot blonde, their only response is "Nice!" Kyle turns to his friends for help and hall-monitor Cartman catches the pair making out in the school hallway, so the authorities finally arrest the teacher. But she pulls out the old Mel Gibson defense, blaming alcohol, and the town promptly forgives her because she too is a victim—a smoking hot victim.

This simple pitch presents a setup and two complications (i.e., the surprise that the police won't help, and the irony that Cartman is the one to force the arrest) and does include the story's resolution. Note that I've tried to weave humor into the springboard, using amusing descriptions and even a snippet of dialogue ("Nice!") to paint a funny picture. This raises a very important point:

> *NOTE: If you're selling yourself as a comedy writer, it's important that you describe your concepts and stories in a funny fashion. Otherwise, why should anyone believe that you can deliver a funny script? (This advice applies to all springboards, pitches, and story outlines that you create!)*

Why might you omit the endings from some springboards? Because some pitches work better if you leave the producer hanging, hungry for more. If she wants to hear the ending, she can always ask. Better yet, she can pay you to write it.

High-Concept Stories

A *high-concept* idea is similar to a springboard, only more compressed and dynamic. In just a line or two, it presents an exciting, crystal-clear story hook. As in "Arnold Schwarzenegger is . . . the nanny!" (Years ago, when Arnold was the world's biggest action star, a writer friend of mine coughed up this idea but didn't follow through. Since then, other writers came out with the films *Kindergarten Cop*, *Mr. Nanny*, and *The Pacifier*. Oh well.)

Some writers like to incorporate titles of hit films or TV series into a high-concept line, such as "It's *Die Hard* meets *The Office*—some computer dweebs from corporate show up to install software, and Jim asks Dwight if they might be terrorists." Nowadays, some people consider these title-dropping concepts cheesy, but if they are the best/funniest way to get your idea across, who cares.

At this point, as you go through your list of story ideas, try to envision how each premise might be developed into an episode. Write the best ideas out as rough springboards, limiting yourself to no more than a few (three? five?) lines for each. Why go to this trouble? Because if you can't articulate the essence of a story in a few lines, it might be too muddled a concept to successfully flesh out (or sell to a producer). So make the effort, write your thoughts down. And don't kid yourself into believing that a horribly confused story concept will magically straighten itself out later. It won't.

Obviously, as you work through your list, you should discard any unwieldy stories. Can't come up with an ending? The plot seems clichéd? Too contrived? Out, next.

And here's a thought: What if you are writing for a show that uses multiple story threads, three to five equally important plots, rather than a single main story? (A show like *Friends* or *Seinfeld*.) Should you create separate, fully developed springboards for each? No, not at this exploratory stage. Two or three lines for each plotline should suffice for now, as you weigh different ideas. Later, when you select several to weave together, you can fill in the gaps.

NOTE: When it comes to writing, everyone works differently. When something important occurs to me but I don't want to interrupt the current focus of my work, I write the idea on a separate page rather than risk forgetting it. Under the heading "CHARACTERS," I might list ideas for visiting characters, funny character bits, unique dialogue traits, etc. Under the heading "STORY," I note story reminders, funny jokes or situations, and alternative story directions. Under the heading "NOTES/QUESTIONS," I list practical to-do's such as reminders to double-check a peripheral character's name or get a producer's email address. Obviously, you should do whatever works for you; this is just one approach to keeping things on track.

Eventually, you will end up with that one perfect idea, a well-shaped premise guaranteed to launch an Emmy-worthy script. But do you really have to write all of this stuff down and go through all of the steps listed above? Some writers do not. Some go through the steps but do it all in their heads, creating/winnowing/structuring without putting a single word on paper. Others base a script on the first idea that occurs to them, and are talented enough to create great material.

Again, do what works for you. Do whatever you need to do to create a great premise. And once you've accomplished that, it's finally time to start writing a story outline.

Well, almost . . .

9

DEVELOPING THE STORY

You've got a great premise and you sort of know where the story goes, so why not start writing the script? Unleash those creative juices!

Well, some writers can. A very talented few can create a wonderful, enthralling story as they work their way through a first draft. But most of us need a road map. Without it, our stories tend to go astray and hit a series of dead ends. We take weird paths to solve story problems and end up with a script that seems disjointed, forced, patched together.

Is this such a big deal? You bet. In my thirty years as an executive, writer, teacher, and consultant, I have come to believe that story is the single biggest reason that a project will succeed or fail. (By my definition, characters are integral to story; they drive the story and their arc of development is realized through story.) In the sitcom business, what determines whether you get a script assignment? The stories that you pitch. What are writing staffs trying to fix when they keep working until 3 a.m.? Flawed stories. What are viewers really talking about when they discuss "boring," "ridiculous," "she'd never do that" episodes? Bad stories.

Recognizing the importance of story, sitcom producers require that an episode's plot be figured out *on paper* before a writer goes to script. Sell that brilliant premise of yours during a pitch, and your first task will be to write a formal story outline. If you are hired as a freelance writer, you might write an outline yourself, and rewrite it, following notes given by the producers during the pitch. Or the producers might sit with you and practically dictate the entire story, which you then clean up and put into outline form.

If you are on the staff of a show, you might write the outline after creating the story with your producers, or pitch a story you created and write the outline after getting notes from your producers. Or the producers might write the outline themselves and just hand it to you (so you can write the script). Or the entire writing staff might sit together and pound out the story, after which someone (probably you) will write up the outline.

One way or another, the story ends up on paper. The good thing is that if a producer asks you to write an outline, you get paid to do so. (More on this later.)

Should you bother doing all of that extra work if you are writing a spec script by yourself? Definitely, you need that road map. In fact, though the standard process when working for a producer is to go directly from story pitch to outline, I recommend that you do another step in between. I recommend that you create a *beat sheet*.

Creating a Beat Sheet

A *beat sheet*, or plot sheet, is a one-page blueprint of the story's structure.

A traditional half-hour sitcom episode features one main storyline which is composed of five to nine plot points, or beats. If the show also features one or two subplots, which occupy less screen time, each of those subplots usually rings in at only three to five story beats.

But that's for a *traditional* sitcom. Since the late eighties, a second breed of sitcom has become popular—sitcoms that feature multiple story threads instead of a single main storyline (that is or isn't accompanied by subplots). Each story thread is a main story in its own right, featuring one of the show's lead characters. However, since all of these threads have to be crammed together into a half hour of television, each storyline incorporates fewer beats and occupies less screen time than a traditional main story. *Seinfeld* is an example of a show that features this *thread structure*: In a typical episode, one story would feature Jerry, another Elaine, another Kramer, and a fourth George. All of these stories would be main stories of roughly the same dramatic weight, but time restrictions limited each thread to an average of three to six beats apiece.

So how do storylines and beats translate into a beat sheet?

First, let's clarify the meaning of *beats*. A beat is a moment, a discovery, or an incident that alters the main character(s)'s goals and/or cranks up a story's dramatic tension. As Linda Seger notes in her book *Making a Good Script Great*, story beats sometimes consist of two parts, an *action* that forces a *reaction*.[1] For example, if one character accidentally blabs another character's secret (an action), the second half of that beat might be that the first character then lies to cover up his blunder (a reaction).

A beat sheet is simply a list of the beats that define your story. By providing a clean, at-a-glance look at how your episode develops, this list enables you to quickly see whether each plotline works or doesn't work. To keep the full focus on story, each beat should be written in the briefest possible form: just a phrase or two, not even a complete sentence, that provides the gist of what happens. For instance, the previous paragraph's example might be reduced to: "Character One blabs secret—claims (*new lie*) to cover up."

Beat sheets are powerful tools because they enable a writer to repair fatal story flaws before it is too late—meaning, before the flaws have been completely obscured by clever scenes and funny dialogue. If you look at that sheet and the story does not build, is not logical, is not funny, does not surprise and seduce, then it's back to the drawing board. And consider yourself lucky for having caught the flaws now, when they are easiest to fix.

NOTE: There is another industry definition of "beat sheet" that refers to a type of written story outline sometimes used by producers of drama series. Those detailed, multi-page outlines are usually distinguished by numbered scenes, truncated grammar, and functional scene descriptions.

Here are three more thoughts about beat sheets to keep in mind:

1. When an episode features multiple storylines, it is probably easiest to sort out the beats for each individual story first, and then figure out how to weave the different stories together later. Of course, if a great sequence of integrated beats suggests itself early on, run with it.

2. Ellen Sandler suggests a way to remind yourself that the main character of a storyline must drive that story: "Start each beat with your Central Character's name ... figure out how that event affects your Central Character; then rephrase the beat in terms of your Central Character's reaction."[2] Of course, in most subplots, a secondary character drives the story rather than a Central Character, but the approach is the same.

3. A sitcom main story or subplot might fully conclude at the end of an episode, or it might serve as one installment of an ongoing *story arc* that is playing across multiple episodes of the show. An example of the latter: An episode of *The Office* might focus on a new female character's first day of work at the Scranton branch, and not only tell that story but also launch a story arc in which Michael courts, dates, offends, and is sued by the woman over the course of several episodes.

Okay, given that stories are composed of beats and that beat sheets are a great way to track a story's development, how does one use beats to create a compelling storyline?

Story Structure: Linear vs. Thread

I once heard (sorry, but I can't remember the source) that "if movies are larger than life, sitcoms are smaller."

At a very basic level, many sitcom stories tend to follow a well-worn path. First, a lead character encounters a new problem or opportunity, and goes to outrageous lengths as he attempts to solve that problem or pursue that opportunity. (If his actions were logical rather than outrageous, there would be no story.) Then, running into an escalating series of obstacles, he takes inappropriate actions to achieve his goal. (That goal often changes and becomes more imperative as events proceed.) By end of story, the character's misguided efforts backfire on him; exposed and embarrassed, he learns the error of his ways. Sort of.

This pattern of development is nothing new. It's the same linear structure model that was described by Aristotle more than two thousand years ago. To paraphrase from Aristotle's *Poetics*, a book that you should have on your shelf, a story is composed of three sections: The "beginning" introduces a complication to a character's life, launching the story. The "middle" section presents developing action, a series of "revolutions" and "discoveries," that drives the story forward. The "end" resolves the story conflict, often through a reversal of fortune for the main character.[3]

Notice the similarities between these two models? The same *linear*, or three-act, structure that you see in a conventional sitcom story is also used in conventional movies, one-hour series, books, myths, fables, etc. (Notice that I use the qualifier "conventional"—not all storylines follow the Aristotelian model, as we will discuss below.)

Looking more closely at sitcoms, we see that the three acts of an individual storyline usually unfold in the following manner:

- The first act, the beginning, is very brief because you don't need to introduce characters and settings; they are already in place if you are writing for an existing sitcom. Within the first few pages, and in just one or two story beats, a complication (the inciting incident) occurs which sends the lead character off on some sort of mission. Typically, she wants to pursue a new opportunity or solve a new problem.

- The second act is the longest. Taking up half to two-thirds of your storyline, it is the journey or quest that your character pursues as she tries to achieve her goal. Dramatic tension should escalate as she goes—jeopardy mounts, stakes increase, the character's actions become more desperate, etc. As Hollywood screenwriting guru John Truby counsels, a writer tackling her second act should "think development, not repetition"; meaning, each scene should build on preceding story, not repeat material that was covered in earlier scenes. Second acts often end with some huge revelation or event that leaves your character facing a major choice or dilemma.

- The third act usually takes up about a quarter of your storyline. The pace picks up and comedic tension builds as the tale reaches its climax—characters confront each other, the truth is revealed, and the story is resolved. The main character loses as often as she wins, but somehow the episode usually manages to close with a happy ending.

Please note that I have described the above model as the structure of an *individual storyline*, not an episode. As previously mentioned, some sitcoms feature only one main story in each episode while others regularly feature four or five *story threads* instead of a single main story. However, each of these threads follows the same three-act structure as described above. The primary structural difference is that, due to time constraints, story threads are shorter—they feature less dramatic development, fewer beats—than a traditional main storyline. (The synergistic effect of multiple story threads being woven together gives them as much dramatic power as a traditional sitcom's single main story.)

How might each of the three acts break down in terms of average number of pages within a script? Well, there are no hard-and-fast rules regarding such things, but for point of illustration only, here is one example: In a typical thirty-page sitcom script (written in *film format*, which is explained in Appendix A), an episode that features a *single main storyline* might break down as follows: one to five pages for the first act, fifteen to twenty pages for the second act, and five to ten pages for the third.

Again, this is just one example, based on a traditional, linear, single-main-story episode.

If you are writing for a show that features thread structure, a typical episode might include four story threads, each taking up roughly a quarter of the thirty-page script (seven to eight pages). Where each act of each thread might appear page-wise is impossible to say here, since the different threads could be woven together in any number of ways. (Remember *Seinfeld*?)

Story Threads vs. Subplots vs. Ensemble Stories

What are the differences between these three elements?

Story threads, as defined in the preceding section, are main stories that feature main characters. Time limitations require that these threads be shorter, less developed, than traditional main stories. Though several story threads are woven together to fill out an episode, and though they connect with each other at various points in an episode, each thread features one of the main characters pursuing a goal that is different from those the other main characters are pursuing in their threads. At the same time, a main character driving one thread will often play a supporting role in another main character's thread. (For example, one character might be addressing boyfriend issues in her thread, while also providing friendly support to another character who just got fired in his thread.)

Subplots are short, secondary storylines that usually feature a show's supporting characters. Subplots sometimes present stories that are totally unrelated to an episode's main story, or that *seem* unrelated until they dovetail with the main story late in the episode. Other times, subplots might present stories that run parallel to the episode's main story; meaning, they explore a similar theme or dilemma, and occasionally provide the key to resolving the main story. Example: A main story might feature a lead character who is acting like an insensitive chauvinist, who finally realizes that he's been a jerk when he scolds his buddy for behaving in a similar fashion (in the subplot).

Ensemble shows differ from shows that utilize *thread structure* in several ways. Take shows such as *Entourage* or *The Office*, for example. Though it might seem that an ensemble show features an interesting cast of equal characters, a second look usually reveals that one of the characters is more equal than the others (e.g., Vincent Chase, Michael Scott). It might feel as if the less-equal ensemble characters get as much story time as the lead, but if you count up the number of episodes that feature each character (or the dollars that each actor rates during contract negotiations), it becomes clear that most ensemble shows are actually wrapped around a single lead character. What is more, though other members of an ensemble cast might be featured in some episodes of the series, they are starring in a single main storyline rather than in one main thread woven in with other main threads. (Of course, the distinctions between thread structure stories and subplots in an ensemble series can be difficult to see, because supporting characters in ensemble shows usually get a lot more screen time than those in a traditional series.)

Stories Without Endings

Some sitcoms will introduce a story thread or a subplot and then just cut it off in mid-stride. We see a beginning and a middle, but no end. *Family Guy*'s Stewie might hatch a plot to kill Lois or take over the world, design his weapon, mutter vague threats . . . and that's all. Nothing else happens, there is no resolution.

Is this a sign of sophisticated writing, a bold decision to mimic the many unresolved threads that occur in real life? Sure. That, or maybe the show was running long so they just chopped out the ending. Either way, occasional unresolved storylines such as these can add a fresh sense of reality to a show—*if* they fit comfortably within the show's creative format.

Serialized Stories (Story Arcs)

Since the form was first created, most sitcoms have been completely *episodic*; every episode told an entire story from beginning to end, tying up all loose ends and answering all questions by the time credits rolled. It used to be that few shows varied from the norm; the aptly named *Soap* series was a rare exception.

Episodic series still exist and thrive—*The Simpsons* and *Family Guy* are two examples—but many modern shows are following a new trend in narrative structure. As mentioned earlier, some of today's sitcoms are driven by *serialized* storylines, or *story arcs*. These are stories, either main plots or subplots, that are spread out over a number of episodes, perhaps even a whole television season. Example? A character meets, dates, and dumps a new boyfriend over the course of five episodes. We still get a beginning, middle, and end in the storyline, and the same number of story beats, but the three acts don't all occur in one half-hour sitting.

To be more accurate, most modern serialized shows are kind of a hybrid: They feature mostly episodic main stories that provide some sense of closure at the end of the half hour, but that also serve as installments in a continuing, larger story (that lasts for multiple episodes). Or a show's main stories might be wholly episodic (lasting for just one episode) while its subplots are the stories that arc across several weeks or months. Examples of both types include Earl's multi-episode stint in prison, Jack Donaghy's long-term battle to reclaim his job at *30 Rock*, and all of the romantic subplots flowing along in *The Office* (e.g., Jim and Pam, Dwight and Angela, Michael and Jan, Michael and Holly, etc.)

In addition to episodic and "hybrid" shows, there are a few true half-hour serials on the air, such as *Entourage* and *Californication*. But nowadays, these shows tend to be dramedies rather than comedies.

Why the recent interest in serialized stories? Many producers and executives believe that continuing story arcs promote viewer loyalty, an increasingly rare commodity. And many writers embrace arcs because they provide additional time to explore characters and character relationships more deeply.

Dramatic Structure vs. Broadcast Format

So far, when we have discussed the three acts of a sitcom story, we have been referring to a script's *dramatic* structure. But the word "act" is also used as a purely technical term, coined by network scheduling types, to describe a segment of an episode that occurs between commercial breaks. This and other elements that interrupt a show define its *broadcast format*.

To clarify, unless your show is on a commercial-free network, that marvelous script that you are writing will probably be interrupted by opening credits, commercial breaks, and closing credits. One of your jobs is to study the series that you wish to write for so that you can duplicate its broadcast format (i.e., its standard pattern of scheduled interruptions) when you write your outline and script.

And here is where things get a bit muddled.

The timing of commercial breaks does not necessarily coincide with the transitions between the three *dramatic* acts in a typical storyline. The commercial break that comes right after the first act (speaking broadcast-format-wise) might actually be located halfway through the second act (speaking dramatic-structure-wise) of your story. So the different uses of the term "act" can seem confusing.

Why do you care? Because when you write your outline and your script, you are supposed to break your story up into segments that reflect the *broadcast format* pattern regularly used on your chosen show. You will be typing "ACT ONE, ACT TWO, etc." at points that do not necessarily coincide with *dramatic* act breaks in your story.

Should you worry about this now? Well, first, you should brainstorm to come up with the primary events that will drive the story (your beat sheet). But then, as you sort out the scenes in a written outline, you should try to position some of the key plot points so that they happen just before the commercial breaks that would normally occur on that show. (These are called *act breaks* or just *breaks*.) You can't always sync them up and that's fine, because many breaks happen right after a smaller bit, a joke or meaningful piece of dialogue. But if you can schedule a big beat to occur just before the commercial break, that cliff-hanger will help to keep viewers tuned through the next commercials. Producers and execs will love you for doing that, and any new writer who puts strong act breaks into a spec script will score major points.

Okay, so how does a show's broadcast format normally play out?

As mentioned, some series always start the half hour off with a brief teaser or *cold open*. They show the first scene(s) of the episode to get viewers hooked, then go to opening credits (the title sequence), then a commercial break, and then they come back for the first act (speaking broadcast-format-wise) of the episode. These openings are popular because that first nugget of story is more likely to grab a viewer's interest than is a credit sequence that he's already seen fifty times.

Other shows might start with the first scene and just run credits over the action, postponing the first commercial break for as long as possible to avoid losing viewers.

After the opening, the main body of an episode is interrupted by one or two commercial breaks, dividing it into two or three acts. Usually, just before each break, an act will end with the sort of cliff-hanger described above, to lure viewers back after the commercials. (Act breaks usually involve a main story but can sometimes involve a subplot—check your show to identify its pattern.) When the next act starts, after the break, that new act sometimes begins by having one of the characters briefly *recap* what has just happened in the story, to reorient viewers.

At story's end, some shows finish the last act, go to commercial, come back for closing credits, and that's it. Other shows just run the closing credits over the final scene and they're done.

Still other shows finish the last act, go to commercial, and then come back with a brief *tag* scene. A tag is a very quick final scene tossed in just for laughs (and to hold viewer interest through the previous commercial break). While tags often play off of one of the episode's storylines, that storyline has already been resolved at the end of the last act. Closing credits sometimes follow a tag scene, and other times they flash across the screen while the tag scene is playing out (making those hard-earned credits practically unreadable).

Other creative twists on the traditional cold-open, no-open, tag-or-no-tag patterns have included *Seinfeld*'s opening and closing monologues (which were eventually discontinued), and variations in the opening credits for *The Simpsons* (that include Bart writing funny phrases on a school blackboard and an ever-changing family-on-the-couch scene).

Story Tips

Here are some more things to keep in mind when building your story:

Your Lead Character Should Drive the Story

A reminder: Even if you use a visiting character to bring a story into an episode, that story should feature your lead character. Your lead character should be the one pursuing the goal or evading the crisis. Her decisions and actions should be what move the story forward. And your lead character should be the one who resolves the story at episode's end, even though her actions will often result in her being exposed and humiliated.

Producer MATT WILLIAMS: Every sitcom episode has to build up to one key dramatic moment, what [the story's] really about. It can build to a key decision that your protagonist has to make. It can build to a key discovery that a character makes. It can build to a key moment of reconciliation. But everything in your story builds up to and away from that moment, which, ninety percent of the time, is in your block comedy scene.

Conflict: It's a Good Thing

Anyone who has graduated from third grade can tell you that conflict is an essential element of drama. Well, good news, conflict is also a great source of comedy. Unfortunately, a lot of inexperienced writers shy away from scenes that feature characters really going at it. They walk their leads right up to the brink of some juicy confrontation, but then pull back. They send the lead off in a different direction instead and we, the audience, are left feeling cheated.

Be brave. Throw your characters into hot water, because that's when things really get interesting. The funny thing is, once you do, sparks fly and stuff starts happening, and those scenes often end up being your favorites. Thanks to conflict.

Milk a Character's Flaws

As in many dramatic stories, sitcom plots often grow out of a main character's weaknesses, his tendencies to get himself into trouble. Cartman pretends to have Tourette's, Earl lies to the little old lady, Michael Scott has the nerve to lecture the very people he's offended—by exploiting a character's flaws, stories such as these generate natural, seamless humor because they grow right out of the show's premise.

One Storyline per Character

While the lead characters of a series usually have some involvement in all of the storylines in an episode, each plot or subplot in an episode should feature a different person. Check to see how your show spreads the stories around. Typically, one character gets the main story, another gets a subplot, maybe another gets a second subplot, and so on.

In a show that utilizes thread structure, each lead character gets only one thread—or perhaps, some weeks, no thread—and might also serve as a supporting character in the other lead characters' threads.

Stories Should Build As You Go

While stories need to be funny and interesting from the very first page, they should become more involving as you go. Typically, your biggest dramatic moments occur at the very end of the second act and in the third act, partly because it takes the first two acts to lead the characters deep into hot water and establish the importance of whatever issues are at stake. You'll help yourself to achieve this (building tension) if you keep our discussions of premise-driven comedy in mind.

Should the Story Include a "Ghost"?

Sometimes you can increase the emotional impact of a story by connecting the main character's current goal with an event in his past, a psychological ghost that still haunts him. Did he pursue a similar objective or face a similar problem once before, and fail miserably? And comically? Is he actively trying to avoid returning to the same situation, or hoping to accomplish now what he couldn't before? Sheldon Bull, in his book *Elephant Bucks*, suggests that including a connection like this can clarify a character's motivation and help audiences relate to a story. "In any good story the audience or reader must understand why a character wants what he wants. This is where rooting interest comes from. How can we root for a character to achieve his goal or solve his problem unless we understand why it is so important to him?" Or, simply put, "Can you find a way to make this goal or problem mean something special to the Main Character?"[4]

Time Frame of the Story

Traditionally, a sitcom storyline lasts for only a few days, a week, or maybe a couple of weeks. The argument given is that a longer time span would dilute the dramatic tension of the story. (How urgent can a story be if it runs for six months or more?) Some episodes, such as a baby-delivery show or a trapped-in-a-space show, are even played out in real time; the story spans only a half hour or several hours, unfolding at roughly the same pace for both characters and viewers.

More recently, adventurous sitcoms have enjoyed success by taking huge liberties with the time frame of a show. For example, *The Simpsons* might interrupt a normal scene to flash forward twenty years for a ten-second glimpse of the future, then cut back to present day without missing a beat. In its final year, *Seinfeld* featured an entire episode that ran in reverse; some critics took shots at what was an obvious gimmick, but viewers had no problem following the storyline. On *Family Guy*, each episode features numerous flashbacks to funny and outrageous events cued by a character saying something as simple as, "It reminds me of the time I . . ."

Does this mean that you are free to ignore time-frame traditions if writing a spec script? No. Some execs and producers tend to mistake innovative story elements for a lack of familiarity with the series. (Or worse, bad writing.) I recommend that you save those cool time-frame ideas for when you are already on the staff of a show. Then, they—and you—will be given more serious consideration.

Check Your Story Logic

As you develop your story, take a moment to check the timing of events in your plot. Does everything happen in a logical sequence? Is there enough time for an action to take place? Have the characters missed a deadline mentioned in the story?

While you're at it, do all of the actions and events in your story make sense? Even reality-bending shows like *South Park* have limits and parameters to which their writers must adhere. So if you previously ignored a contradiction here or promised yourself you'd come up with a more believable solution there, now's the time to stop and fix it.

Comedy's Impact on Story

In sitcoms, how are storylines affected by comedy? Typically, we see the following:

Characters and Events Are Frequently Exaggerated

Think big! When *Two and a Half Men*'s Uncle Charlie tries to keep Jake from being expelled from school, he doesn't just try to charm the teacher. He seduces her . . . and discovers that she's a religious wacko . . . and freaks when she reveals that God has told her Charlie and she must never part!

Goals and Strategies Are Often Silly or Outrageous

If a character's plan for reaching some goal was rational and logical, there wouldn't be a story to tell. Unless a series is deeply rooted in realism, audiences are usually happy to suspend disbelief and accept the idea that sitcom characters almost always ignore obvious solutions.

The Stakes Are Usually Small . . . or Not

Sitcoms aren't about abortion debates or nuclear holocaust. Sitcoms are about bad hair days and battles with Soup Nazis, small issues that we can relate to, and that don't cost millions to portray on the small screen.

Though, scratch that. Animated shows like *South Park* and *Family Guy* frequently do serve up fantastic stories such as battles with Satan, alien invasions, evil government conspiracies, and Barbra Streisand robots going on a rampage. So, actually, the size and nature of a story's dramatic stakes depend on the individual show. A traditional live-action sitcom is likely to feature mostly credible situations and deal in human truths; its comedy comes from funny situations, amusing characters, and clever dialogue. But for some broad sitcoms, almost anything goes as long as you follow the parameters established for the show, and remember that even a fantastic or outrageous story must build and resolve in a compelling manner.

How the Production Process Affects Your Script

While this chapter is about the art of turning a promising episode premise into a solid story, there are a few realities of television production that you should be aware of when writing a script. Meaning, your creative instincts often must be tempered by budget and time constraints, and the following:

Locations and Sets

Ever notice how most traditional sitcoms seem to take place indoors, in just a few rooms? It's a money thing. Those rooms, called *standing sets*, are crammed together on the floor of some big Hollywood sound stage (or, on rare occasions, a New York sound stage). Most traditional sitcoms are shot in *multi-camera* style, meaning that three to five cameras shoot each scene simultaneously, covering different angles of the action; production pauses only to redo parts of a scene, start a new scene, or move to a different set.

A multi-camera show usually employs three to five regular (standing) sets and perhaps a couple of *swing sets* (sets that are used only once or just on rare occasions, that can be swung out from the stage wings or pulled from storage when needed). And that's it. An office, a coffee shop, a living room, a bar where everyone knows your name—those are the familiar spaces where most of a multi-cam show's scenes take place.

Though producers of a multi-camera show will invest in new sets if they are critical to a strong script (e.g., a hospital room, the interior of a subway, a gate at the airport), they're usually not happy to spend that extra money. And they are not impressed when they see spec scripts or freelance scripts that call for several expensive new sets; the perception is that the writers of those scripts are uninformed. So be thrifty. For multi-camera shows, try to direct your storylines so that they can take place in the show's regular (standing and swing) sets. If you must venture elsewhere, fine, but limit yourself to one or two new sets, tops.

But what about those episodes where the characters travel to Hawaii or Italy? Those staff-written episodes are usually stunts dreamed up to attract viewers during network *sweeps* months. (*Sweeps* refers to a critical audience rating period that influences how much a network can charge advertisers for commercial time.) Costly? Sure, but the producers see the trips as a way to attract new viewers and perhaps land a free trip to Hawaii while they're at it. Are such travel stunts a good idea for a spec script? No. Again, their use in a spec script would only serve to indicate that the writer is either out of the loop or just not very bright.

Multi-Camera vs. Single-Camera Shows

While traditional multi-camera sitcoms shoot mostly on a limited number of sets in an indoor soundstage, in recent years networks have also aired a number of *single-camera* productions, series that use one camera to shoot on both standing sets and a variety of off-the-lot locations. (Rather than simultaneously cover several angles as a scene plays out, a single camera is used to shoot one angle of a scene, and is then moved to get a second angle as the same scene is re-run, and then another angle, and so on.) An example is *My Name Is Earl*, which regularly featured scenes in familiar settings like Joy's trailer home and Ernie's Crab Shack, but also included scenes shot at numerous other interior and exterior locations. Why do this? Because it opened up all sorts of great story options. (How far could Earl get if all of his good deeds had to take place in his own den, kitchen, and garage?)

Many writers, producers, and executives are huge fans of single-camera production because they believe that adding locations makes a series seem more fresh and realistic. We don't just hang out in our dens all of the time, unless there's an Xbox there, so why would a show's characters?

Other differences between the two formats include: Multi-cam shows tend to feature fewer, talkier scenes; less character movement; and few exterior scenes. Single-cam shows tend to use more and shorter scenes to tell their stories, and they often "open up" stories by using new locations and minor characters at those locations to provide story conflict (and humor). Multi-cam shows provide more continuity of movement (because we see instantaneous cuts between cameras), while single-cam shows usually feature more dramatic lighting and camera shots. Lastly, multi-cam shows are usually cheaper to produce and take less time to shoot.

Which form is best? Will one become dominant in the future? Each has its own strengths, and their relative popularity seems to change based on which has had the biggest recent hits. (Ratings equal revenues.) So both will probably be around for a long time.

As far as writing for one type of show versus the other, don't over-think the matter. As long as you've done your homework when studying a show's format, you'll have an excellent idea of how your story should unfold—its pacing, scene length, types of locations, use of minor characters, everything.

How can you tell if a show is multi- or single-cam, so you can pick the right script format for your spec? Use the resources in Appendix B to obtain a copy of a produced episode, or identify the show's production style by checking websites dedicated to the series and then follow the generic script guidelines provided in Appendix A.

One last note: Some producers and executives do believe that there are HUGE creative differences between the two production formats, and will only want to see single-cam specs when hiring for single-cam shows, and multi-cam specs for those shows. So arm yourself. As you create a portfolio of brilliant scripts to send out, make sure that you have samples of both.

Locations in Animated Shows

Sets? Locations? It's a cartoon! So when writing for a series like *Family Guy* or *South Park*, you can use whatever exotic settings you want as long as they are appropriate for that show's premise.

Halt, make note of that last qualifier—by now, you know that if you send characters to a time or place that seems odd for that show, your script will seem off target.

Special Effects in a Live-Action Series

Special effects are expensive to produce and time-consuming to shoot. Sure, you can call for some basic *mechanical effects*, effects that can be produced by a prop person or effects technician right there on the set, including things like smoke, breakable mirrors, and levitating objects. And there are a number of flashy electronic effects that can be created if the show is being shot or edited on digital media, such as objects radiating light and images superimposed over other images. But otherwise, live-action sitcoms are not the place for car crashes, exploding buildings, and morphing monsters. While the rare sci-fi or fantasy sitcom might call for exotic effects on a regular basis, most shows never use the stuff.

Stunts

As with special effects, stunts cost money and time. They require trained personnel, a coordinator, performance fees, etc. Unless a show has regularly employed stunts in the past, you probably should avoid including them in your spec script.

Nail the Story, the Rest Is Easy

Building a story is hard work. That's why many writers prefer to jump right into dialogue, arguing that a story should unfold naturally, that it should come "from the writing."

Well, that sounds good, but I side with a guy named William Goldman who, having chalked up a couple of screenwriting Oscars, has proclaimed the following:

> For the most part, the public and critics have come to believe that screenplays *are* dialogue. Wrong. If movies are story, and they are, then screenplays are structure.[5]

But sitcoms aren't movies? Sure they are, just shorter and funnier. Their other differences aside, both forms are hugely dependent on story structure.

My point is that if you take the time to nail the story up front, the rest of the writing will be a breeze (or at least breeze-like). You will have your road map, and your story will drive forward in a purposeful fashion. No wrong turns, no wasted motion.

What's more, if you create a fresh, compelling story, your producer will be very happy. He can always punch up a script's dialogue and add jokes—that's what his staff of twelve writers are paid to do. But show him that you can cough up great stories and you might suddenly be deemed a very valuable commodity.

So, think story, study story. Read books, take classes, and analyze scripts to enhance your story building skills. And remember two things: Stories are driven by characters (their discoveries, decisions, and actions), and they must remain true to the overall series premise.

NOTE: Will you ever be asked to change a brilliantly structured story, to redesign that masterpiece that you have worked so hard to develop? Yes, always, almost without fail. With so many people involved in the creative process, just expect that it will happen. But if you start out with a good story, you will (usually) receive fewer meddlesome notes. And people will remember that your original story—however much it might change—was crafted in a solid, professional manner.

10

CREATING FUNNY CHARACTERS

You are trying to achieve two goals when working on characters in your script: First, when writing for an existing series, you must remain true to the voices and personalities of the show's continuing characters. Otherwise, your script might be funny and compelling, but . . . something's not right, Homer just doesn't sound like Homer. (People notice the difference. Especially producer-type people.)

Second, when creating visiting characters for a series or original characters for a pilot, you must make them both fresh and three-dimensional. Besides helping your story, this is a great way to convince producers that your writing skills go beyond an ability to mimic an existing show's format or recycle worn-out character types.

Where do you start when working with existing characters or creating new ones? You start with your gut. When you think of an *existing* character, what strikes you first? If you had to describe her personality in one sentence, what adjectives would you use? Why exactly does that character work or not work for you? Why and when is she funny? What role does she play in driving stories forward? (Be specific. Write it down if you have to.)

And when you're creating a *new* character? What traits came to mind when you first conceived him? Did you picture him only in terms of how he could facilitate your story, or as a living, breathing personality? Why did he seem funny to you? (Again, be specific.)

Then, look a little deeper. Lajos Egri, in his book *The Art of Dramatic*

Writing, suggests that characters are best defined by their "physiology, sociology, and psychology." He lists different traits for each of these three dimensions in an effort to help writers get a feel for a character:

> For physiology, he tics off traits such as sex, age, height, weight, posture, appearance, and physical defects.
>
> For sociology, he lists items such as social class, occupation, education, familial history, religion, race, politics, and leisure-time activities.
>
> For psychology, he lists morals, ambitions, frustrations, temperament, attitude, complexes, IQ, etc.[1]

Must you take the time to explore all of the traits that Egri describes, for all of the characters that will appear in your script? No, of course not. The point (mine and, I speculate, Egri's) is that an examination of *specific attributes* can provide valuable clues to a character's personality. *You decide which traits are most telling*, for which characters, and develop those. Personally, I usually focus on the character's emotional base—his dreams, flaws, fears, and goals, the things that make him most human.

How do you develop traits that will make a character *funny*? Good question. The answer is different for every character in every story. Fortunately, most of the time, some amusing traits will automatically occur to you when you first dream up a character.

If you want to develop more of that character's humor, or if you can't see any humor in a character, try exploring traits that make a character seem *incongruous within his environment*. (Remember the important role that incongruity plays in humor?) Here are some examples: In the classic *Taxi* series, Louie De Palma was a little man who belittled taller people— the show got lots of laughs by capitalizing on Louie's short height, a *physiological* trait. In *The Beverly Hillbillies*, the Clampetts were millionaires living in a community of millionaires—but their lack of education and social standing, *sociological* traits, made them incongruous and funny. Within the Clampett clan, Jethro's complete lack of an IQ rendered him even more unique in his elitist environment—a *psychological* trait that generated loads of humor.

So explore incongruities between characters and their environment. The tension created by these dissimilarities can make your characters seem fresh and distinctive, and should suggest a lot of comedy.

Remember the Mix

In addition to deciphering an existing character's traits, or creating an interesting blend of traits for a new character, remember to assess his role *in the character mix*. While we come to know characters by observing their decisions and actions, the manner in which they interact with others is just as enlightening.

Most sitcoms are star vehicles that feature a single lead character and a supporting ensemble, but some other series feature a *split-lead* (e.g., *Two and a Half Men*) or multiple leads (*Seinfeld*). Whichever the case, the continuing characters in a show frequently act as a family unit. This unit might be led by a strong parental figure (e.g., *Everybody Hates Chris*'s Rochelle) or by the biggest baby of the bunch (e.g., *Family Guy*'s Peter) And the family ties might be more figurative than literal—witness the groupings in *Earl* and *30 Rock*.

Whatever the mix, the show's continuing characters should be the ones who drive the stories forward. They should have the same types of emotional problems that the show's viewers have and they should be anything but perfect. (Perfect is boring, and most sitcom storylines grow out of characters getting themselves into trouble.)

How should the leads interact with each other and the rest of their sitcom family? Actively, dynamically, with sparks a-flyin'! As in life, a sitcom family is most interesting when everyone is going at it. Nobody cares if a lead character is debating global politics with an outsider, a character whom we don't know. But get two series regulars arguing over which way to hang a toilet paper roll, and that we'll watch.

Character Arcs

While *story arc* refers to a plotline spread out over multiple episodes of a series, *character arc* refers to a character's emotional growth as he moves through a story. The two concepts are usually directly related—in a strong story, the main character's psychological development shapes her decisions and actions, and that is what drives a story forward.

Do *sitcom* characters grow to new levels of maturity and enlightenment as a result of their weekly adventures? Yes and no. Structurally speaking, sitcom characters will frequently follow the same pattern that we expect to see in drama. They often start off an episode by behaving in a selfish or self-centered manner regarding some issue. During the second act, they take inappropriate actions as they try to achieve some goal. At story's climax, they realize the error of their ways and finally do the right thing. A lesson is learned, all is well, "The End."

Until the next episode.

While long-term psychological growth is usually an important dramatic element in movies, books, and other forms of fiction, you don't see much of it in a series like *South Park.* The characters are who they are, and by next week they will have forgotten any lessons that they supposedly learned this week.

There are rare exceptions. For instance, sometimes the producers of a domestic sitcom will have their characters—most often the kids—learn from their mistakes as they mature. They will still make and remake mistakes over and over again, but the *types* of mistakes that they make will change as they and the series evolve. The issue is no longer "Will the son cheat on that test?" but rather "Will the son cheat on his girl-friend?"

Character Types

Interestingly, one can often spot familiar character types in television sitcoms. In his critical essay, "Comedy, Its Theorists, and the Evolutionary Perspective," Robert Storey identifies four personality types that are commonly found in comedy: "the fool, the wit, the rogue, and the hero." While these types can be found in all forms of fiction, Storey suggests that the first three keep recurring in comedy because audiences are happy to laugh "*at* the fool, or *with* the wit, or (ambivalently) in complicity with the rogue's transgressions."[2]

Of course, the concept of recurring character types is nothing new in drama. Remember Joseph Campbell? Character archetypes in world mythology? Well, you can find a few in sitcoms too. See if some of these sound familiar:

The Supportive Parent

As previously mentioned, many sitcom families are led by a wise, insightful, supportive parent type. Since this character is usually more sensible than other family members, many of her stories grow out of problems that others have caused. And much of the comedy that comes from this character type is generated by her reactions to funny situations around her. Often, this is the character that provides the guidance that another character needs when making some important decision. Marge Simpson and *30 Rock*'s Jack Donaghy are examples of a supportive parent.

The Idiot Savant

Often playing the child to a "supportive parent," the idiot savant is a character who makes up in insight what he lacks in IQ. This person is the trusting, innocent simpleton whom the others deem lovable but inferior—even though he is usually the one who blurts out a simple-but-brilliant solution when disaster looms ahead. Idiot savants come in all shapes and sizes. They generate a lot of their humor by giving literal responses (punchlines) to joke setups, and by stating truths that nobody else dares to mention. Both Darnell and Randy of *Earl* are examples of an idiot savant.

The Idiot Idiot

Another childlike character, this type rarely provides an insight to compensate for his idiocy. He is just dumb, funny, and lovable, a constant source of trouble. (Trouble which, happily, spawns lots of funny predicaments.) Idiot idiots are usually featured in broader comedies, and their antics often involve a lot of physical humor. (They are the "comic fools" noted above.) Think Barney Fife of *The Andy Griffith Show*, Joey Tribbiani of *Friends*, and Johnny ("Drama") of *Entourage*.

The Clown

The clown is usually an intelligent, rational adult—who falls down a lot. She generates stories and comedy by being inept, clumsy, and awkward.

Clowns often stumble into outrageous physical predicaments, which are made all the more funny by their frantic efforts to extricate themselves. The greater the potential for embarrassment, the more a clown is guaranteed to screw up. Classic sitcom clowns include Lucille Ball and Dick Van Dyke; *Two and a Half Men*'s Alan is a more recent example.

The Operator

The operator is a close cousin to the "rogue" mentioned above and the "trickster" frequently featured in ancient myths. This character is always on the make, looking for some golden opportunity. Not only do his ill-conceived schemes create funny predicaments, but his seeming inability to quit when he is ahead keeps the stakes rising and the comedy coming. Think young Bart of *The Simpsons* and Stewie of *Family Guy*.

The Mentor

The mentor is a source of wisdom for other characters. However, those other characters usually don't seek his advice until they have already screwed up a situation big-time. Mentors, unlike supportive parents, sometimes are peripheral characters in a sitcom family. In these cases, their distance from the main story action enables them to be more objective when assessing a dilemma. (Which is just as well, since, wise beings that they are, they are less likely to become ensnared in the type of snafus needed to drive a sitcom episode.) Wilson of *Home Improvement* and Brian of *Family Guy* are examples of a mentor.

The Confidant

The confidant is another source of advice, though their advice, unlike the mentor's, is often bad. Taking the role of a best friend, a trusted associate, an uglier sibling, confidants are usually a bit of a loser compared to the show's lead; they get fewer dates, have worse jobs, and are a degree less intelligent. However, they are always eager to discuss the lead's schemes, suspicions, fears, or what she should wear to the ex-boyfriend's wedding. Think Jenna of *30 Rock* and Robert of *Everybody Loves Raymond*.

The Irritant

Some characters exist solely to make other characters miserable, which creates conflict, which leads to comedy. The irritant might range from merely being an obnoxious person, to having a specific hostile agenda (directed against another character). Examples include Newman of *Seinfeld* and Dwight Schrute of *The Office*.

The Romantic Interest

Per our earlier discussion of stories driven by sexual tension, the romantic interest is a character that makes another character "tense." Typically, a lead character desires the romantic interest, but that person is unobtainable because of a gap in social status, a career conflict, or some other obstacle. The couple belongs together but—as was the case with *Earl*'s Randy and Catalina—only we, the audience, can see that. In other shows, two leads both serve as romantic interests to each other and have a healthy relationship. They frequently question and test their relationship, but always reconfirm the strength of their bond by story's end. Jim and Pam of *The Office* are a good example.

The Critic

Many sitcoms feature a character who is always criticizing the people around him. This critic—the "wit" named above—is usually very clever and blunt, and often dead-on in his comments. He gets some of his laughs by dishing out snappy insult humor, and some by having his own wisecracks (born of pretense) backfire on him. In the latter case, either his target gives back better than the critic gave, or the critic discovers that his crack was unintentionally cruel ("That'd almost be funny—if her dog wasn't dead!"). Examples of this character type include Cartman of *South Park* and Stewie of *Family Guy*.

Do recurring character types like the above appear in every show? No. Do producers, when they create a new show, just pick one character type from column A and two from column B, etc.? Let's hope not.

In fact, to describe these behavior patterns as character types is probably too restrictive. While some characters do stick to a particular mold pretty closely, most share a blend of these and other traits. And that blend can shift from week to week, and even *scene to scene*. Frasier would play *supportive parent* to his dad in one episode, and then childlike *idiot* to the man in the next. *30 Rock*'s Jenna might play *confidante* to Liz for two-thirds of a storyline, and then switch to Liz's worst *critic* during a third-act confrontation.

So it is probably most useful to think of these types as just another way to get a handle on how a show's characters might interact during one storyline. Or as a way to describe a character's temporary mode of behavior in a particular sequence or scene.

Visiting Characters

Many sitcom stories feature one or more *visiting characters*, individuals who appear in only one episode or in a string of successive episodes. (Characters who pop up irregularly throughout a season, or over the life of a series, are usually referred to as *recurring characters*.) While, as noted above, you should try to make visiting characters fresh and exciting, there are a few things to remember:

Not Too Fresh and Exciting

Visiting characters should not outshine the series regulars. If a newcomer gets too much screen time or seems too appealing, the show will feel off balance. (And you can bet that the show's producers will get a nasty call from their star's agent, proclaiming that her client is suddenly feeling used, abused, and undervalued.) After all, America tunes in to see the series regulars, not some stranger. Does that mean that you should write low-key, boring visitors? No, just remember that while an outsider might bring a story into an episode, that story should quickly become a regular character's concern. And keep a lid on how much dialogue you throw to your (fresh and exciting) visiting characters.

Regarding Opponents

Stories come from conflict between people, which makes dramatic opponents—half of said people—very important characters. If you are going to tell a juicy, compelling story, and the opponent is a visiting character, that opponent should be as powerful as or even more powerful than the series regular who is featured in the story. Otherwise, there won't be much of a story to tell; the series regular will quickly trounce his opponent and the conflict will be over.

Should a series regular always beat his opponent? Hardly. Remember, in comedy, the third act of a storyline often climaxes with the lead character losing a fight and being humiliated. Which is funny.

Who serves as the opponent in a romantic storyline? While there are often a number of parties who present obstacles to true, if temporary, love, the biggest opponent is usually the romantic interest him- or herself. Whether a love relationship spans the life of a series or only a single episode, the two characters that belong together frequently start out as rivals or enemies. They are made for each other, but are too busy doing battle to realize that fact, at least at first. The pleasure of the story comes from seeing them go through hoops until they finally succumb to their happy fate.

Lastly, as with all characters, the opponent in a story should have human dimensions, his own value system, goals, fears, point of view, etc. A bad guy who is simply bad for bad's sake seems poorly drawn and uninteresting. Consider *South Park*'s Satan, fearsome ruler of all that is unholy, who is most fun to watch when shown struggling with the same personal insecurities and relationship issues that regular people face.

Avoid Repetition—Again

As with story structure, one should think development rather than repetition when creating characters. Avoid introducing visiting characters who are merely a carbon copy of a series regular, *unless* that similarity is part of the episode's comedy. An example using *Two and a Half Men*: What if Charlie discovered that he might be the father of a kid who looks just like Jake, but who is smarter, more helpful, and more fun to have around?

Serving Your Story

Lastly, here are some practical questions to consider when creating a visiting character:

- Who might be the best person to introduce the story?

- Who might help to keep the story moving?

- Who might help to relay important *exposition*? (Exposition, or *pipe*, means information that a viewer must have if she is to understand a story.)

- Who might serve as the best foil to the regular characters?

Moving On

So far, you have dreamed up story ideas, created springboards, selected a great premise, developed your characters, and beaten out the story. The next step? It's time to write an outline.

11

WRITING AN OUTLINE

An outline is a selling tool.

Sure, it provides a description of your episode and aids in the writing process. It helps you to take that wonderful story that you have developed and break it down scene by scene. It forces you to pick the locations and times in which the beats of your script will unfold. You still have holes in the story? Loose ends to tie up? Problems integrating plotlines? It's hard to overlook these details when writing an outline.

But, in addition to helping you refine your story, or helping a producer understand your story, an outline must be interesting to read. And since you are writing for a sitcom, it should be funny. (Here is another instance when your efforts to incorporate humor into the story premise will pay off.) After all, you are trying to sell a producer on the idea that he should invest thousands to have you write a script, and then maybe a million or two to produce an episode, all based on a few skimpy pages of story description. (Which is kind of cool when you think about it.)

What are the exact steps in this process, just to review? If you are a freelance writer, you are trying to land an invite to come in and pitch your ideas, your springboards, to the show's producers. If you are fortunate, they pick idea number six, and give you from two to seven days to come back with a written outline. Or they might invite you in and just dictate a story to you, or develop one with you, and then send you off to put the formal outline on paper. (And, great news, you do get paid for this step.)

When you submit the outline a few days later, the producers usually will give you notes for changes and send you off to revise the document. Two to five days later, you submit the revised outline, and if all goes well, the producers give you more notes and tell you to "go to script." (Congratulations, now you'll be paid even more.) Other times, the writing staff and you will rewrite the outline together, and then you will be told to write the first draft. Or you might be invited in to write the first draft *with* the staff. Still other times, the producers might cut you off and have someone else write a script based on your outline, either because they have already paid for that person's time or they think—based on your outline—that you are a weak writer. (Their mistake, obviously!)

If you are on the staff of a show, the whole process might occur in a less formal fashion, with shorter deadlines, and it might involve group writing and rewriting efforts at different stages.

Fine, so that explains how an outline fits in when you are writing a script *on assignment*. But why waste time writing an outline when working on a spec script, since no producer will ever see the thing?

Fair question. As long as you have beaten out the story as described in previous chapters, you should be in pretty good shape to begin a first draft. However, you probably still haven't translated all of the beats into individual scenes or sewn up assorted loose ends. It would help to at least rough out an outline to clear up some final issues—scene chronology, locations, times, characters present, entrances and exits, and a description of what transpires during each segment. Write it in crayon, in Swahili, use poor grammar and funky punctuation, who cares, but make those last big story decisions before diving into the first draft. If you don't, it's likely that you'll take some wrong turns and stall halfway through the script—which will cost you a LOT more time than writing an outline would have!

Writing to Sell, Not Educate

How do you make a scene outline entertaining? The thing is only five to seven pages, single-spaced—not very long considering all of the story information it has to convey. How can it not seem purely functional?

Well, write it as if it is an amusing short story. Or take the approach that you would use if describing the episode to your best friend. Stick to the main story points and present them with sizzle. Bring the story to life by including *specific descriptions* of the key dramatic moments and funny situations. (Not lengthy, just specific.)

And here's a tip: *Don't be afraid to leave out less-than-critical information!* Because you cannot describe everything that happens in your episode in an outline, *nor should you*. In fact, a sure sign of an inexperienced writer is that he feels compelled to educate the reader. He wants those producers to know every damn detail that he, the writer, has dreamed up. Because only then can the producers fully appreciate the story and him. Right?

Wrong. Excess information slows down "the read." Sure, if you use the tiniest of type fonts, maybe you can fit every single detail into those seven pages. But who wants that? The producer, who has fifty other things on her desk that require her immediate attention, will not appreciate your thoroughness. You want to sell her? Give her just enough to want more. Give her just enough to follow the beats, to get a handle on the characters, to see how the storylines end. Along the way, when you can, leave a little mystery in the air. Leave the producer hanging and let her fill in a few blanks. Make her want to see the script!

No question, it's an art. How much is enough? Or too much? Developing this sense takes a lot of practice, diligent trimming, maybe some feedback from writer friends. A helpful rule of thumb is to frequently ask, "Does the reader absolutely have to know this detail in order to keep up with the story?" Every time you come back with a no, *phhht*, dump it.

Another way to get a handle on what will sell a show's producers is to ask for copies of outlines that were written for the staff's favorite episodes. (Obviously, you should do this *after* the producers have heard your pitch and hired you to write an outline.) Production secretaries are usually helpful about providing such materials if they know that you have actually been hired to develop an episode of the show.

What might they hand you? Just what goes into one of these things?

Building an Outline

An outline breaks your story down into an ordered sequence of individual scenes. It should be only five to seven pages long, single-spaced. (Some producers prefer eight to twelve pages, *double-spaced*, as we will discuss in the next section.)

er, outlines are all about headings and paragraphs: headings line, identify the location and time of a scene; and paragraphs that, sitting below each heading, describe what happens in that scene.

Usually, each scene is described in one paragraph, maybe two. Most of the space is devoted to main storylines, with subplots just getting a line or two here and there. (Some writers prefer to describe the main story developments first, and then end the paragraph with a line describing any subplot developments that also occur in the scene.)

Does each scene in your outline have to feature one of the dramatic beats in your story? No. Sometimes beats are spread across scenes. Let your instincts regarding pacing of the story dictate how you divide it up among scenes.

Here are some additional points to consider when building your outline:

Broadcast Format

As mentioned earlier, a scene outline must reflect the broadcast format regularly used for the series. As you develop and order scenes, now is the time to factor in the scheduling of commercial breaks, the number of (broadcast format) acts in each episode, and whether or not the show uses cold opens or tags. Remember, the timing of commercial breaks might have little to do with how you have structured your story dramatically, but *you should try to position an important plot point or key story moment just before a required break*, to keep the audience tuned during the commercials that follow. (Of course, half of the time, someone higher up will opt to insert an act break at a different point in the story than you originally indicated, but there is nothing you can do about that.)

Unique Aspects of the Show

Now is also a good time to review any unique aspects of the series format that you discovered when you researched the show. Do the episodes always open with a scene from a B Story? How long do the cold opens tend to be? How long are most scenes? Do the acts always end with a huge cliffhanger? Etc. Always follow the show's lead.

Hook the Reader Quickly

By the time a reader gets two or three pages into your script, he should be hooked by at least one storyline. Meaning, he should know what someone is trying to accomplish and why, what is at stake, and what stands in the way. Jokes and clever dialogue are certainly important, but story is what keeps eyes on the screen. Take too long to establish a core conflict and the reader will become frustrated and disinterested.

You say that you can't reveal the story hook early because it would ruin the structure of your episode? Then, at the least, create an air of mystery about the soon-to-be-launched story by hinting that something big is in the works. (Better yet, realize that you probably can adjust your episode's structure and get that story moving right at the beginning of the outline.)

Foreshadowing Story Beats and Jokes

As suggested in the last paragraph, foreshadowing an upcoming beat by hinting that something big is in the works is a great way to keep readers (and viewers) involved. Suspense holds an audience's attention, and the eventual unveiling of the foreshadowed beat provides a satisfying reward.

On a different level, foreshadowing can also aid with *exposition* (i.e., the information that an audience needs to have to keep up with the story). If the audience is to believe that Liz Lemon's new neighbor is truly a dangerous pyscho, it helps to foreshadow that discovery by having that character behave in an increasingly bizarre manner early on.

Whether you are dealing with a plot point or a simple bit of humor, an event sometimes carries more weight if it has been deftly foreshadowed. When that event finally occurs, it can even earn bonus points because the audience is impressed when it realizes that it has been set up.

At the same time, if you reveal too much about an upcoming event or joke while foreshadowing, you'll ruin the surprise, right? So proceed with care—a vague hint is all that's needed.

NOTE: If you plant a seed, remember to harvest it. Otherwise, it might seem that your story is cluttered with unfinished business.

Scene Development

Most scenes develop in much the same way that conventional storylines do. Short or long, they usually feature their own beginning, middle, and end. Characters start the scene with an agenda or particular perspective in mind, and engage in some sort of conflict or discover surprising information (dramatic acts one and two). Then the scene is resolved by having the characters make a decision or take an action that moves the story forward (act three). When the characters proceed to the next scene, the dynamics of the episode's story (and perhaps the characters' goals) have somehow changed. If the scene was strong, it propelled the reader forward to a new point in the story, and/or it raised the stakes of the story. If the scene was weak, it did nothing to develop the episode's story and only served to slow down the read.

Keep Scene Descriptions Brief

In keeping with our make-'em-want-more philosophy, each of your scene descriptions should be lean and mean. When writing an outline for an existing sitcom, that should not be hard to accomplish because the main characters and settings are already familiar to the reader. Simply focus on keeping the story moving and avoid bogging down in minutiae. As in, don't choreograph every detail of that food fight at *The Office*—just start the thing, describe the crowning moment when Angela catches a pie in the face, and move on.

Don't be surprised if the first few scenes of your outline come out a bit longer than the rest. Opening scenes usually contain a lot of exposition (e.g., visiting characters being introduced, the story premise being established, perhaps a new set/location being described, etc.) that has to be gotten out of the way at the top of your episode. Just convey the information in as entertaining and concise a manner as you can.

How It Should Look on Paper

It seems that every producer has a different opinion of how an outline should look on paper. Fortunately, most want to see the same basic elements included in the document. If you've sold a pitch to a show, it is always best to obtain actual samples from a producer's assistant so that your outline can look just like the ones written in-house—the familiar appearance will make your piece more appealing.

There are several software programs that help with outline and script formatting. The best even have templates for specific shows, though you might have to turn off some functions (like scene numbers and special-effects slugs) that belong only in a production draft and not in a spec script. I recommend both of the leading programs, Movie Magic's Screenwriter (available at stores and www.screenplay.com) and Final Draft (at stores and www.finaldraft.com). Each goes for $200–$250 and is well worth the investment.

If you are unable to obtain a sample outline from the actual show, and so that you can double-check to make sure that a software program is providing the correct formatting, here are standard guidelines for writing a professional looking outline:

Fonts, Margins, and Page Numbers

Outlines should be typed in a classic serif typeface, nothing fancy or ornate. The Courier New font has long been the industry standard for screenplays, so I recommend using that or something similar. For ease of reading, the type should be pica size, or 12 point, meaning that you can fit ten letters into an inch of horizontal line space. (Avoid using funky type styles or a variety of type sizes—the pros don't, so you shouldn't.)

As for margins, leave an inch all around—sides, top, and bottom.

As for page numbers, type them way up in the top right corner of every page—say, a half inch in from the top and side of the paper. Every page should be numbered except for the cover page (if you use one) and page one of the actual outline. Some writers also like to include identifying information at the top of every page, directly across from each page number, in the form of a slug like [*Series Title*, "Title of Your Episode"] or ["Title of Your Episode," Your Name].

> NOTE: *Do not include the brackets in your slug—I am using them throughout this section only to indicate the information that you should type.*

Single vs. Double Spacing

Some producers prefer five-to-seven-page, single-spaced outlines, and others prefer eight-to-twelve-page, double-spaced outlines. As always, you should use whichever length and style is used by the producers of the show. If you can't find out which they prefer, I recommend the single-spaced version. (Almost everything we read in life is single-spaced, so why stray from the familiar?)

Cover Page

Some producers prefer that outlines start with a cover page, and some don't—either way is fine. If you want to include a cover page, start by writing the title of the television series a third of the way down the page, centered, in all caps, and either underlined or in bold.

Then skip two lines and type the phrase [OUTLINE: "Title of Your Episode"], centered, with your episode's title encased in quotes and typed in upper- and lowercase letters.

Next, skip four lines and type the word [by], centered, in lowercase.

Then, skip a line and type your name, centered, in upper- and lowercase.

Next, skip down to the lower right corner of the cover page to insert a *block* of contact information. Start by typing the word [CONTACT:] in all caps, flush left *within the block*. On the four or five lines beneath that, type the name, address, phone number, and email address of the person—either your rep or you—whom the producers should contact for follow-up; these lines should all be typed flush left *within the block*, single-spaced, in upper- and lowercase.

Lastly, if you wish to include a copyright notice or a Writers Guild registration notice, type it in the lower left corner of the cover page, directly across from the lowest line in the block of contact information. However, note that many writers advise against placing a registration notice on the title page of a TV series outline or spec script, for two reasons: First, since you created only the story and not the series premise, characters, and settings, it's probably fruitless to even register the material, because you own too few of its creative elements. Second, because of the first argument, placing a registration notice on a title page might make you look like an insecure or inexperienced writer.

NOTE: See "Protecting Your Work" in Chapter 16 of this book for a discussion of copyright and Writers Guild registration issues. See Appendix A for an example of a cover page used for complete scripts, which is similar to the layout used for outlines.

Body of the Outline

If you are going to attach a cover page to your outline, skip to the next paragraph for instructions on how to begin writing the body of the document. If you *do not* wish to attach a cover page, your first step is to provide contact information on page one of the outline. Simply type your name, address, phone number, and email address in an upper corner of the first page, in a single-spaced block, flush left, in upper- and lowercase letters.

Skip down three or four lines from the top of the page and type the series title centered, in all caps, and either underlined or in bold.

Then, skip one line and type [OUTLINE: "Title of Your Episode"], centered, with your episode's title encased in quotes and typed in upper- and lowercase letters.

Then, skip two lines and begin the body of your outline. As previously discussed, a sitcom script always starts with either a *cold open* or the first act. So, type the appropriate heading—either [COLD OPEN] or [ACT ONE]—in all caps, underlined, flush left.

Then skip one line and type the *scene heading* for the first scene. A scene heading (or *slug line*) is typed in upper- and lowercase, underlined, flush left, and consists of three elements. The first element indicates whether the scene will take place indoors or outdoors; the abbreviation [Int.] is used to indicate an interior scene, while [Ext.] indicates an exterior scene. The second element identifies the scene's location—a street, a room, an elevator, a boat, a bus. And the third element, which is separated from the first two by a dash, names the daypart during which the scene takes place. Traditionally, writers are supposed to designate either [Day] or [Night] here because, when it comes down to it, most scenes do not require a more specific time designation. However, there are rare times when you might have a compelling reason to indicate [Dawn] or [Dusk], or a specific clock time, or that the next scene is occurring [Moments Later] or, simply, [Later] than the scene that came before. If there is no gap in the time between scenes, type [Continuous] instead of a daypart or, better yet, just leave that third part of the scene heading blank.

Examples of scene headings? [Int. Hank's Car–Night] means that the scene literally takes place *inside* the car, at night. [Ext. City Bus–Day] means that the bus is part of the scene but is seen from the outside. [Int. Hotel Lobby–Continuous] and [Int. Hotel Lobby] mean exactly the same thing—we are in the lobby, and there is no gap in time between this scene and the previous one.

NOTE: Be sure to take a look at the script guidelines in Appendix A. They include several nuances that also apply to outlines.

After each scene heading, skip one space and then describe the action of the scene in a paragraph or two, typed in upper- and lowercase.

When beginning the next scene, skip two lines before typing the new scene heading.

When you reach the end of a cold open, skip four lines and start your first act, by typing the act heading—[ACT ONE]—in all caps, underlined, flush left. Then, proceed with the next scene.

When you reach the end of the first act, skip two lines after the last scene and type [END OF ACT ONE], in all caps, centered, and underlined. *Then, start the next act on a new page*. Indicate the new act by typing [ACT TWO] at the top of the next page, flush left, in all caps, and underlined. Then, just as before, skip a line before typing the next scene heading. This pattern is repeated if your episode also includes a third act.

If your episode includes a tag, skip four lines after writing [END OF ACT TWO]—or [END OF ACT THREE], if you have one—and type [TAG] flush left, in all caps, and underlined. Then skip one line and describe the scene.

To indicate the very end of the episode, skip two lines after the very last scene and type [END OF EPISODE] in all caps, centered, and underlined.

Here's an example of how an outline might look on paper. This excerpt comes from a *Family Guy* script developed by a talented student of mine,

Maggie Fremont. In this story, Peter Griffin is inspired to produce his own version of the *To Catch a Predator* show, and has no qualms about entrapping innocent people in his hunt for child predators. Note that the scene descriptions are simple and brief, and they include some of the jokes that we'd see.

EXCERPT *of an Episode Outline:*

ACT TWO

Int. Parked Van — Day

Brian and Stewie man the controls for the hidden cameras. Stewie plays director, threatening to go all Christian Bale on the dog if he screws up a shot.

Int. The Griffins' Kitchen — Continuous

Peter gives Meg a pep talk as they wait for the predator to arrive. They've got an easy first target—Quagmire. Peter puts a Zac Efron mask on Meg's face, saying that he looks more like a girl than Meg does. Meg is about to protest, but realizes he's right.

Peter hides as Quagmire enters. Meg starts to flirt. Quagmire is okay with the face but something about the body just isn't working for him. Luckily, he brought his own blindfold. Before he can put it on, Peter strolls in. He asks Quagmire to sit down, then stand up, then sit down. This continues awkwardly until . . .[1]

Stylistic Tips

Here are some stylistic pointers to consider when writing your outline:

"Play It, Don't Say It"

This well-worn phrase suggests that one should avoid having characters enter a scene and tell us about an important event that has happened elsewhere. Rather, we should *see* the big stuff (e.g., confrontations, decisions, tender moments, etc.) happen. That's why we tuned in, right?

Write in the Present Tense

Outlines and scripts are written in the present tense, partly because they must be shot in the present tense. (Laws of physics.) Also, it is far more compelling to envision actions unfolding right in front of us rather than to picture them as dated events. So type that "Peter jumps for joy" rather than "Peter jumped for joy."

"And It Will Be Really Funny Here"

Remember when I said that a sitcom outline should actually be amusing to read? Sorry, but pointing out where funny things *might go* does not count. Either cough up a bit of humor when needed or quickly move on, hoping that the reader himself will fill in that blank with an imagined joke.

Including Dialogue in an Outline

Sometimes the best way to illustrate a story beat or draw some comedy from an outline is to include a *very brief* snippet of clever dialogue. Fine, great idea. But only if the dialogue is really, really good—funny, true to character, just enough and no more. Many an outline has ground to a halt because a writer tossed in a chunk of dull dialogue, serving only to give his producers second thoughts about assigning him the first draft.

Describing Characters and Scenes

If a character or setting is a standard component of a television series, you do not need to describe him or it in your outline. Just tell us that "Charlie enters" and we'll get the picture.

When introducing a visiting character, a new setting, or the original characters in a new series, just give us the essentials. We only need a phrase or two that describes appearance and current attitude, to catch on. The character's subsequent actions will clue us in on his personality, and superfluous details about a setting will only slow down the read.

How do you slip that character or setting description into the outline? Smoothly. Integrate it into the story rather than set it apart so that it distracts the reader. Nobody wants to see a separate paragraph, a list, an asterisk, or italicized type that points out some boring, functional exposition.

Lastly, format-wise, many producers prefer that a new character's name be typed in all caps the first time, and only the first time, that he is mentioned in an outline. Others don't care. You decide.

Avoid Using the Royal "We"

Some writers tend to describe actions and events by using phrases like "*We see* the door open" or "*We hear* a door slam." This is no crime, but it does strain the reader's suspension of disbelief by reminding him that he is reading an outline rather than witnessing live events. When possible, just go with "The door opens" or "A door slams"—no more description is needed.

Paint the Picture

An outline is supposed to be an entertaining read, right? Make it so by using active verbs and specific details to paint compelling pictures of the story's events. No, you do not want to overdramatize quiet moments or inflate descriptive phrases. And you definitely do not want to pile on purple prose (i.e., showy adjectives and adverbs, metaphors, etc.). But you can sometimes improve a line by writing "Homer inhales the donut" rather than "Homer eats the donut."

No Camera Angles

You are the writer, not the director. Unless a specific camera angle or move is *absolutely necessary* to your story or a featured joke, do not include it in your outline.

ptions? Sure. Material written for animated series often con-
a judicious selection of camera angles, since those shows enjoy a
shoot-anything-we-want flexibility. But it's better to include few rather
than many of these directions—less is almost always more.

Leave Lots of White Space

Producers and executives love white space. Blank areas at the bottom of
pages mean that there is less reading to do, and they make a script seem
like a quick read since the pages fly by faster. So do not crowd your margins or forgo traditional spacing to squeeze something in. If something
doesn't quite fit at the bottom of a page, even if it will leave a bit of a gap,
just move it to the next page. You will make some producer or executive
very happy. (This does not mean that you should use extra-wide margins
or space out the script elements in a nonstandard fashion.)

Don't Get Funky

You can have lots of fun with exotic paper stocks, funky typefaces, wacky
formatting—just don't do it here. The pros don't, and you want your outline to look just like theirs, right? So stick to standard fonts, plain white
paper, and a trusty staple.

Be a Perfectionist

Believe it—spelling, grammar, and punctuation matter. Sloppy writing suggests that either you don't care or are not capable. So proofread, ask others
to proofread, and rewrite the thing until you are 100 percent satisfied.

Rewriting an Outline

As mentioned earlier, producers usually ask that an outline be rewritten
per their notes before they will authorize a writer to begin the script. (They
might give you notes in a meeting, over the phone, or via a fax or email.)
Since you care about your work, you might find yourself becoming a tad
defensive—okay, homicidal—when they ask for these changes.

Well, try to keep your cool and focus on two primary goals: You want them to ask you to write the script based on that outline, and you want them to enjoy working with you so much that they hire you to write another (freelance) script or put you on staff. Your job is to show that you are a professional, a can-do type of person, and that you are fun to have around. *Never underestimate the value of personal chemistry when it comes to getting work!*

Sure, you can lobby against changes that you think will hurt your story, but the moment that you see a producer's jaw clench or his eyes glaze over, back off. And smile while you're doing it. Get the notes, salvage what you can, and make the changes work. Most times, as much as it will irk you, the producer's suggestions will actually improve your story.

What if you are writing an outline for a spec script and don't have to impress any producers? Well, unless everything you write is always brilliant the first time out, you should consider passing the thing around to get feedback from friends, family, and associates in the business. (Often, the most insightful comments come from people who *aren't* in the business.) And take a second look yourself. Because it is a lot easier to identify and correct story problems at this phase than when you are knee-deep in dialogue.

Advice from Our Producers

What else should you know when writing an outline?

MATT WILLIAMS: Rarely does a writer come in and pitch an episode with an A story, a B story, a runner, and lay it all out the way the staff would. So what we usually do is, we may like one element of the story, or we may say, "You know what? This B story is wonderful. Let's find an A story that we can wrap around this B story." And then, usually, we'll have them go off and think about it, but rarely do we have them go off, beat out the story, and then we look at the outline and send them off to write a first draft. We almost always spend at least half a day, a day, sometimes as many as three days in the room beating out the story together. . . . Usually, to actually write an outline, we'll work with them for a half a day. Then, we'll give them two days to write the outline. Again, this will vary depending on where you are in the [television] season. At the beginning of the season, you've got the time. If we're on episode twenty, we'll say, "Bring it back tomorrow."

Then, what we look for in an outline is clarity. That in every scene there is some dramatic progression to the story. That it's clear what the characters are doing and what they want. . . . In a bad outline, the characters will jump from one track to another to another to accommodate the story. "I don't understand. At the beginning of the episode, he wanted to rob a bank. How come he's buying a used car? And then he's picking up a lost puppy?"

Nine times out of ten, you get to that two-thirds mark in an outline, that sweep up to that final turning point, and that's when most outlines will fall apart, because the writer doesn't really know where they're going. They know how to set it up. They know how to complicate things. And then they get two-thirds of the way there, and they kind of peter out and go, "Oh, I'm not sure what this episode's about or where I'm going."

MICHAEL REISS: When producers are working with you to develop an outline, don't be afraid of parroting back just what they gave you. Often a new writer will say, "Well, gee, they don't want to see exactly what they told me to write"—Yes, we do! We want to see that! Exactly! If you can improve on what was decided, great, but don't be afraid to regurgitate. And the flip side is, if the producers tell you don't do something, DON'T do it.

MAXINE LAPIDUSS: Generally, for that first assignment, [a freelancer's story outline] is going to be pitched out to within an inch of its life. I mean, it's got to fit into a slot between episodes five and eight, so certain things are going to have to be accomplished [in that story]. . . . We'll say, "Okay, the germ of this idea is great. We want to do this episode, and this is how we think it should go." And then the writer will go off and work on that, and come back to us with another pitch—a full-blown pitch—which would constitute the story meeting. And then we would take maybe a day or two or three, to really beat out the story [with that writer], beat by beat.

IRMA KALISH: You don't want to put too much dialogue or too many jokes into the outline because by the time the producer reads the first draft, he'll be saying, "I know I've heard this joke before. This must be an old joke." So you can put a little touch here and there just to make sure that the producer knows that you can do comedy. But don't put all the jokes in.

SANDY FRANK: When something happens with a character, what is his emotional reaction? You should probably even put that into your outline. He's scared. He's upset. He's annoyed. He decides he wants revenge, whatever. Because, otherwise, what happens a lot is that you force the characters to do things that don't come naturally.

IAN GURVITZ: If they pitch you a story that you really like, or some combination of your ideas and their ideas turns into a story, you talk about it for a few hours and then at some point, maybe because of time restrictions, you say, "Do you think you have enough to just bang out an outline?" And usually the person says, "Yeah. Let me go with it." (Secretly you're hoping they say yes, because you're sick of talking about it and have other work to do.)

If you sit with a writer all day and you break the story, the outline you get back better reflect exactly what was said in the room. If they've added their own jokes to it or if they say, "You know, we talked about such-and-such this way, but it doesn't really seem to work. What about if we go another way," that's fine. . . .

If you short shrift the story process, you're going to be in for late hours and a nightmare production week when that story falls apart.

12

WRITING THE FIRST DRAFT

Once your outline is done, and redone, congratulations—you are finally ready to tackle that first draft. If you are working on an actual assignment, your producers will usually give you one to two weeks for this step. That's seven to fourteen days to write about thirty pages (if writing in film format) of quality primetime television.

Where do you start?

Producer MAXINE LAPIDUSS: You sometimes only have four or five days to write a first draft. Now, my sister, who's a comedy writer too, once worked on a show with a gentleman named Robert Blair. And so he, we, have something that we call the "Blair System." The first day, when I'm sitting down and I have to get the script out, rather than craft the first page, and make sure that the descriptions are perfect, and that there are five really sharp jokes on that page – now I "Blair" through the script. I try to write two to three scenes, a whole first act, the first day. Because it's much easier to go back and rewrite later. It's not just a blank page.

Just Do It

Just start writing. You have done all of the prep work. Now let the creative half of your brain cut loose and go crank out a rough draft. Naturally, you should consult your outline regarding story development and scene structure. And you can use the same page layout that you saw when you studied scripts from the show. Just mark this page of the book and set it aside, turn off the editor in your head, and come back in thirty pages. Then, use the information in this chapter and the script format guidelines in Appendix A to clean up your rough draft.

You don't feel ready to dive in just yet? That is fine too. This a creative process and we all create differently. If you prefer, read the rest of this chapter first and then tackle your script.

What if, halfway through the first draft, you come up with a new story direction or some different scenes that would greatly improve the script? If you are writing a spec script, then great, run with it. The Sitcom Police won't arrest you if you stray from your original outline. However, if you are writing a script on assignment, check with your producers before you make any radical changes; those people don't like to receive huge surprises when reading a first draft.

If you do decide to make big changes halfway through a draft, my advice is that you should take the time to create a new beat sheet and perhaps a revised outline before plunging ahead. Otherwise, you might wreak havoc on your episode's structure.

Writing Scenes

Here are some thoughts to consider when writing the scenes of your script. Linda Seger, in her book *Making a Good Script Great*, makes the following points:

> Through the use of images and dialogue, a great scene advances the story, reveals character, explores an idea, and builds an image. A great scene will do all of these. A good scene will do more than one.... Film is dimensional. A scene can accomplish many purposes, all at the same time. The background might be showing an image. The actions might reveal character. A piece of dialogue might advance the story. And the combination of all of these can explore the theme.[1]

While not all scenes can accomplish all of the above goals, each scene should be unique and have purpose. Being funny, by itself, is not enough.

Here are some other thoughts on writing scenes:

First Scenes Are Critical

Agents, managers, writers, producers, and executives are busy people. If your first few scenes are weak (i.e., slow, not funny, clichéd), none of these folks will keep reading long enough to discover that "the script really picks up in the second act." By then, the thing will have been tossed onto the "don't call us, we'll never call you" pile.

Avoid this by grabbing your reader immediately, right in the first few pages. How? By opening with a solid story hook and fresh humor. Remember: Sitcom scripts average two to four solid jokes per page, starting with the *first* page. And I don't mean clever scene descriptions or minor wordplay—I'm talking real jokes. If you're not sure you're hitting the mark, get a red pen and check off the full-fledged jokes in those first pages (or the whole script). If you come up short, you know what to do—fix it.

Scene Length

Sitcom scenes can range in length from an eighth of a page to five or more pages. If you are writing a spec for an existing series, follow whatever patterns or trends are used by that show. (You should have noted such patterns when you first studied the series.) While there are no formal rules regarding lengths of scenes, most probably run two to four pages (when writing in film format). Longer scenes are fine, but once you head north of five pages, you might want to consider how that scene affects the overall pacing of your script.

Start Late, Finish Early

Today's audiences are so sophisticated, having watched thousands of hours of television and film, that they require very little orientation when viewing a program. Open a scene with two characters in the middle of a raging argument and viewers will catch right on—they don't need to start out by seeing two minutes of a conversation turning hostile. If you start a scene too early, it will seem drawn out and dull. Start a scene as late as you can, and it will open with momentum and sweep the viewer right along with the story.

Similarly, once a scene is done, once the story points have been covered, get out of it. End the thing. Allow its momentum to carry us into the next scene. Don't linger to rehash an issue or squeeze in extra jokes.

> *NOTE: For some great examples of how little scene information an audience requires, watch the film* Pulp Fiction. *The Oscar-winning screenplay for this movie required the audience to fill in numerous blanks concerning everything from locations to character backstories.*

How do you judge starting a scene too early versus starting too late? Use the old exposition test—"Does the audience *really* need to know this stuff? And, does it need to know it *now*?"

Are there any exceptions to this "start-late-finish-early" maxim? Of course. You might deliberately prolong a segment to establish a particular mood (e.g., young lovers struggling through a first dinner date). Or to build dramatic tension (e.g., young lovers struggling through a first dinner date, at *her folks' house*). Sometimes a more languorous approach is just the ticket, though you are more likely to see that tack used in straight drama than in modern, keep-it-moving sitcomedy.

Character Entrances and Exits

How many times have you seen this: One character says her good-byes and exits a scene, just as another character oh-so-conveniently enters through a second door to pick up the conversation. The obviousness of this maneuver reminds viewers that they are watching a staged (poorly staged) show.

Characters should have a good reason to enter or exit a scene. If you will need them later but want to avoid an awkward entrance, give them a good reason to be present at the beginning of the scene and then engage them when the time is right.

Same goes for exits: If a character has a dramatic need to exit, then have him exit dramatically. Or keep him handy and use him during the rest of the scene.

End with a Button

A *button* is a clever line or small dramatic twist located at the very end of a scene. (If it's a joke, it might also be called a *blow*.) It is used to provide closure before moving on to the next story segment. Buttons can range in weight from a simple punchline for a joke, to a revelation that affects the story.

Buttons are compact, clever things—a big story beat that ends a scene is not the same animal. While most writers always aspire to be clever (and compact), it is not always desirable to end scenes with a button. Sometimes it is better to close with a big revelation, a note of mystery, a quiet moment, or a simple reaction line.

Of course, if a scene ending is also an act break (heading into a commercial), it's best to close with a cliff-hanger based on a new plot point, to keep viewers tuned until the episode resumes.

Using a Montage Sequence

A *montage* is a string of very short scenes—three, five, or more—that provides a quick view of someone going through a sequence of steps. In sitcoms, you might see a montage of *Family Guy*'s Peter Griffin stumbling through a series of exercises as he prepares for a competition, or Earl doing a variety of favors to placate one of his past victims. While a writer shouldn't overuse this device, it can be a remarkable tool for compressing time and actions. Most montage sequences incorporate little, if any, dialogue, and all (sitcom versions) feature a healthy dose of visual humor. One or two montage sequences in a script is fine, but it might seem distracting to incorporate more—unless you are intentionally repeating them as a joke. (Details regarding the page layout of a montage sequence are provided in Appendix A.)

Pacing of Scenes

If you have developed a well-structured story and kept your scenes lean and mean, you should be in pretty good shape regarding the pacing of your script. Otherwise, it's a matter of just going with what feels right. Sometimes you will want to trim here or indulge in a moment there. As long as you give preference to decisions that serve the overall script rather than those that favor merely one scene, you will probably do just fine.

Don't Overdo Visual Humor in a Spec

I believe that it is a mistake to base too much of a spec script's comedy on *visual* humor. Some writers would disagree with me, but my reasoning is this: Visual humor is meant to be seen, right? Producers and execs giving your script a ten-minute read are more likely to catch dialogue jokes than funny images crammed into a scene description. In my experience, a surprising number of industry pros aren't even able to appreciate visual jokes (in a script) because they just don't have an aptitude for translating written type into images. (This is not a dig, just a different-people-have-different-strengths thing.) So, unless a series is all about physical gags, I advise against writing a spec script that relies too heavily on visual humor. Once you get the job and have more leeway, you can go wild with the stuff.

Harvesting Comedy Built into the Premise and Scene Levels

Guess what—you've already done the hard part. You have created a funny story, composed of funny scenes, and you have studied the art of writing seamless jokes. The humor is all there, just write the words. And have fun. This phase of the job is the reason people get into sitcom writing.

What if you hit a bump and the jokes just aren't coming? Flip back to Chapter 6 for a quick review, and see if that shakes things loose. Also, think back to the elements that made the episode premise seem funny to you in the first place.

Professional Script Format

Let's not do this here. For details of how a professional script looks on paper, turn to Appendix A. There you will find complete instructions for writing in three different styles, *film format* (the page layout used for shows shot with a single camera), *tape format* (the layout used for shows shot with multiple cameras), and *animation format* (for shows created via some animation process). When you first research a show, one of the things you should find out is which shooting style it uses, so you'll know which script format to use.

Please understand that script format is very important. If your script doesn't look just like a professional's, the reader will be reminded, on every page, that you are not a professional. Who wants that? Sure, once you have racked up a few Emmys and are producing your own show, you can get creative. But until then . . .

For now, all that you need to know about format is that half-hour, live-action sitcom scripts are about thirty pages long if written in film format, and forty-five to fifty pages long if written in (the more loosely spaced) tape format. Half-hour animation scripts are written in sort of a mix of the two formats, and usually run forty to fifty pages.

Whichever format is used, the two primary elements that appear on a script page are scene descriptions and character dialogue. Let's talk about them.

Writing Scene Descriptions

Scene descriptions are very brief paragraphs that depict the setting of a scene. They describe the physical layout of the space, the characters who are present, and any important actions that occur during the scene. While scene descriptions found in movie scripts are sometimes lengthy and dramatic, those featured in sitcom scripts are short and sweet. They frequently consist of no more than a single line like "Chris enters and plops down on the couch." Why the minimalist approach? Most of a sitcom's scenes take place in a finite number of familiar sets and involve limited doses of physical action, so there is little need for elaborate descriptions. (And, of course, viewers at home will never read or hear a script's scene descriptions.)

Where do scene descriptions actually occur on the page? An opening description can usually be found immediately following each scene heading in a script, since readers need at least some information about the setting of the coming scene. Additional descriptions are inserted between dialogue segments whenever the story requires them—a new character enters the room, the phone rings, two characters start wrestling, smoke pours out of the oven, etc.

Here are a few stylistic points to consider when writing scene descriptions. (You will remember some of these from our discussion regarding story outlines.)

Write All Scene Descriptions in the Present Tense

. . . because scripts are shot in the present.

Paint the Picture

Though scene descriptions are supposed to be brief and functional, they should not be boring. When appropriate, use active verbs and specific details to describe the action in a scene. But leave out those adverbs and adjectives when you can.

Avoid Using the Royal "We"

Just describe the action as you would in a short story. Otherwise, using phrases like "we hear" and "we see" reminds the reader that he is reading a script.

Viewers Won't Get to Read the Scene Descriptions

. . . so don't cram them with exposition or backstory (e.g., "It occurs to Earl that his mother once had a bunion just like it."). If viewers need to know or see something, reveal it through actions or dialogue.

Grammar and Punctuation

Use proper grammar and punctuation in your scene descriptions unless you are deliberately writing in a loose conversational style. Which approach is better? Both work. But if your attempts at conversational prose occasionally seem stilted or forced because you haven't yet found that voice in your writing, stick with the more formal approach. Better to be safe than awkward. (Naturally, *dialogue* should be written in a conversational style—make that a variety of conversational styles—since each character speaks in a unique voice.)

No Camera Directions

Unless you *absolutely must* indicate a camera angle in order to describe a joke or moment, do not include one in your script! Most times, a good writer can accomplish the same goal by directing the reader's attention through artful scene descriptions. You want a close-up to show Liz's surprised face when she opens that door? Just write "Liz's jaw drops" when you describe her reaction. The reader will picture Liz's face *in close-up*. Mission accomplished, without camera angles.

Choreographing Big Action Scenes

As with camera directions, it is not your job to choreograph every little detail of a big action scene. Just launch us into the food fight or the mud-wrestling match, describe a few key moments, and tell us how the thing comes out. Trust the director and his actors to connect the dots, or you will end up with a thirty-second scene that takes up three pages of your script.

No Maps, Pictures, or Blueprints

Do not draw on your script. If you can't describe the essence of a location or an action via a scene description, it's time to find a new career.

Indicating a Pause

There will be many times when you will want to indicate a brief pause in a scene. Perhaps you want to suggest an awkward moment between characters, or that a character is taking a beat to react to something that another has said or done. To indicate such a pause, simply type either [Pause.] or [Beat.] as a line in the scene description. (In fact, that one-word sentence, by itself, often serves as the *entire* scene description.) Then resume the action or dialogue.

NOTE: Obviously, this new meaning of the word "beat"—as in, "she takes a beat to respond"—is not to be confused with a story beat.

Indicating a Reaction

There will be times when you will want to indicate that a character gives a particular reaction—she looks stunned, frustrated, dismayed, whatever—but the type of reaction seems so obvious that it would be lame to actually describe the thing. To indicate that the (obvious) reaction does occur, simply type a line of scene description that reads [Character Name reacts.]. As with [Pause.] or [Beat.], this two- or three-word sentence often serves as the entire scene description.

Writing Dialogue

On paper, a character's dialogue is written as a block of sentences positioned directly beneath his name. As described more fully in Appendix A, his speech might begin with or include a *dialogue cue*—a word or several words that describes the character's mood or an action that he performs while speaking.

If you have studied the characters in a series and have a good ear, your dialogue should ring true. If you don't quite feel that you have captured a character's voice, you might find it useful to look at two things: speech patterns unique to that character, and ways in which emotions might affect his speech.

Unique Speech Patterns

Everybody speaks in a unique voice. To get a handle on how a particular character talks, you might try looking for clues in his or her . . .

Sentence Structure

Does she use proper grammar, or talk in double negatives and mismatched verbs? Does he describe himself in the third person ("George is not happy!")? Does she speak in complex sentences thick with haughty references (as some of Jack Donaghy's snooty girlfriends do), or is she a short-sentence, monosyllabic type (like *Two and a Half Men*'s Berta)?

Vocabulary

Does the character use big words, small words, right words, or wrong words? (Compare Tracy Jordan to Jack Donaghy, or Stewie Griffin to his brother, Chris.) Does the character swear or use vulgar language? (Cartman does, Bart Simpson doesn't.) Are his words appropriate for his age, education, and cultural background? (How many times have you seen a kid character walk on stage and start talking like a grown-up?) Does he use a unique vernacular inspired by his interests, career, or environment? Does he concoct his own words or labels? (Many a love-struck character addresses his romantic interest by using cuddly, made-up names.)

Pronunciation

Some characters regularly mispronounce words, either because they lack a strong vocabulary (Homer Simpson) or English is not their native tongue (*Earl*'s Catalina). Others are distinguished by the pains that they take to pronounce every syllable clearly (*30 Rock*'s Kenneth). Similarly, some characters tend to use contractions ("he's," "they're," "don't," etc.) while others would never do so.

> NOTE: *When writing for characters that speak with an accent, avoid slowing down the read by including too many corrupted spellings in your dialogue. Just insert a funky mispronunciation every line or so and the reader will remember that the character talks in fractured English.*

How Emotions Affect Speech

Not only does every character speak with a unique voice, but each person's emotions affect his speech in unique ways. Depending on the context of a particular scene, you might find it helpful to consider how your characters would act if they were . . .

Arguing

When arguing, people tend to yell, stumble over words, omit words, swear, and start slamming things. But that's the norm. How would your characters act? Do they grow quiet? Become martyrlike? Babble incoherently?

Depressed
Depressed people often become monosyllabic, speak negatively, talk in short sentences, and reach for chocolate. Your characters?

Happy
Happy people tend to talk exuberantly, use glowing adjectives, view everything in a positive manner, and speak in run-on sentences.

Fearful
Frightened people tend to use short sentences, curse, exclaim, and repeatedly call for help or mercy.

Anxious
Anxious people often chatter to themselves about their concerns, repeatedly ask for reassurance, focus on negative consequences, and overanalyze comments made by others.

Other emotional dynamics that affect speech include a desire to seduce, placate, manipulate, impress, terrorize, and so on. An artfully drawn character will act (speak) differently in each circumstance.

Comedic Nuances

One thing that every writer wants to hear a producer say is, "You really nailed the characters' voices." Part of the trick to achieving that feat is to develop a feel for the little comedic nuances that distinguish a character's dialogue. Here are just a few examples of the many traits that might shape a character's voice:

The Understated Response
No matter what's happening, characters like *Earl*'s Darnell and *Californication*'s Hank always give a low-key response. The house could be burning, thugs threatening, the sky falling, whatever, they just don't seem

to get very excited, and their incongruous reactions almost guarantee a laugh.

Exaggerated Response
Think characters like *Earl*'s Joy or *30 Rock*'s Tracy Jordan. Outrageous, flamboyant, sometimes a touch wacko, these types generate laughs by overreacting to even the most ordinary of events. (Another incongruous response.)

Irony
Some characters love to play the caustic commentator or misunderstood martyr, and others are so dumb they don't even know when they're putting their own foot in their mouth. All three types deliver speeches that feature dry irony, which Webster's defines as the "use of words to convey a meaning that is the opposite of its literal meaning." Think Ari Gold from *Entourage*, when he offers someone a truce with "Let's hug it out, bitch!"[2] or Johnny ("Drama") bungling a boast with "I've been working steady the past twelve years, minus the last three."[3]

Nervous Babbling
When the going gets rough, some characters get babbling. *30 Rock*'s Kenneth will do brief spurts of this when stressed, while *The Office*'s Kelly drones on about trivial issues or relationship problems so often that the habit has become a primary trait of her character.

Pulls No Punches
Some characters astound and amuse by being brutally honest and frequently offensive. *Californication*'s Hank is always blunt and sometimes rude: "Well, you should've called. I wouldn't have answered, but you coulda left a message, which I would've quickly erased."[4] But *Entourage*'s Ari Gold will always hold the prize for being openly aggressive and hostile: "Hey, Adam. . . . Just so you know, your girlfriend, when she was in the mailroom, offered to blow me. True story."[5]

Space-Shot POV
Some characters see the universe from such a different point of view that their comments and responses frequently consist of twisted but funny

logic. Their words make sense, but only if you live in a different dimension. Creed of *The Office* is an example.

Wordplay

Jerry Seinfeld is an example of a performer who can get a string of laughs just by juggling a word, or several words, for an entire speech. Wordplay involves repetition, juxtaposition, and playing off of different meanings of a word. For instance:

> How do they do it? How? Do they know people I don't know? Or do I know the people they know, but I don't know it—because I know the right people, but those people are holding out on me. I don't know![6]

Double Entendre

Some characters are always on the make (e.g., *Two and a Half Men*'s Charlie and *Family Guy*'s Quagmire). Their speeches frequently feature a sexual connotation, and they often interpret other characters' (innocent) lines as having a second, risqué meaning.

Again, these are just a few ways that a character's dialogue might be distinguished by comedic nuances or traits. Obviously, the best way to develop a feel for an existing character's voice is to watch episodes and read scripts from his show.

Miscellaneous Tips

Here are a few more points to consider when writing dialogue:

Speech Length

The average character's speech—in a sitcom, not Shakespeare—probably ranges from one to five sentences in length. If a character is lecturing, ranting, or emoting, it might go on for half of a page, maybe three-quarters of a page. But if that character is still speaking after a full page, shoot him.

Or at least, trim his speech, or have another character interrupt his speech with questions or punchlines. Though the dialogue might be enthralling, it could cause a break in pacing that will call the audience's attention to the fact that they are watching a show. (Make that "a soliloquy.") Usually, the only times that such overlong speeches make it to the screen are when an Emmy-lusting star has bullied the producers into letting him wax dramatic, or the show is a hit and suddenly the head writer thinks he *is* Shakespeare.

Superfluous Dialogue Cues

Unskilled writers often include too many dialogue cues in their scripts, which slows down the read. If the dialogue is good, the reader won't need any help in figuring out what moods the characters are experiencing when they deliver their lines. And the writer should trust the director and his actors to interpret the script; often, they will put a fresh spin on the material that gives it a whole new dimension.

Overusing Character Names in Dialogue

Avoid having characters use another character's name every time they address that character. They only need to say the name once or twice early on in order for the audience to remember it. The exception is if you are writing for a character whose nature is such that she frequently addresses other people by their names when she speaks.

Offensive Language

Adult sitcoms, particularly on cable television, often include a lot of coarse language in character dialogue. That's fine as long as that language is true to character. However, language and moral views *included in scene descriptions* reflect on the writer, not the story's characters. Unless you wish to risk offending a sensitive producer or executive—some are more conservative than you would think—you might want to keep your scene descriptions clean. (Hey, I am not your mother or the Sitcom Censor—I only mention this because I want to see you employed.)

Too Nail-on-the-Head

Avoid having a character deliver a line that is too *nail-on-the-head*, or *on the nose*. Meaning, don't let a character blurt out an important statement or fact in so blunt a fashion that his speech seems fake and the tension of the moment is lost. ("I don't want to propose because she might reject me.") These blunders are hard to catch, but if a line seems too stiff, abrupt, or dramatically convenient, see if you can come up with a less direct, more realistic way to handle the speech. You've heard of "dramatic subtext"? Where characters hold back feelings, lie, or say the opposite of what they mean? Often, that's a better way to play a dialogue exchange because it automatically creates tension and it reflects human behavior.

Signature Lines

Some characters are distinguished by a signature phrase that they frequently use (e.g., Michael Scott's "That's what she said."). These phrases wear thin quickly, so use them once or twice in your script, if you must, to demonstrate familiarity with the show's character, and then take evasive action.

Planting Exposition

Exposition can be defined as information that an audience needs to know in order to keep up with a story. As always, less is more—your job is to entertain, not educate. As mentioned earlier, you can't go too far wrong if you remember two questions: "Does the audience *really* need to know this stuff?" And "Does it need to know it *now*?"

When you choose to reveal exposition, it should be seamlessly integrated into your story. Avoid having a character run in to tell us about some critical event that happened elsewhere. Instead, *show us* the event—that's why we tuned in.

Screenwriting guru Robert McKee points out that exposition can sometimes be served up as a plot point, thereby performing double duty. He names an example from the film *The Empire Strikes Back*: "You can't kill me, Luke. I am your father." By using a piece of exposition to drive the story forward, the writers created a powerful moment; the audience must deal with both a huge revelation about two primary characters and the impact that this news will certainly have on the rest of the film's plot.

McKee also points out that sometimes one can disguise exposition with jokes or an argument. The audience still gets the information, but is too involved in the material to notice.

Another technique deals with characters or actions that seem too incredible to believe, such as a three-year-old who knows karate or a horse that talks. A writer has a better chance of selling an outrageous idea if she has one of her characters proclaim that "That's crazy!" The fact that someone has acknowledged the outrageousness of the idea reassures viewers, helping them to maintain their suspension of disbelief. (This used to be referred to as "hanging a lantern on" an implausible piece of information.)

Similarly, an unlikely idea goes down a lot easier if you foreshadow the information. You want to have a character suspect that his new chum might be dangerously psychotic? When you introduce the newcomer, start by creating a little mystery about his background. Then, reveal a string of increasingly ominous facts as you go, so that it later seems reasonable to accept the idea that this chum is actually a homicidal maniac. The audience will usually go along with a fantastic notion as long as you don't just spring it on them at the last moment.

Another important type of exposition involves *characters expressing their emotions and beliefs*. Some writers shy away from having characters state how they feel about other characters or emotionally charged situations. True, such deeply personal dialogue can be difficult to write without getting gooey or lapsing into clichés. However, viewers want to see these moments—they represent the heart of a story's conflict. And viewers need to hear characters express their feelings in order to keep track of where the story is heading. So be bold and reveal your characters' emotions and beliefs through dialogue. As long as you keep an eye out for clichés and stay true to the characters' voices, the clarity of these statements will strengthen your story.

On a more functional level, *characters should also state their goals*. You're the writer, so you know what the character wants to accomplish. But if someone doesn't clarify those goals for the audience, your story might appear unfocused. Of course, if you can't figure out what words a character should say to describe his goal, then you have a bigger problem—your story *is* unfocused. If even you can't explain what your characters want at any given point, there is no way that an audience will be able to keep up.

Advice from Our Producers

What are producers hoping to see in a spec script, or in the first draft of an assigned script?

MATT WILLIAMS: I look for three things. First, is the voice true to the series? In other words, are the voices those of the characters in the series? In a really good spec script, you read the first three, five pages, and you know instantly that the writer has captured the voice of the regular characters. There's a certain tone, a certain world that's established with each sitcom, and the first thing is, has the writer tapped into that world?

Secondly, I look to see if the story is moving along. For a lack of a better word, does the plot work? Sometimes what will happen is that we stop for a scene or two to do a bunch of jokes about toast or something, and you go, "This doesn't have anything to do with the story." . . . I want a story that's driven by character motivation. I want to understand why characters are doing something. I think one of the big things that happens in spec scripts is that you have characters doing incredibly wacky things, but you stop and go, "But why would they ever do that?" And the writer's answer usually is "Well, it's funny." [Wrong answer.] You have to be real within the parameters set up in the sitcom.

The third thing I look for is just—I guess the best label would be "punch." Are there any really funny, unexpected moments, situations, or lines? Anything that surprises me? Because, after you've done this for awhile, you kind of know the rhythm. You know there's going to be a setup, setup, punch. . .

I'm less concerned about individual jokes or moments. Is the story working? Are the characters clear? Because if the structure's right and the story's working, you can rewrite every line of dialogue in four hours. . . . If you get to a Monday table reading and you're up there trying to figure out what act two is about, you're going to be there [rewriting] until four o'clock in the morning.

MAXINE LAPIDUSS: The one thing that's very important for a comedy spec script is that it's really funny and that it really makes me laugh. Any script that comes across my desk that makes me laugh out loud more than once, I'm generally going to call that writer in for a meeting. . . . It's also important that the characters' voices are really clear and clean.

A lot of writers don't even do a spell-check. You know, they don't even take the time to check grammar, to see if the periods are in place, the commas are in place. I think, at the very least, that a script should look like a script, be written in the correct format, and have a professional appearance.

Recently, a guy sent me a bunch of spec scripts. And they were all really mediocre. And his whole thing was, "Well, I've got this and this, and if you don't like this, I've got this." [Your career] shouldn't be a car dealership. If you're going to put the time into four spec scripts, it's much smarter to take that time and put it all into one spec script, and really hone it and make it fantastic.

IRMA KALISH: I would hope they would have studied the show and know that we don't have such and such characters in it because they died two years ago, or that we would never in a million years go to someone's house (because we never had before), or that we can't have twenty acts in a half hour, or seven changes of scenery and six changes of wardrobe. . . .

I always asked to see first drafts. That's where a writer's work is best represented. If you look at a produced script, you're looking at the work of a staff or a rewrite by another person who didn't get credit. You have no idea. So you ask to see a first draft. . . . When you turn in what's called a first draft, it should never be *your* first draft. You should always go over that first draft and do your own rewriting before you're given notes on it. Be your own worst critic. Go over it again. . . . Sometimes you are disappointed that a writer whom you had in, because you liked the previous scripts he or she had done, does not deliver on the first draft. And you have to suspect, one, that they didn't put the time into it or, two, that they were busy doing a lot of other scripts and they just gave this one short shrift.

LAWRENCE KONNER: If you have a pile of a hundred [spec scripts] on your desk, which you often have, there are liable to be twenty that are just clearly unprofessional. Just people who don't really have a clue. Wrong format, sloppiness . . . I mean, it seems silly, but . . . it's got to look like it's a professional script, cleanly typed and spell-checked. (I have read more than one spec script in which leading character's names were misspelled.) And then you have probably forty or fifty scripts that are just . . . that feel like they've been transcribed from an already existing episode. They feel like last week's leftovers. Properly done but no spark. That makes about 70 percent. (And don't forget, these are the hundred scripts that made it in through agents or some other recommendation. These are presumably the best of what's out there.) So, then, of the 30 percent that are left, these now are pretty good. These have met the first requirement, which is that they're professionally done. And they meet the second requirement, which is that they have a new idea, they feel fresh. This is the group that you look at. . . . [Out of the hundred scripts, you end up with] two or three that have an inexplicable shine.

Number one, and underline this: I want the work that the writer does when they leave my office to reflect what we talked about in the office. I don't want them to go home and have a new idea. And this is a very difficult thing because often the new idea is better. Certainly the writer thinks it is better. But, generally speaking, I'd rather you call me and say, "You know, I did what we said. But it occurred to me that if we take the grandmother out of the show, it could be a lot better. Let me tell you why." That I can work with. I can look at the decision we made, which was to give this business to the grandmother, and then at your new suggestion, which is to take the grandmother out, and I can weigh it. But don't take the grandmother out without telling us. . . .

And number two, which might seem like a contradictory note, I wouldn't mind being surprised a little bit in the script. No big surprises; little surprises. Little-big surprises.

It's not your job to change the show. It's not your job to improve the show. It's not your job to be the savior of the show. You know, "If only I was the guy in charge, boy, this would be a whole lot better." You can think that, but you can't behave as though you think that. When you're doing an episodic job, you defer to the bosses. You give them what they want and you try to make it the best you can make it even if you think the story shouldn't include the grandmother.

[If you come back two weeks later with a script] that simply doesn't reflect what was discussed in the room, that's the worst sin you can commit. Because now, it's useless to me. Now, I have thirty pages that I can put in the shredder, and a guy whose name I'm going to cross off my list.

SANDY FRANK: Most spec scripts are not very good. But most scripts are not very good. I just read about forty pilots that were produced this year. These were the produced pilots—the best, the cream of the crop. And most of them were quite dull. Some will look better when they're produced, because the actors will do something good and the sets will look nice, etc. But in general, it's very hard to write a good sitcom. . . .

If the jokes in a script actually make me laugh, that's a good thing. Because most of them are just, "Yeah, yeah. Okay, I've seen jokes like that before. Okay, that one, that one, that one."

The plots you see are usually like those from that list of the hundred most common plots, in that big, pink book about sitcoms. You know, two dates for the prom, or the high school reunion, or someone is hit by lightning and becomes just like some other character. You see them all the time. . . .

Avoid including a lot of internal direction [dialogue cues]—you know, like "slyly" or "quietly." That's stuff for the actor and the director to figure out. And, you know, a lot of people—[executives and producers included]—don't read action cues. So don't put many in. . . . Also, you don't want to have any weird logic bumps in your story, where it's like, "Wait a minute. Why did . . . Huh?"

I read someone's spec script recently—a friend of a friend asked me to—and it was in this weird format that I had never seen before. The margins were a little bit weird and such. And it threw me. And I know it shouldn't. I know it's not that big a deal, but. . . . You just don't want to throw the person who's reading your script. You don't want the person for one second to think, "Huh?"

When That First Draft Is Finished

Once you have completed the first draft of your script, you should pause and pat yourself on the back. What human on the planet hasn't said "Aw, I could write a better show than that"? Well, you actually tried. And whether it ever gets produced or not, whether it's your first script or fifti-eth, you have accomplished something that most others just talk about.

You have written. You are a writer. Neat, huh?

Of course, your work isn't quite finished yet. Before collecting that Emmy, there's one more step that every writer has to go through....

13

REWRITING THE SCRIPT

As discussed in the first section of this book, an unfortunate truth of the sitcom world is that "three-quarters of all writing is rewriting." If you are a staff writer, you are expected to participate in many rewrites of many scripts. If you are a freelancer, writing one episode for a series, your (industry standard) contract obligates you to write both a first *and a second draft* of your script. The process runs something like this: You usually get one to two weeks to write a first draft. You submit the script, and within a day or two, the producers meet with you or call you to discuss their notes for revisions. (Or, you and the show's staff might decide on changes during a group rewrite session.) You are given two days, five days, maybe a week to do the rewrite—less time than for a first draft since most of the story is already laid out. You submit the second draft, the producers say thanks, and then they shoot your script word-for-word.

Okay, I'm lying.

They take your second draft and, as often as not, rewrite the heck out of it. It might be handed to a staff writer for the first overhaul or it might go straight into *the room*. The "room" is a conference room where some or all of the show's writing staff meet to work on scripts. (This group effort is referred to as *roundtable writing*, *tabling a script*, and even *gang-banging* a script.) These sessions consist of five, ten, or fifteen writers and writer-producers sitting around the room, rewriting a script line by line. Everyone tosses out script fixes and jokes, the senior producer decides which go into the new draft, and someone—a producer, writers' assistant, or low-level writer—writes down the changes. An assistant prints up a hundred copies of the new script, circulates those for additional notes, and then that draft is rewritten. And rewritten again. It is not uncommon for the staff of a show to rewrite a script five or more times.

Are they doing this just to torment you? At times, you will be convinced that they are. But their goal is simply to make your episode the best that it can be. To complicate their efforts, they must address mountains of script notes from executives at the production company, the studio, and the network. Plus notes from the cast, the star's girlfriend, his agent, her agent, and Carl the caterer. In Hollywood, everyone thinks that he's a writer. And giving notes is just like writing, except that you aren't the one who has to stay up until three in the morning, trying to fix that second act.

Naturally, different producers operate in different ways. On some shows, producers strive to preserve a writer's creative vision by putting tremendous effort into guiding her work on the story outline and the first two drafts. On other shows, a producer might take a writer's first draft but not require a second, though he will still pay for one, because he prefers to have his staff do all of the rewrites. On still other shows, the producers will sometimes have different writers rewrite different scenes of a script and then patch those scenes together. Whatever the dynamics, many writers consider themselves fortunate if half of their original dialogue makes it into the final shooting script. Of course, if you are a member of the show's staff, you are in a better position to champion your material than a freelancer is, because you are right there, part of the team.

Just what types of script notes are given?

Vague Notes

Some people are not very good at identifying and describing script problems. (Not surprising, since many of the people who are empowered to give notes are not, and could never be, writers.) The worst of them will dish out some power-lunch clichés like "You need more of that whole contra-oedipal, boy-hates-dad-loves-mom-but-*is*-dad type of thing, you know? Go there, that's the fix. And it's *true*."

Uh-huh. What??

You've got a scene in a basement and they're telling you that it's not funny. But some people can't just say "needs more jokes here." And most people can't see that the real problem is located *three scenes earlier*, when you failed to establish the predicament that is supposed to get paid off in the basement scene. Oh well. Smile, nod, and listen. Though vague notes can be frustrating, they often point toward a flaw in the script. It's up to you to identify the real problem and fix it.

Notes Required by Budget Limitations

On occasion, producers will give notes designed to reduce a script's production costs. They might ask you to move the scene on the ski slopes to the interior of a chalet. Or to have the argument that occurs in the courthouse take place in the lead character's kitchen. Or to replace a proposed expensive guest star with a celebrity-blocked-from-view-by-his-entourage. Hey, fair is fair. Not only do your producers have an obligation to keep costs in line, but you, as a professional writer, should avoid putting costly elements into your script.

Good Material Gone Stale

As previously discussed, once the surprise of a joke is lost, it just doesn't seem as funny. One unfortunate byproduct of extensive rewriting is that good material is often tossed out because, after twelve readings, it no longer gets a laugh. An added frustration is that its replacement sometimes creates other script problems; while the new joke might be just as funny, the wrong choice can screw up some other part of the story. Which means more rewriting.

What can you do? Not much. You can try to convince your producer that the original material is worth saving, but if you push too hard, he might conclude that you are either difficult to work with or short of ideas. A professional writes, and rewrites, as required.

Rewrite Maniacs

Some writers are so prolific that they can come up with a joke anytime, anywhere, on any subject. As impressive as this is, if that writer is also a producer, he can make other writers' lives hell. It is so easy for these talented people to cough up new jokes that some of them tend to change script material at the drop of a hat. Unfortunately, the new jokes that they come up with—or ask you to come up with—do not always improve the script. Sometimes they are just new, not better. And sometimes the substitution creates new story problems, which someone—you?—then has to fix.

Of course, other times, these comedic volcanoes are the geniuses who drive the funniest, best-written shows on the air. What to do? Grab hold, hang on, and try to learn from these people. For as much as rewrite maniacs might burn through your best material, working with them is a tremendous way to hone your own comedy writing skills.

Producer SANDY FRANK: A lot of times, when you're down on the stage and you're shooting the episode, some people are still trying to punch up every joke. And it actually has a big psychological effect; everyone thinks it's really making the episode so much better. But in reality, the script is 98 percent done. You're really just killing yourself for that extra 1 or 2 percent. But performers, especially if they're stand up comedians, really like it when you give them a new joke because that is a laugh and therefore good. And executives tend to like the frenetic activity ... It makes them feel like you're earning your money.

Conflicting Notes from Different Bosses

Once, when I was writing a freelance episode for a CBS series, my boss was replaced midstream. I had gone off to write the first draft after getting outline notes from the executive producer. When I showed up to get notes for the second draft—Gulp!—a different producer was now in charge. (The first one had gotten a development deal, or been killed or something.) Unfortunately, but predictably, my new boss just didn't see things the way the other producer had. This meant that I had to do a *page-one rewrite*. Meaning, the entire script had to be drastically restructured and rewritten, from the first page. And, as is usually the case, the new draft was due in half the time allotted for the first draft.

Yippee. But the new boss had a right to his creative viewpoint and it was my job to make the changes.

A bigger problem occurs when you receive conflicting notes from different bosses who are both still on staff. Say, a co-producer instructs you to change a scene even though you distinctly heard the executive producer declare, in an earlier discussion, that said scene was perfect. You've got a problem. Piss off either the big boss or the lesser guy by ignoring his notes and you might create an enemy who sees that you never get more work on that show. Probably the best solution is to get on the phone to one or both parties and be honest—point out that you have received conflicting input and ask for a final ruling. (Even better, suggest a brilliant compromise.) Then, proceed per your instructions and try to keep your head down. If someone confronts you later, apologize, explain the confusion, and offer to rewrite the scene again.

The most confounding script notes of all? The notes you get most often? A producer will have the nerve to suggest changes A, B, and C, and much to your dismay—she's right. They all work, they greatly improve the script, and, dammit, why didn't you think of them? Oh well. You'll get good notes and bad notes, notes that fix and notes that create havoc. The one silver lining is that even if the show's staff completely rewrites your script, you usually get full credit for the finished teleplay. This is a traditional courtesy paid to TV series writers, partly in recognition of the fact that they have limited control over what happens to their work. Why do you care? Because your reputation is built on script credits, and the amount of residuals that you collect from reruns of an episode is determined by your credit.

Pointers on Rewriting

Here are some pointers regarding rewrites:

- Fight for the really big points but let the others go. Professionals don't get bogged down in minutiae, and the producers won't hire you again if you're always arguing.

- Follow orders graciously. If you have made your point but the producer still says to make a change, smile and do so. Often, you will discover that he was right. And you do not want to alienate a producer who thought enough of your writing samples to hire you, and who might hire you again.

- Don't offer to do more rewrites than are required by your contract. Your gesture is likely to come off as a desperate effort to curry favor rather than an earnest desire to improve the script.

- If someone offers notes on your script but is not paying you to write it, you should not feel compelled to incorporate his ideas. At the same time, if a reader suggests changes and you do choose to incorporate them, that does not entitle that reader to part ownership of your script. Some unscrupulous types might claim that it does, in a very loud voice, but if you haven't entered into a legal agreement with them, and they didn't type out portions of the new draft, then you owe them nothing. And, in view of their behavior, you would be wise to avoid them in the future.

When Rewriting by Yourself

The above section describes the rewriting process involved when you are writing a freelance assignment or working on staff. But what if you are working on a spec script all by yourself? The good news is that you don't have to deal with reams of script notes. The bad news is that you don't have ten to twenty seasoned professionals offering advice on how to improve your script.

What should you do? First, be a perfectionist. If you can't honestly say that a draft is the very best that you are capable of writing at this point in your career, then it's back to the keyboard. Find the flaws, explore the moments, make the script sing. Trim out everything that's repeated or not needed, and see if you can pull a few more excellent jokes out of the story. Because that script is the ultimate proof of your writing talent. You usually get just one chance to impress a rep, producer, or executive, so the sample that you hand her had better be the best that it can be.

Even at that, expect that you will skim through the thing in four months and see room for further improvement. If the script is still fresh enough to use as a work sample, rewrite it again, and again, for as long as you keep circulating it.

Are you doing all of this in a vacuum? You don't have to. Solicit feedback from friends, family, teachers, and other writers. While few of them are likely to have a professional sitcom writing background, civilians are often good at locating weak points in a story, even if they can't explain why an element doesn't work. Conversely, they can be just as helpful in identifying script strengths that you might want to explore in greater depth.

Should you hire a professional *script consultant* to evaluate the material? While there are some excellent, experienced screenwriters who offer this service, be aware that many of the people who sell script consulting services (providing *coverage* on your script for a fee) are ill equipped to perform the work. See Appendix B for more on this subject.

When receiving input from others, try to not get defensive. Try to not talk, period. Instead, listen, take notes, and then discuss their points *after* they have finished listing them. If you interrupt their thoughts to defend your creative decisions, as most writers instinctively want to do, your readers might forget to mention other points or become reluctant to speak further. For that matter, if you have to defend or explain a creative decision, it probably needs a second look anyway, because you certainly won't be around to defend or explain that decision when some producer is reading your script.

When reviewing other people's notes, avoid letting your pride get in the way. If you can't take constructive criticism, you should not waste other people's time by asking them to evaluate your scripts. If all you want are ego strokes, then offer copies to Mom and assorted doting relatives, and pray that the producers you approach are as easily impressed.

At the same time, always take other people's notes with a big grain of salt. If you still feel that an original choice was valid, don't change it. It's your work, your decision.

If you or your readers find numerous faults in the writing, have the strength and wisdom to do a major rewrite. Preserving flawed material might save you some short-term effort, but it can also ruin your chances of getting work. (A real shame after all of the time that you have already invested.) The best way to start making big changes is to redo your beat sheet and outline. I repeat: *Start by revising your beat sheet and then building a new outline from that.* It's critical that you fix the broad story beats *before* rewriting dialogue. Otherwise, you risk being so focused on punching up lines that you overlook fatal structure flaws. Or you might become so enamored of a scene or some joke that you can't see that it should be cut.

In other words, your rewriting priorities should be story first, then sequences, scenes, moments, and dialogue. And at every step, comedy, comedy, comedy. Reverse the order of your priorities and you risk ending up with a bad patch job; yeah, you sort of fixed everything, but the read is uneven and the script feels weak.

Advice from Our Producers

What else do producers want to see during a rewrite?

SANDY FRANK: When you're given a note, you basically have to do it. Now, you may think, "All right, this is a terrible note." It's a good thing to say, "Well, wait a minute. If you change A, isn't that going to change B, C, and D? And now the ending won't really work if we make that change." That's fine. You should say that. It's your job to say that. But if the producer then says, "No, it's okay," you just have to shut up and basically do it. Because if you continue to fight—first of all you may be wrong, the other person may be right—if you continue to fight, it will not be good for you. You become an annoyance.

MAXINE LAPIDUSS: You might have the most brilliant idea in the world, and you might have executed it in the most brilliant way possible, but if the executive producer thinks it should go a different way, then you have to be flexible enough to let go of your idea and accept the changes that are being made. . . . The hardest thing for me as an executive producer is if somebody's being really resistant and holding on to something that I know either I can't sell to my actor—because they absolutely don't want to wear the funny hat that day or dress up like a chicken, or whatever—and I'm saying, "It's not going to happen," but they're fighting and fighting and fighting to hold on to that idea. All they accomplish is that they make it tougher, I think, to get recommendations for their next job.

IAN GURVITZ: There's a reason why you have seven to ten people in a room and are going to run-throughs every day. It's not just to constantly walk around going, "This is a great script. Boy, is it great. It's still great." It's to constantly be thinking and making it better.

If you go to the shoot to see your episode and it bears no resemblance to what you wrote, or if there are, maybe, two jokes left from what you wrote, it's going to sting. Be prepared for the experience. In the course of the week, drafts get changed and rewritten. It's not always that they didn't like what you did. More often than not, it's just that that's the nature of it. . . . You're going to feel like, "I didn't do a good job." But if they say you did a great job, accept it.

LAWRENCE KONNER: Laziness shows in rewriting. If the worst surprise of the first draft is to turn in a completely different story [than was discussed], then the worst of the second draft is to demonstrate laziness. You do token changes, a line here, a line there. Okay, the producer said to put the grandmother in, and so you write, "Grandmother enters, says 'Hello,' and leaves." That's not what he meant. . . . You should use the second-draft notes as an opportunity to rethink things. Remember that once you've gotten the first job, your goal is to get another job. And one of the things that's going to impress people is your willingness to put some effort into the second draft.

IRMA KALISH: There's no point in saying—because they've all heard this before—"Do you want it good or do you want it tomorrow?" Forget it. Make it good and hand it in when you promised.

MATT WILLIAMS: There are two extremes that you don't want to go to as a beginning writer. One is the give-it-up mode. Those writers just give up on everything. They have no point of view. The room says paint it green; "Okay, it'll be green." And the other one is, holding on to every word you've written. Somewhere in between those two extremes is the ideal. Express your opinion. Justify why you think something works, and if the room is still resisting and the head writer says, "I'm sorry, I don't see it," give it up. And then listen. Listen, listen. Because in sitcom writing, in the ideal world, the room becomes one mind. Not a collection of minds; it becomes one mind. As the outside writer coming into the group, listen and try to tap into what that single mind is, so that you can understand what the room is trying to do.

Once the Script Is Finished

Writing a script requires that a million-and-one creative decisions be made, and all in the course of three to five weeks! Look at the average schedule for a freelance script assignment:

Two to five days to prepare a verbal pitch
Two days to a week to write an outline

Two to five days to rewrite the outline
One to two weeks to write the first draft of the script
Two days to a week to write the second draft

If you are working on the staff of a show, you might be given even less time, depending on production deadlines. If you are writing a spec script, you get to determine the schedule.

Once your latest writing sample is finally finished, polished, the absolute best that it can be, you are ready to send it out into the marketplace. But what exactly does that mean? How do you land work as a sitcom writer?

You get work by selling, by taking aggressive action. If you are serious about making your living as a sitcom writer, you have to get up from the keyboard and make something happen. If you do it right, it's a little bit like going to war. . . .

Part 3

A Battle Plan for Launching Your Career

14

STEP ONE: DEVELOPING A STRATEGY

Most writers absolutely hate to sell, but selling is how a writer gets work. Since there is no avoiding the process, the best alternative is to attack it head-on. The following chapters present an aggressive, focused, take-no-prisoners strategy—the quickest way to get a writer employed and back at the keyboard where she belongs. This strategy is broken up into a series of finite, doable steps, to make the job search less overwhelming.

Let's begin with an overview of the job market and an assessment of career goals.

The Job Market

First, it helps to understand how the network development process works, since it dictates what writing jobs become available.

In the old days, most sitcoms aired on the big broadcast networks (ABC, CBS, NBC, FOX, and later, UPN and WB, which later morphed into CW). The networks rarely produced these shows themselves, due to government regulations that limited their right to own the shows that they aired. Instead, networks would pay *license fees* to outside producers in exchange for the right to air selected shows that they, the outsiders, agreed to produce. (The outside producers, who actually owned the shows, could later make money by re-running them in syndication.) Occasionally, some television syndicators and station groups would band together to create an original series for syndication, and the cable networks managed to put a few original shows on air. But back then, everyone pretty much conformed to a traditional series development schedule that runs something like this:

From early summer to midwinter, pilot scripts for new series are pitched, commissioned (by the networks), and developed.

From January to April, the networks pay for a handful of the best scripts to be produced as pilot episodes or *presentations* (less expensive partial pilots—just a few scenes to give the network an idea of how the show would look).

In May, the networks announce which shows, old and new, will be given production orders (*pickups*) for the coming year, and producers start scrambling to hire their writing staffs.

From June on, the writing staffs work like dogs to get their episodes produced.

In August and September, new series premiere and old series return with new episodes.

In midwinter, failing series are replaced with *midseason* entries that have been held in reserve.

If a show seemed very promising and its producers or star had leverage, it might be given a full year's order of twenty-two or twenty-four episodes. (Repeats and preemptions occupied the remaining thirty weeks of the year.) If a show seemed weak or its principals didn't have leverage, it might receive a short order of only four, six, or thirteen episodes. And it might be relegated to midseason replacement status—meaning, it might never make it onto the network's program schedule. If a short-ordered series got on the schedule and proved successful, the network would give it a new pickup order requiring that additional episodes be produced to carry it through the full broadcast season.

That was then. These days, all bets are off. The broadcast networks still stick mostly to the traditional development schedule, but they are airing far fewer sitcoms. Fortunately, pay- and basic-cable networks have stepped in to pick up the slack, producing a variety of original sitcoms aimed at their target audiences. Series are being developed and launched at all times of the year. In fact, some cable programmers prefer to premiere their shows in early summer, to take advantage of the broadcast webs' habit of burning off less appealing reruns during those months.

Additional changes include the following:

- The (previously mentioned) regulations restricting network ownership of programming were, for the most part, eliminated. In response, the broadcast networks now produce a number of their TV series in-house in order to maximize control of, and profits from, the shows that they air.

- As the broadcast networks have lost viewers to cable networks and the web, they've sought to reduce development costs and now are even willing to consider homegrown pilots produced by nonprofessionals. (More on this later.)

- When a network orders a series from an outside producer, it usually demands that it be given a piece of the show (partial ownership) as part of the deal. Since the network then has a greater financial stake in the project, it takes a more aggressive role in controlling its development and production.

- The series development process has become more *deal-driven*. Meaning, many new shows are given a production order or promised a time slot on a network schedule simply because that network owes someone a deal or wants to entice a top talent into working for it.

- New shows are given very little time to find an audience. Series usually start out with very short production orders—four episodes is not uncommon—and some have been pulled off the air after only one or two airings. If this strategy had been applied years ago, we never would have had *Cheers* or *Seinfeld*, series that took months or even an entire season to establish themselves.

- Recognizing the marketing potential of the Internet, the networks now host fan sites for most series, promoting viewership by offering interactive content and free downloads. When producers pitch a new show, it helps if they include innovative ideas for making interactive connections with their audience.

What does all of this have to do with you getting work as a writer?

First, the traditional network development process described above has created several different *hiring windows* for writers. We will identify these and explore ways to capitalize on them later, in Chapter 16.

Next, though the recent success of reality programming has reduced the number of sitcom writing jobs in broadcast TV, growth in cable television has created new jobs as those networks get into original production. The good news is that cable networks seem more willing to hire new, untested writers than the broadcast networks are, and more new writers are landing staff positions as their first jobs, without having to earn their stripes by landing freelance assignments first.

The bad news is that cable networks usually pay writers much less, and shorter pickup orders for shows mean a higher turnover rate. In addition, producers prefer to hire writers whom they know and trust when assembling a staff; they are reluctant to deal with unknown talent, particularly when struggling to get a new series up and running.

In short, today's job market remains in flux as the new media technologies sort themselves out. There are still jobs, but the pay is less and job security fleeting.

As for the material being written? You've seen *Entourage* and *South Park*. The creation of new media outlets has given writers the opportunity to explore all types of subject matter, from profound to lurid.

The question is, where might you fit in?

How the Writer Fits In

The great thing about the television industry is that *the writers run the show*. Okay, yes, they get loads of input, pressure, and—many would say—interference from the executives who control the money. (The network suits, studio suits, and production company suits.) But happily, the executive producers of a sitcom, the individuals who have the most creative control, are usually *writers*. (Unlike in the movie industry, in which creative control is usually held by the director, or sometimes the star.)

Top-level producers who have proven that they can manage production of a network-quality television series are called *show runners*. This is an exalted, highly paid position, achieved by very few. (An executive producer title does not automatically qualify one as a show runner; that honor usually goes to producers who have previously held *primary* responsibility for delivering a show, preferably a hit show, week after week.) A show runner might create a new series or be brought in as a hired gun to help with someone else's project. If a lesser writer-producer creates a new series but has not, in a network's eyes, achieved show runner status, he will be forced to work with an established show runner if he wants to see his series produced. With so much money at stake, sometimes millions of dollars per episode, network executives are understandably reluctant to trust unproven talent with their investment.

How do you get to be a show runner, so that you can see your own series ideas become a reality? How do you get any job as a staff writer?

The hiring-and-promotion sequence for staff writers usually goes something like this, working up from the bottom of the ladder. Term Writer, Story Editor, Executive Story Editor, Co-producer, Producer, Supervising Producer, Story Consultant, Consulting Producer, Co-executive Producer, and Executive Producer.

A sitcom might employ anywhere from five to twenty writers and writer-producers, though shows probably average a staff of eight to twelve. Not all job titles are used on all shows, and a writer being promoted might skip one or more titles—say, go from Story Editor to Co-producer—if she is a hot commodity. As a writer climbs the ladder, she gains a greater say in creative decisions and is eventually given responsibility for aspects of the show's production. However, otherwise, job duties vary widely from job to job and show to show. The few constants are that all staff writers write scripts, join in group writing sessions, and attend read-throughs, run-throughs, and final shoots.

If most of a show's producers are writers rather than production types, who takes care of the technical stuff? Titles vary, but most shows employ a technically proficient producer whose job it is to manage the facilities and crew needed to produce the series. Most of these producers have little to do with creative issues such as scripts, casting, and direction. From low to high, their titles might be Associate Producer, Unit Production Manager, Line Producer, Supervising Producer, Producer, and Executive Producer. They are assisted by Production Coordinators and Production Assistants, and, of course, a large production crew.

A Writer's Workweek

As romantic as the title of Hollywood writer sounds, exactly how do you spend the hours of the day? Is it all ego-boosting meetings with fawning executives, chatty lunches at overpriced bistros, basking at the beach as you pound away on a laptop? Not quite.

You already know the routine for a freelance writer, from our discussion in Part Two of this book. A script assignment means three to five weeks of intense writing. You pitch, write, get notes, rewrite, and pray—because if you do a great job, you might get another assignment or land a staff job. (Most freelance writers want to join a show because staff jobs pay more, offer longer terms of employment, and are the primary route to eventually achieving some level of creative control, via a producer's rank.)

If you are a staff writer, you probably put in sixty, seventy, or more hours per week. You work in the show's production offices on a studio lot, crammed into one of many small writers' offices. In fact, it is usually a production company or studio, not a television network, that pays your checks.

When the show starts gearing up for production, the writing staff gathers to develop (or *break*) stories for the season's episodes. Each show works differently. The writers might pitch story after story, then everyone separates to develop the beats of the story assigned to each of them, then they all come back for group revisions before going off to write the scripts on their own. Or the writing staff might all work together, figuring out the beats for each episode and then sending individuals off to write the scripts. Or the staff might figure out the beats together and write the scripts together too, scene by scene.

If the show is a serial or features serialized storylines, this is the stage when much time is spent figuring out how each story arc should develop in the coming season. Then segments of those arcs are spread out over the episodes that are to be written.

On most sitcoms, one episode is produced each week, with a week taken off here and there to allow for catch-up. Traditionally, the actual production season lasts nine to ten months: Producers prep and staff a show during early summer, start producing episodes in July or August, and shoot until the following March or April.

Most shows always shoot the final versions or segments of their episodes on the same day of the week, usually Tuesday, Thursday, or Friday. Here is one (multi-camera) model of how the five days preceding a final shoot might break down:

- DAY ONE often starts with a *table reading* attended by producers, writers, cast members, department heads (from the crew), and assorted (network and studio) programming executives. Everyone except the executives literally sits around a large table, or circle of tables, as the cast reads through a draft of the script being produced that week. Notes are given and the writers go off to rewrite the script while the director and department heads start prepping all of the physical elements needed to produce the show. If the script looks bad, the writers face a very long night.

- DAY TWO often features another reading and more notes. If the script looks good, the director starts plotting camera moves and re hearsing the cast, and might stage a complete run-through so all can see how the lines play out on stage. Some producers schedule a regular *rewrite night* on this day, regardless of what shape their scripts are in.

- On DAYS THREE AND FOUR, the actors get serious about memorizing lines as the script settles into its final form. The director rehearses the cast and blocks out camera movements. More notes are given, more rewriting is done.

- DAY FIVE, the shooting day, might culminate in two run-throughs of the episode: first, a formal dress rehearsal; then notes, last-minute changes, and perhaps dinner; and then, the final shoot. Afterward, it's off to editing, where the best elements of both run-throughs are combined to create the finished episode.

The above steps describe just one of several five-day models used to produce sitcoms. As mentioned earlier, some shows use multiple (three to five) cameras to shoot an entire episode straight through, simultaneously covering different angles of the action in each scene and pausing only to redo something or prepare for the next scene. Other shows use a single camera to *block and shoot* the scenes of an episode over the course of several days, covering only one angle of a scene at a time, moving the camera to get different angles as the scene is re-run. Some shows shoot on film, which provides a rich look but can be more difficult to produce; others shoot using video cameras, usually high-definition, which are easier to use but, some claim, can result in a flatter look. Some shows shoot before a studio audience and others, primarily single-camera operations, do not. Some shows record dress rehearsals to provide additional footage for editing, and others only record the final performance. Some smother their audio tracks with canned laughter, others do not.

As noted earlier, single-camera shows also differ from multi-camera shows in that they allow the writers to include a variety of location scenes in a script, which can make a story seem more open and fresh. But the show's staff must still adhere to a tight weekly production schedule to get its episodes completed on time.

Every production team runs its show differently, but all engage in read-throughs, rewrites, rehearsals, blocking, run-throughs, and shooting. When not helping to repair or punch up the script currently being shot, a staff writer is usually busy performing other writing functions. Perhaps she is generating new story ideas to pitch to her producers. Or she is writing the first draft of an episode that she has been assigned, or rewriting someone else's script. Or she is joining other staff writers in the room to *break a story* (meaning, to figure out the story beats and act breaks of a future episode). Or she and the other writers are punching up the script that is scheduled to be produced next week, or the week after. Or she is sitting with a producer while a freelancer makes a pitch, or helping to beat out a story that the freelancer will then write.

Did I say "or"? Make that "and." Because that writer will probably do most of these tasks during the course of a week.

It can be tons of work, but it's also a real rush. Because being a staff writer means driving onto a studio lot every day, bumping elbows with celebrities, earning big bucks. And getting paid to sit with funny people, creating funny stories. And getting to see your words come out of actors' mouths, on camera, en route to an audience of millions. (Including Mom, Dad, and that jerk who dumped you in college.)

How do you get to be a part of this?

Writing Is a Business

As glamorous as it might seem, sitcom writing is a business. If you want to succeed, you must treat it as *your* business.

Yes, you must have talent. And you must produce consistently, writing script after script. But you also need to attack the sitcom-writing job market as you would any other highly competitive career field. Many a talented writer has failed to get work because it was just so much safer and easier to stay at home, typing away. That doesn't cut it in a field where:

> Formal education means little.
> Employers erect barriers to deflect job applicants.
> Hiring decisions are often based on personal friendships.
> Thousands of talented, charming people are competing for a handful
> of jobs.

If you are serious about launching a writing career, a big chunk of your day should be spent thinking in terms of meetings, schedules, deadlines, contacts, and follow-up. *Selling your material and yourself.*

It helps to have a master plan of sorts, which is why the following chapters were written. Assuming that you already have at least one terrific spec script in hand—make that two—your next goals are as follows:

1. Keep writing. "Writers write." And it might be that next script that finally gets you hired.

2. Land the right agent and/or manager.

3. Get your spec scripts to the right people.

4. Turn pitch meetings into jobs.

5. Turn jobs into a career.

Those are the broad goals. But before you plunge ahead, there are three important matters that we should discuss: the age factor, how to keep eating, and moving to Los Angeles.

Ageism

Remember when I mentioned, at the beginning of the book, that a surprising number of sitcoms are run by thirty- and thirty-five-year-old producers? And perhaps I mentioned that many television executives are that age and younger? It's true. And to be frank, that is bad news for those of us over forty. Why? Because young producers do not always feel comfortable giving orders to people who are older than their dads. And TV execs seem convinced that anyone over thirty is out of touch with the latest trends. (And therefore can't relate to the youthful audience demographics that television advertisers seek.)

What can you do if those gray hairs are starting to come in? Besides going the Nice-'n-Easy, Grecian Formula route? Well, if you are already an established writer who thinks and looks young, you're probably in pretty good shape. For a while.

But if you are forty years old and just starting out, the going could be very rough. If you feel a tremendous drive to write sitcoms and would not sacrifice much by making an attempt, then okay, take a shot. Life is short, so go for it. You can always try something else if this doesn't work out.

On the other hand, if you don't think it wise to buck the age bias, there are alternatives. You want to write comedy? Write screenplays—age is much less a factor. Or write funny books, or articles, or plays, or short stories. Nobody ever said that sitcoms were the only road to a comedy writer's fulfillment.

It's your call and I regret tossing out a wet blanket. But I did promise that this would be your comprehensive, all-in-one guide to the field.

Putting Food on the Table

Unless you are rich, you will probably need a paying job to put food on the table. Launching a writing career can take many months, even years—and that is assuming that you are successful. How will you eat during that time?

My suggestion: Marry a very rich, very old person. (Just a thought.)

Or, get a proverbial "day job" if you don't already have one. There are two basic types. First, if you live in Los Angeles, you can get a job in the industry—working as a production assistant, writer's assistant, executive's assistant, producer's assistant, tape librarian, runner, or in some other entry-level capacity. The advantages? You are right there, part of a production team, rubbing shoulders with people in the business. You can make contacts, learn the production process, show people your work, and maybe even impress someone enough to be given an assignment.

The disadvantages? You're not really rubbing shoulders with those people—you bring them coffee. And you type, deliver scripts, type, place calls, order Thai food, pick up dry cleaning, and type. And because everyone wants to work in show biz, you work very long hours for very little pay. Which leaves you little energy to keep writing the scripts that you need to write.

Hmm, dilemma. A job in the industry might give you access, but it can eat up all of your free time.

How about a less demanding job in another field, just to pay the bills while you write? The advantages are that you will probably work fewer hours and make more money. But you are out of the loop. While you are playing receptionist in some lawyer's office or waiting tables at Chez Bistro, you might miss out on an important connection that you would otherwise have made while working as a lowly PA.

What to do?

As long as you can find a way to keep writing and circulating your material, either path can serve you well. An ideal compromise is to get a job as an assistant to someone who works in the business but isn't a slave driver—maybe a producer who is between shows or an executive who blows out of the office at six every night.

Or some people land jobs as *floaters*, temp secretaries employed by a studio or network, or that are sent out via referrals from a temp agency that focuses on entertainment clients. Working as fill-in assistants and gophers, floaters are dispatched to help out when needed at different shows, the studios, production companies, and the networks. This enables them to meet a large circle of contacts. At the same time, their temp status usually means that they get decent pay without having to face all of the job pressures that their full-time counterparts face.

In short, the ideal day job provides you with industry access and leaves you time to write.

If you live in Los Angeles, how do you land one of these food-on-the-table industry gigs? That's a whole other book. Fortunately, there are already a number of publications that address that subject—check your local Barnes & Noble. And, to toss my two cents in, I will suggest the following:

Check the Trades

Every week, Hollywood's daily trades, such as *Daily Variety* and the *Hollywood Reporter*, list projects that are starting into production. Grab a phone book, call the companies involved, and talk your way into an interview for any job that they might have available.

Call the Big Companies

Networks, studios, and large production companies usually have a Human Resources (or Personnel) Department. While these departments have no say regarding which writers, producers, or other creative types are hired, they sometimes do fill secretarial positions within the company. Call and request an interview.

Check the Industry Directories

Several publishers put out industry directories that list everything from production companies to animal trainers. Sold at entertainment-oriented bookstores and through online retailers, these guides are available to everyone. (See Appendix B.) Buy a couple and start dialing. Call every company that seems to be connected to the sitcom world and ask who hires their secretaries, runners, PAs, whatever.

Call Your Cousin's Wife's Brother

Everybody knows somebody in Hollywood. Call that person and ask that she keep her ear to the ground.

Clearly, my advice is to *canvas everybody*. As for style of approach, I suggest the following:

1. **Use the phone** rather than mailing out a ton of résumés or shooting off emails. It might be scarier to just call people out of the blue, but it prevents them from cutting you off with a standard rejection letter.

2. **Be polite and prepared.** When you call, have your thoughts in order. And know what type of job they might have available rather than blurting out, "Gee, I'll take anything!"

3. It is often better to **position a cold call as a request for an informational meeting** rather than a plea for a job. Don't worry—if an employer has an opening, she won't be shy about mentioning it if she thinks that you'd be a good candidate. Also, **be prepared to ask intelligent questions** when you call to request that meeting; the employer might put you on the spot when you first call to see if information is what you're really after.

4. **Do your homework.** People are always flattered and impressed when you bother to learn who they are and what they have done.

5. **Start at "A" and go to "Z,"** and keep calling until someone says, "You're hired!" Do not let someone's negative response (or words of encouragement) slow you down. The best thing that could happen is that you suddenly end up with three job offers, putting you in the driver's seat.

6. **Keep good records.** Names, job titles, phone numbers, dates that you called, dates that they said to call back, strategies that occurred to you, etc. Think that you'll remember everything? Think again. And no, those scraps of paper piling up on your bureau don't count.

I hope that these suggestions help. In the end, it all comes down to knocking on doors until someone hires you.

On a related subject, you probably noticed that I keep referring to day jobs *located in Hollywood*. Which brings up another big question—do you have to move to Los Angeles if you want to write sitcoms?

Must You Live in Los Angeles?

Yes. Sorry.

Not that Los Angeles is a bad place to live—it is known for its balmy weather, sunny beaches, and friendly folks. But balmy and friendly aren't for everyone.

Unfortunately, if you want to write network sitcoms for a living, you may not have a choice. Hollywood is where almost all sitcoms are produced. Yes, a couple are done in New York City, but they represent very few jobs. And many of the writers on those shows came from L.A., and none of them are anxious to hand their coveted spot over to you.

True, some already-established, top-level writers manage to land occasional gigs from out-of-state. But unless you have a lot of clout, it would be a mistake to think that you can charm producers into making that exception for you.

The good news is that *you do not have to move to Hollywood right away.* In fact, I recommend against it. First, find out if the work is for you, and if you have a legitimate shot at earning a living as a sitcom writer. How? We will discuss a strategy for testing the waters, long-distance, in the next chapter.

Let's move on to the first phase of your job search—landing an agent and/or manager.

15

STEP TWO: LANDING AN AGENT AND/OR MANAGER

Do you really have to have representation? Yes. Most producers and executives won't read your writing samples unless they come through an agent or manager. It's a weeding process. If you are a psycho, you probably can't get representation, which means that you can't get to the producers and executives. (Whew!) If you are untalented or lack drive, you probably can't get representation. If you are a gold digger looking to sue someone for stealing your ideas, you are less likely to get representation. In short, agents and managers screen out large portions of the bad writing samples and weak writers that would otherwise end up in the offices of those producers and executives.

What's the difference between agents and managers?

An agent is primarily a salesperson. He might work for a big multinational outfit headquartered in expensive Beverly Hills digs, or a specialized boutique agency employing ten or thirty people, or a one-person company (his) operating out of an apartment bedroom. An agent spends the day canvassing the industry for information regarding job opportunities, and pitching his clients to prospective employers. He does most of his work on the phone but also frequently gets out for meetings, business meals, and production run-throughs. When he closes a deal, he usually negotiates the basic terms himself, and then either he or his agency's lawyer sorts out the formal contract.

Agents live by their contacts and the quality of their client lists. They usually specialize, focusing in an area like feature film actors or television

Producer LAWRENCE KONNER: The cliché is that your agent works for you, that your agent is your employee. It's just not true. You need to relate to them as another employer. You need to be in their good graces.... Take every meeting that they get you seriously. Don't show up unprepared. The last thing you want is for the producer to call your agent and say, "The guy came in here and he had nothing to say." Then your agent will stop sending you out.... Your agent has to believe in the future of your career, because 10 percent of [a new writer's income] is not enough to justify their time. They actually call new people development clients— as in "research and development"— because it's, "Well, this person could pay off in five years, so I'm willing to take this chance." So you have to present yourself to the agent as that person, the one who's going to eventually become a million-dollar-a-year client.

series writers. (Agents who handle TV and film writers are called literary, or *lit*, agents.) Sometimes, especially at a big agency, different specialists team up to service a client. You might have one agent for TV writing, another for new media work, and another for film—though, usually, one member of that team is your primary agent, the person that you deal with the most. Often, on the selling side, an agency will assign particular agents to deal with particular networks, studios, and production companies, so that those companies aren't constantly being deluged with calls from twenty agents at the same firm.

What does an agent get for his troubles? Ten percent of your up-front writing fees. Agents who are affiliated with the Writers Guild of America work strictly on commission—they do not charge you money in advance and they do not get a cut of your *residuals* (i.e., additional money paid to you if a show is distributed after its initial airing). If you never earn money as a writer, you owe your agent nothing. If a prospective agent tries to charge you an up-front fee in exchange for representing you, pass him by—such a requirement is forbidden by the Writers Guild and the guy is pulling a fast one.

NOTE: An agent might earn fees in addition to the standard 10 percent if a deal involves more than basic writing services, such as agency packaging or a complex production financing arrangement. And an agent might be due additional money if he has negotiated above-scale fees for the writer. However, newer sitcom writers are rarely involved in such deals, and those who are don't begrudge the larger fees since those mean that the writer is making more money.

Are agents worth 10 percent of your earnings? Most are. In addition to helping you find work, good agents also do the following: negotiate your compensation, job title, and working conditions; go after fees that are owed to you; provide career guidance; provide information about people that you will meet; provide produced scripts and episodes to help you prep; and serve as a buffer between you and your producers when there is a problem.

NOTE: I did not say that a good agent also serves as a writing coach and a shoulder to cry on. While some are very helpful in these respects, it is a real bad idea to waste their valuable selling time by asking them to play couch-therapist. That's what friends and family (and coaches and therapists) are for. You need your agent to be on the phone, all of the time, trying to get you work!

How are managers different from agents?

Managers, rather than constantly hunting jobs for a client list of twenty to forty people, focus on honing the careers of a shorter list of clients. They provide more personal attention than an agent can, doing everything from generating networking opportunities, to connecting you with other people's projects, to circulating your specs, to giving you script notes, to offering up that shoulder to cry on. In exchange for 8 to 20 percent of the client's earnings, they attempt to groom her for success. Though managers are not officially licensed to seek writing jobs for their clients, they do so all of the time, frequently working hand in hand with the client's agent. (Of course, there are also rare cases in which a writer's agent and manager are constantly battling over which paths the shared client should take.)

Which is more important to have, an agent or a manager? Do you need both?

Your first goal should be to land an agent. But, hard as that is, you might end up by landing a manager first. That's fine, because that lends you credibility, and sometimes a manager will be the one to hook you up with an agent!

Is it worth giving away up to 30 percent of your earnings because you signed with both? Maybe. What would you rather have, 70 percent of something or 100 percent of nothing? And hey, if you sign with someone and he's not getting work for you or you end up not liking him, it's usually not that hard to end your business relationship with that person.

What about getting an *entertainment lawyer* to represent you instead?

Yes, some entertainment attorneys will agree to work on a deferred commission basis. However, though you should retain a lawyer if you are closing a complicated deal or if he can provide unique access to someone needed for a high-profile project, a lawyer is no substitute for an agent or manager. Lawyers spend their days doing law things—drafting contracts, taking depositions, going to court. Agents and managers spend their days calling producers and executives, and pushing clients. Which do you want working for you?

Developing a Hit List

Okay, so you need to land an agent or a manager. How do you get one? Better yet, how do you get the right one?

First, you need to collect individual names, not just company names, and specific contact information. And while you can't be too picky if just starting out, there are a few criteria that potential representatives should meet:

- **Any agent you approach should be a signatory to the Writers Guild of America.** Most legitimate film and television agents (not managers) sign a signatory agreement with the Writers Guild of America, the screenwriters' primary union, that requires them to conform to certain standards that protect writers. (For details about the WGA, see Chapter 16.) Ask if the agent is a Guild signatory or call the WGA's Agency Department at (323) 782-4502 to check.

- **She should be based in L.A.,** probably not in NYC, and definitely not in Boise. For reasons that you already know.

- **He should specialize in sitcom writers** or, at least, television series writers. Some representatives whose clients specialize in a different form, like feature films, are happy to sign television writers even though they (the reps) have no television connections themselves. They hope that you will find your own work so that they can collect a commission for merely closing the deal, and that you will help to open up some television doors for them—thanks for nothing! Unless you are desperate to have *any* representative just so that producers will read the stuff that you submit, keep looking.

■ **Some of her clients should have staff jobs.** The best test of a rep's abilities is to ask which of her clients are now working, particularly in staff positions. On a related note, if some of her clients have attained producer status, they might be in a position to hire some of the rep's other clients; the advantage here is that since those producers want to keep the rep happy, they are predisposed to favor any writers whom she recommends.

■ **Should he work at a big firm or a small firm?** Hard to say. The big names at any firm are not likely to take on new writers—they've got their hands full servicing established clients. You might benefit by signing with a newer person at a big firm because she has access to that firm's massive intel network, and your work will be associated with a very successful company's name; of course, a rep at a large firm might also feel so much pressure to produce that she is inclined to drop any client who doesn't quickly find work. Many believe that you are more likely to get personal attention and loyalty from reps at a small firm, and that you will face less competition from that firm's other clients; on the other hand, a small firm might lack the leverage of having a bunch of clients already ensconced as producers around town, who are predisposed to hire their own rep's clients.

Upon reflection, if you are fortunate enough to have a choice between a rep at a big firm and one at a small firm, you should base your decision on who best meets the following requirement:

■ **She should love your work!** Here's a news flash: If a rep isn't knocked out by your writing, she will not push you as hard as her other clients. Who needs that?

Now that you know what to look for in an agent or manager, how do you find these people? You start by gathering names and contact information.

- **Get a copy of the WGA's "Agency List."** This is a *partial* listing of the agencies that have become signatories to the Writers Guild of America. (Some firms opt to keep their names off the list to cut down on the number of would-be clients who contact them.) The list contains basic office addresses and phone numbers, but not the names and titles of individual agents (which you need). It indicates which agencies have said that they would be willing to accept unsolicited scripts from writers, and it is updated every few months. You can find this list published on the web, at the WGAW's home page at www.wga.org.

NOTE: There are two branches of the Writers Guild of America—the WGA, west (based in Los Angeles) and the WGA, east (based in New York City). Each is an independent organization, and the two branches don't always agree on issues, but both try to act in concert when it comes to important matters such as industry-wide negotiations on writers' contracts. Usually, if you live west of the Mississippi, you are expected to join the WGA, west, and if you live east, the WGA, east. Of course, if you want to write sitcoms, a form produced mainly in Los Angeles, you will probably end up in the WGA, west. Requirements for joining the Guild are discussed in Chapter 16.

- **Check industry directories.** As previously mentioned, several industry directories are available at your corner bookstore and online. The best ones identify individual agents and managers and even provide their job titles, and are updated every few months (an important point given the rapid job turnover in Hollywood). For details on where to find these directories, see Appendix B.

- **Read the trades.** I recommend either *Daily Variety* or the *(Daily) Hollywood Reporter* (not the weekly editions). Aside from informing you about what is going on in the industry, which is kind of important to know, the trades often report on representatives being hired or fired, and on who is representing whom. Plus, both publications are available in an online version, which means you can also access past articles in the site's archives (very handy when researching someone's background!). Of course, when you trip over a useful news item, you should write the subject's name and related details down because there is no way you'll remember them otherwise.

- **Create a database.** This is your new business, right? Then you'll need to manage all of the information you're starting to accumulate if you're going to get ahead. That means creating a system for logging "data" and using some sort of calendar to remind you of *next steps*. Index cards or computer software, it doesn't matter what you use, as long as you create some method for keeping written track of things. For each listing, note the contact's name, address, information revealed, what you submitted, when you submitted, leads they provided, and *future actions you should take*. It is critical that you transcribe that last detail to your calendar and follow up diligently—do so and you will *greatly* increase your chances of finding work.

- **Cruise the web, often.** Make it a standing date. Every week, set aside a couple of hours to cruise the web for information about industry developments and job leads. The Internet makes it incredibly easy to stay on top of the business. Make regular visits to the sites recommended in Appendix B and add to my list as you discover new resources.

- **Who represents your favorite writers?** This one is a bit harder, but worth the effort if you are trying to impress a particular agent or manager. The idea is to jot down the names of the writers who work on your favorite shows. (Obviously, these names are listed in the shows' on-air credits.) Then, find out who represents those writers, either through resources such as those noted above, via those listed in Appendix B, or by calling the WGA, west's Agency Department at (323) 782-4502. For a small subscription fee, you might even use a website dubbed "whorepresents.com" (seriously, that's the name!) to identify writer-agent connections.

The goal is to get the names of specific reps, not just the names of their firms. Having this information serves two purposes: You have identified reps who apparently appreciate writing tastes similar to yours, since they represent writers whose work you like. And when you call later to seek representation, you might find an opportunity to impress their assistants and them by showing that you do your homework; meaning, you might flatter each of these reps by mentioning that you have sought him out because he represents great writers like so-and-so (his client), who's written for such-and-such shows. It doesn't always work and you'll look like a kiss-up if you're too obvious, but a well-played approach could improve the odds that a rep will consider taking you on or give you a referral to someone else.

■ **Network to create contacts.** There are many excellent books and courses that can do a better job than I of telling you how to network your way to new business contacts, but here are a few thoughts on the subject. First, networking does not mean just weaseling your way into industry events and trying to schmooze bigwigs at parties. Some people are good at this, most aren't, and Hollywood professionals are skilled at deflecting such overtures because they've been approached many, many times in the past. Instead, I recommend that you make a *long-term investment* in networking. (Of course, this assumes that you live close enough to come into contact with industry folks.) Get involved in the types of groups and activities that might appeal to Hollywood professionals. Go out and join a softball league, rent a kid and start a play group, take your dog for walks in upscale parks, join a hiking club, an environmental group, take yoga lessons, start a book club, a weekly card game, attend a church or temple, learn to surf, learn to jog, start a band. Buy the latest online gaming console and blast your way into alliances with some Hollywood young guns.

Join any cool group that does cool things, that might attract cool contacts like agents, managers, producers, and execs.

My point is that you are more likely to make productive connections through casual, regular gatherings than through onetime encounters at industry functions. Of course, you're doing this for business reasons, so if you find that an activity isn't providing the types of contacts you need, you should pull stakes and try a new group. I know it sounds superficial, probably because it is, but

Producer **ELLEN SANDLER:** Your community is your support. You need to be generous and kind to your fellows. You need to build a network that you contribute to, not just take from.

you're on a mission here and you have limited time to invest in net
working.

Once you do make a connection, wait patiently for the right moment when you can ask that new contact to read a script. If he balks,
back away and let him off the hook—you tried, it didn't work. If he
agrees to read it and does, but he then seems uncomfortable—meaning
he didn't like it—let him off the hook and don't corner him by demanding reasons why. (He might still be willing to read another
script.) If he responds positively and forwards you to someone else,
take great pains to not embarrass your first contact when dealing with
the second contact, and remember to express sincere thanks for the
opportunity.

Lastly, check out as many screenwriting courses, seminars, and panel
discussions as you can, especially the free ones. Bring prepared questions if appropriate and go with a promise to yourself that you will
introduce yourself to at least three (five? fifty?) people. Like-minded
souls attend these events and you never know when you might meet
a future mentor or make an industry connection that can aid your
career.

- **College connections.** Every college has some alums who work in
the entertainment industry and most schools maintain a database that
tracks their alums. See if you can gain access through your college's
career development center, and maybe you can find some names to
add to your hit list.

Also, many schools have alumni clubs in L.A. and NYC, and some
of these have entertainment industry committees that schedule social
gatherings and business seminars for their grads. If you live in one of
those cities, become a regular attendee to see if you can make some
connections, or if your school doesn't organize such events, why don't
YOU volunteer to do so? That way, you're the one contacting and hosting guest speakers of your choice—a great way to meet someone who
wouldn't otherwise take your call.

- **Enter screenwriting competitions—carefully.** There are a few television writing competitions floating around that you should consider. Most
charge an entry fee, but they typically award winners cash prizes, promises that their material will be submitted to industry pros (agents, manag-

ers, execs, and/or producers), and maybe even admission into a select mentoring program. The Warner Bros. Comedy Workshop and the Disney–ABC fellowship program are good examples—investigate these opportunities and others by going to websites such as www.donedealpro. com, www.hollywoodlitsales.com, and www.moviebytes.com, and by checking the other resources listed in Appendix B.

Perhaps the biggest benefit of screenwriting contests is that if you win or place in the finals, you can humbly mention your success when contacting agents, managers, execs, and producers, greatly increasing the chances that they will read your material. You are no longer just one out of a million hopefuls; professional judges have declared your work worthy.

One word of caution, however: Do take the time to check out a competition before submitting. Many don't really have any connections to industry pros and are merely scams created to pull in entry fees, and some will try to lock up rights to the script you submit as part of the application process. Find out who the contest's judges are and how past winners have fared (or not) before writing a check.

- **Investigate all possible referrals!** Do you know *anyone* in the business, or anyone even remotely associated with the business? Cruise through your Rolodex, check your yearbooks, ask friends and family. You might be surprised to find out that Aunt Sally's friend Bob's wife once dated an agent, and would be happy to make a call on your behalf. (Don't be shy—people in the entertainment industry rely on personal referrals all of the time.)

If you take all of the above steps, you will eventually end up with a long list of legitimate agents and/or managers to contact. Of course, not all of these people are right for you, so you should winnow the names down a bit to create your final hit list.

Not that there's much winnowing though. Any agent who is a WGA signatory and who represents working sitcom or television writers should be on your list. Any manager who represents working sitcom or television writers should be on the list. Avoid the temptation to rule out people because their company seems too small or doesn't have a fancy address—you might be desperate for them to represent you if bigger names don't pan out. Also, though a resource might indicate that a company will only respond to query letters or personal referrals, *ignore these restrictions* and add it to your list. (When calling these firms, you will often connect with someone who isn't aware of or doesn't bother to enforce his company's policies.)

Then, I suggest that you prioritize the hit list by order of preference, going from most desired rep to least. While doing this, don't be timid. If the guy you'd most like to have represent you is some hotshot who probably won't even return your calls, *put him down anyway*. Take the shot. Because, what if he did return the call? And became your rep? Or referred you to someone else, just to get rid of you? Hey, it happens. But it can't happen for you if you won't even call, right?

Once you have gotten your hit list in order, and have at least one great spec script (or two, or several) under your arm, you are ready to start dialing. But first . . .

Before Picking Up the Phone

Landing an agent or manager can be an arduous process, sometimes taking months and months. Are these people waiting for your call? Do they even want you to call? No, not really, because hundreds of other writers are already banging on their doors. So you need to prepare before reaching for the phone.

- **Don't call until you have something great to show them.** Agents and managers do not sign clients just because they have a charming personality or they have a script in the works. If you haven't got at least one great script ready to go, don't call. Otherwise, they will think that you are either a rank amateur or a nut, or both.

- **Don't send unsolicited scripts.** Some writers, desperate to land representation, will mail a writing sample to an agent or manager before being invited to do so. This is considered rude and is a waste of time, since that person's assistant probably has standing orders to return such scripts unopened or simply toss them in the trash. Not only does your ploy fail, but they are likely to remember your name—in a bad way—should you contact them again in the future.

- **Check the web.** Before contacting your target, go online and see what you can learn about the representative and her company. A few minutes with a search engine and you might find all sorts of information about her background, goals, and clients—details that could prove useful in a conversation.

- **Know your goal.** You have only one mission when contacting an agent's or manager's office: You want her to read a sample of your work! Period, that's all. Sure, a meeting would be great, but nobody is going to sign you until that person has read your material. So keep focused on your goal. Once she says that she'll read something, get off the phone and send over a script.

- **Use the phone.** Notice that I keep saying "phone." While it might seem easier to just mail out a bunch of query letters, *don't do it!* At most of these companies, part of an assistant's job is to respond to unsolicited query letters by mailing back a standard pass letter that says, "Thanks, sorry, no can do." It is much harder for them to turn away a pleasant, intelligent human being (you) speaking on the other end of a telephone line. Yes, all representatives prefer that you send query letters—it's easier on them. But making their lives easier is not your job; your job is to land one of these guys.

Won't they be offended? How do you think they get their business done? On the phone! Because it is a much stronger sales tool than snail mail or email. In truth, any agent or manager who turns someone down simply because she called his office wasn't going to sign that person anyway. So nothing lost. (Of course, if you call first and they insist that you send a query letter, then you have no choice. But do so, and then follow up a week later with another phone call.)

Still too pushy for you? If you are serious about launching your career, you need every advantage you can get. The sooner you land representation, the sooner you can stop chasing these people. So use the phone.

NOTE: What exactly is a query letter? It is a brief note, just one or two pages long, that describes your background and the script you wish to submit. It usually includes the following: a one- to three-sentence introduction that reminds the rep that you called and he invited you to submit the letter; a short recap of your background—basically a written version of the phone spiel I'm about to describe; a compelling springboard for the script you're hoping he'll read; and a closing line that asks if you may submit the script. Include a self-addressed-and-stamped envelope or postcard for his response, and keep the letter brief! The longer the query letter, the more likely it is that he'll find a reason to pass on you. Also, remember that this is a sample of your writing abilities; spelling, punctuation, and grammar count.

Prepare a Phone Spiel

Once a rep gets on the line, you've got only a few seconds to win him over. He's busy, you're nervous, there's a lot at stake—why leave things to chance? Figure out what you should say *before* you pick up the phone. Prepare a clever little spiel that quickly introduces you and the purpose of your call. We're talking five or so sentences that spark his interest enough so that he asks for additional information or says the magic words, "Okay, send it over."

What goes into this spiel? The answer is different for everyone because the pitch has to sound completely natural, but here's one approach. First, give your name to introduce yourself. Then, quickly describe two to three *hooks* that make the other person want to hear more. These hooks are tangible facts *about you*, your writing background, and your achievements. *They are NOT a description of the script you want to submit.* (Sorry, but if you toss out a logline or springboard now, it's just too easy for the other person to pass based on that brief story description.)

What hooks might you use? Especially if you're a new screenwriter and have no professional credits? Well, if you've been referred to this person by someone he knows, that's the best hook of all. The first words out of your mouth should be, "Hi, I'm Evan Smith. JOE BIGSHOT at Paramount suggested that I call. . . ." Odds are that, unless you're rude or you sound like a nut, this approach will result in a positive response.

Or, if you don't have a referral, you might mention:

- Your publications, produced plays, or other writing credits

- Writing awards you've won

- Writing contests you've won or placed in

- A homegrown series pilot you've written that can be viewed on the web, emailed, or delivered on a disk (more on this later)

- Web shorts you've written

- A script of yours that has already generated interest from a producer or exec (who would confirm that in a phone call)

- Stand-up comedy work you've done (sitcom producers love hiring writers who've performed comedy)

- Your degree from a top film school

- Any unique expertise that could give you an edge on a show that deals in a particular genre (are you a lawyer, a cop, a doctor?)

Or perhaps you've discovered some personal connection when re-searching the rep, such as having graduated from the same college, being from the same hometown, or sharing a mutual acquaintance.

If you can't come up with any sort of hook or connection—meaning that you better start work on creating those things!—then a clever but unassuming pitch might still do the trick. There is a lot to be said for sim-ply being earnest, passionate, determined, and articulate (without being pushy, boastful, or cutesy). If you can also be amusing—after all, you are selling yourself as a comedy writer—so much the better.

Once you've presented your hooks, end your spiel by politely asking for the sale: "May I send you that *Office* script that won the contest?" Or "... the pilot script that Joe Producer expressed interest in?" Remember, you have one important goal: You want them to read your best sample.

Here are some thoughts about *how* to present your spiel:

- **It must not sound rehearsed.** If any elements seem false, awkward, or pretentious, change them—the last thing you want is for your carefully structured phone spiel to sound like a canned speech. Work from an outline if necessary, but definitely practice the pitch enough so that it sounds relaxed and conversational.

- As for **tone of voice**, your spiel should give the happy impression that you are a cheerful, confident professional, not a nervous wannabe. Call only when you are feeling upbeat and are at your most personable.

- **Tailor the pitch** for each recipient based on what you've learned about him and his clients. Again, hit the Internet to get a sense of the person you're calling.

Making the Call

Your hit list in hand, your phone spiel at the tip of your tongue, you pick up the phone and start dialing. (You're reaching for a regular, wired phone, not a cell phone—no sense annoying these folks with poor reception.)

When a person answers, try to sound polite, confident, and pleased to be talking with that individual. You need to sound like a winner.

You might have to go through an agency's receptionist to get to a representative or her assistant. If you don't have a specific rep's name, the receptionist will probably refuse to forward you to "the person who handles sitcom writers." So do more research, get a specific name, and call back another day.

If you do have a specific name, ask for that person in a brief, businesslike, even bored fashion (e.g., "Joe Agent, please."), to reduce the chance that the receptionist will try to grill you. If he does ask why you're calling, respond with "About a script" or "About a submission." Both responses are honest, which you must be. If he presses for more, you'll have to briefly explain why you're calling or he'll end the call. At this point, if he refuses to forward you, say bye and hang up . . . and call back in three weeks to try again.

Once you reach a rep's assistant, ask if you might speak to the rep whom you are pursuing. (And make note of the assistant's name.) Unless the assistant is incompetent, he will ask if he can help you instead. Should you blow him off and insist on speaking with the rep? Of course not. That assistant is a powerful gatekeeper; alienate him and he will shut you down, charm him and he might champion your cause. (Plus, the guy is a person too and deserves some courtesy.) Instead of being pushy, just say, "Yes, absolutely," and then proceed to pitch your spiel *to the assistant*.

At this point, any of several things might happen:

- If you are very fortunate, the assistant might interrupt you to say, "Please hold"—and the next thing you know, the rep is on the line! What should you do? Just start your phone pitch over from the top, remembering that you have only one goal—to get that person to agree to read your material. Be aware that sometimes a rep will listen in on the phone line when her assistant first picks up a call, so when you restart your pitch for the rep, change it up a bit so it does not sound rehearsed.

- The assistant might simply invite you to send the script in, without checking with the rep. Great! Get the assistant's name, express gratitude, and follow through ASAP. There'll be plenty of time to meet the rep later, *if* she likes your material.

- The assistant might shut you down with a blanket "Sorry, we're not taking on any new clients right now." Or "Sorry, but we only sign clients who are already established writers." Or "Sorry, we only see people who have been referred by someone we know." You have several options here. You can:
  - Try to small talk your way into getting the assistant to make an exception in your case.
  - Ask if the rep would be willing to meet so that you can ask some questions about how to get started in the business; a pleasant informational chat might lead to the rep reading your script or offering you a referral to another rep.
  - Flatter the assistant a bit and ask *him* to read the script. Most will say no, but some will agree, and if he loves the material, it's likely that he will forward it to his boss—bingo!
  - Larger companies often have newly christened reps who are looking for their first clients—ask the assistant if he knows of any new reps at his company that might talk with you. If the assistant gives you a name, you now have a referral that should get you in the new rep's door!

- The assistant might insist that you submit a query letter before they will consider reading your spec script. Without seeming pushy, try to talk your way out of this one for the reasons described above—it is far better that they read a polished script than a brief summary of your story.

   If they still insist that you send a query letter, do so and then call in a week to (ostensibly) see if the assistant received it, and again try to talk him into letting you submit a complete script. (Who cares if he ever reads the query letter?) Remember, the goal of a query letter is to get the rep to read your script, not tell him so much that he needn't bother.

- The assistant might just blow you off and even be rude. Big deal, it happens. Call back in a month and you might catch him in a more receptive frame of mind. Or someone else might pick up the phone.

Start at the top of your hit list and keep calling until you reach the last candidate. Then update the list and go through it again.

Remember to update your database and calendar each time you connect with a contact, noting what was said to whom, when, and, most importantly, the next steps that you should take with that person.

Keep calling until a rep signs you. Do not slow down just because ten people have agreed to read your scripts—it might be the fifteenth person that finally says yes. And nothing could be better than to suddenly get calls from five reps who want to represent you; whoever signs you would work harder on your behalf because you seem to be a hot property.

If you are having trouble getting reps to read your material, revise your pitch.

If you are having trouble getting past a rep's assistant, try calling after six p.m. Sometimes the assistant will have already gone home and the rep herself will pick up the phone.

Keep calling, keep honing your pitch. When someone agrees to read a script, get off the phone before he changes his mind and deliver the thing pronto.

Finally, remember that this is a business and launching any business takes time. Many new writers lose heart because they spend a few months trying to contact people and get nowhere. Be tenacious and bold, and you will get people to read your material. And that's half the battle.

Submitting Your Material

When a rep agrees to read one of your scripts, here are the steps you should take:

- **Send your best work.** You've only got one shot at impressing this person, so submit your strongest writing sample.

- **Signing a legal release.** Many reps will insist that you sign a one- or two-page legal release before they will read your material. This protects them, to some extent, in case you later try to sue because they profited from a project that seems very similar to yours. Should you sign the release? You have to or else they won't even consider you. But don't worry too much—most agents and managers aren't in the business of stealing material. And if you do run into an obvious infringement problem, you can still pursue the matter through the Writers Guild and the courts.

- **The package.** You should send in a clean, new copy of your script, enclosed in a standard manila envelope. (See Appendix A for professional script format guidelines.) Include a brief, two- or three-sentence cover letter that thanks the rep for agreeing to take a look at the script. This note, another sample of your writing, might reiterate something said in your phone conversation or a highlight from your phone pitch, but keep it short. Make it engaging and concise.

  Some people prefer to handwrite such notes on personalized note cards—small (3 x 7 inch?), blank cards, cut from standard card stock, that bear the owner's name (in a conservative font) in one corner. I recommend that you have your own batch printed up; they are handy when it comes to submissions and follow-up letters.

- **Enclose a self-addressed, stamped return envelope (SASE).** Agents and managers have no wish to pay return postage on the scripts that they reject. In fact, if you don't include a proper return envelope in your script package, many will just toss the script into the trash, un-read. After all, if you don't know enough to do them that courtesy, you're probably not someone they'd want as a client.

One positive note is that, while you will want to mail your scripts to a rep via first-class mail, you can select fourth-class (Media Mail) for return postage—much cheaper.

An alternative to having used scripts returned to you is to ask, in your cover letter, that the script be recycled if the rep chooses to pass on you. (After all, you probably won't use the script again once some-one has bent its corners and spilled coffee on it.) While you might lose the psychological value of showing that you value your work by paying for its return, you will save a tree or two. However, the disadvantage here is that an assistant who doesn't check your cover letter might think that your submission lacks a SASE, and toss the thing out. But if you keep track of your submissions, you will probably discover the screw-up and can resubmit.

Can't you just email the script to save time and money? Well, how much do you value the countless emails that land in your in-box? Sorry, but unless the rep specifically instructs you to submit via email, this shortcut is likely to irritate the person you're trying to impress.

- **Deliver it in person.** Mailing a package can take a lot less energy than driving it over in person. *However*, if you deliver the package yourself, you might luck into some very valuable face time. You could get a chance to chat up the assistant in person, or the rep herself might cruise through the reception area while you are standing there. Bingo! Now you are a real person to these folks rather than merely a disem-bodied voice on the phone. Well worth the drive over, huh?

Of course, it's hard to hand-deliver scripts if your home is three thou-sand miles away. What should you do if you don't live in Los Angeles?

Testing the Waters If You Don't Live in L.A.

As mentioned before, if you already have a successful career or family obligations, I strongly recommend that you test the waters before packing up to move west. There are several steps that you can take to help you make an informed decision:

- **Write those spec scripts first!** You can write anywhere, and it's far easier to write when the rest of your life is settled. So don't get on a plane unless you already have a couple of dynamite spec scripts in hand. If you find it difficult to knuckle down and write in your current (comfortable, familiar) environment, you should ask yourself how productive you'd be if you had just moved to a new city and acquired new financial burdens. Frankly, you might even find, after cranking out a couple of scripts, that you don't really enjoy the work—better to learn that now rather than after you have already moved to L.A.

- **Try to land an L.A. rep via long distance.** Before moving out, use the techniques described above to launch an agent/manager search. Many of the people you contact won't realize that you are calling from out of town. If someone does question you about your location, be honest, but at the same time, if you have decided to move to L.A., mention that you are in the process of relocating. Because the competition in Hollywood is intense. If you aren't passionate enough about the work to move to L.A., it is just as easy to find someone else who is. Plus, television writing involves a lot of face-to-face meetings and group writing—what rep needs the hassle of pushing someone from out of town?

  Some out-of-town writers, believing that their non-L.A. location is hampering their search, go so far as to create a Los Angeles presence for themselves. How? You funnel calls through a cell phone that has an L.A. number, and funnel mail through a friend's or relative's home in the L.A. area, or a local post office box you've rented. Mail comes to you via forwarding from L.A., and you use that address as the return on outgoing mail. Sound like a pain? Definitely. But it can serve temporarily while you check out your prospects. (Another phone alternative is to sign up with a phone answering service in L.A.)

- **They want to meet.** If a rep loves your material and knows that you haven't yet moved to L.A., you'll probably have to fly out for a meeting before she'll even consider signing you (on the condition that you will soon relocate). However, the odds are greater that she will refuse to do even that until after you have made the move. Should you ask her to finance a flight out for that meeting, or some of your moving expenses? Don't even kid.

In either case, if an agent or manager is interested in signing you, you have arrived at the crossroads of that big move-to-L.A. decision, because a rep is not likely to circulate your material until you actually relocate. How would she look if a producer asked to see you the next day, but you were living in Wisconsin? You might plead that you would gladly fly out, but honestly, how often could you spring for a last-minute plane ticket that costs $500, $1,000, $1,500? Just for an introductory "hello" meeting? Sure, you could *try* to schedule a bunch of meetings together to make a trip cost-effective, but the odds of several producers all wanting to see you during the same few days are pretty slim. And, sorry, but producers are not going to hire you while you still live out of town so that you can then feel justified in moving to L.A.

So it's time to make a choice. At least by going through the steps of writing scripts and securing representation, you are in a much better position to make an informed decision. If prospects look good and your responsibilities are few, perhaps you should take the shot; you can always hop a plane back home if things don't work out, satisfied that you gave it a try. But if Hollywood has given you a lukewarm reception or other obligations stand in your way, think twice; perhaps you should try writing in a form other than sitcoms to avoid disrupting your life.

Following Up on Submissions

Once you have submitted a script to a rep, what next? You wait. Give her about three weeks before calling the assistant "just to make sure that they received the script." Be pleasant, not pushy, and use this opportunity to chat up whoever answers. Odds are that they have received the script but haven't read it—reps often take one to three months to get to a new submission. Fine, say thanks and good-bye, and call back in two weeks if you haven't heard. And again two weeks after that, and two weeks after that, until you get a response. Don't fret about the time frame; good reps have stacks of scripts to get through. Of course, sometimes a writer will call after waiting for weeks, only to hear that—oops—they lost his submission. Oh well. Graciously tell them "no problem" and rush a new copy over. Sometimes their goof works in your favor because they then feel obligated to give you more attention.

> *NOTE: You should know that even when someone in Hollywood absolutely swears that he will read your script, that often means that his assistant or a professional reader will do the reading. Then, if that person thinks that the submission is brilliant, the agent/manager/producer/executive himself will read it. It might be disheartening to hear, but this is how people get through the mountains of scripts sitting on their credenzas.*

Remember, be a charmer during all of your discussions with the rep and her assistant. Be sharp, courteous, clever, prepared, fun, and funny. Most of all, try to appear confident. In Hollywood, if you seem desperate or needy, people run the other way.

And again, keep detailed records. Write down anything that might help you to connect with a person, from mutual acquaintances to shared hobbies. Keep track of names (correctly spelled), job titles (some people are very touchy about these), phone numbers, fax numbers, addresses, dates that you called, dates that they said to call back, strategies for following up, etc.

If You Fail to Land Representation

One after another, your scripts come back, some preceded by a rep calling to let you down gently and others accompanied by a friendly pass letter. You've been through your entire hit list three times but nobody has offered to represent you. What can you do?

You regroup. First, take a hard look at the quality of your scripts. Are your samples good enough? Get some feedback from people whose opinions

Producer LAWRENCE KONNER: Avoid bitterness. Avoid the kind of negativity that sometimes swirls around this town and around this industry, including envy and jealousy. It simply doesn't serve you well. It doesn't serve your mental health or your professional health, because you're just focused on the wrong things.

you trust, and try sending out different samples. And, as always, keep writing new samples.

Then, though you should have already done this, revise your phone pitch and update your hit list. Are you getting enough reps to agree to read your material? Are the *right* reps reading your material?

When a rep does pass on you, here are a few other tactics that you might try:

- **Ask if you can submit more samples down the road.** Many reps, anxious to avoid being negative, will cheerfully agree. Which means that you get another shot at them once you have written a new spec.

NOTE: The more times your scripts hit someone's desk, the better. After a while, that person will recognize your name and perceive you as someone who is serious about writing. If your scripts are good, your perseverance will make her more inclined to take you on.

- **Ask for a referral.** Though this rep has decided to pass on you, he might know of other reps who are looking for new clients. If you don't ask, you don't get.

- **Strike a deal for passive (agent) representation.** If a desirable agent is encouraging but does not feel that he can sign you at this time, ask if you can use his name to get your material read. (Some people refer to this arrangement as a *hip-pocket deal*, though that more accurately describes an agent agreeing to represent a particular project rather than sign the writer of that project.) The agent won't have to do anything, but if you land a job on your own, he gets to close the deal and collect 10 percent. And he might then be impressed enough to sign you as a full-fledged client.

Give away 10 percent when the agent hasn't done anything? Yes. By letting you say that he represents you, he is making it much easier for you to get your material to producers and executives. Plus, if it only costs you one commission to get a good agent, it is well worth the price.

- **Approach an agent with a deal in hand.** Sometimes the best way to get an agent's attention is to approach him with a deal in hand.

Meaning, you use other methods to land a job and then offer to let that agent close the deal, *if* he agrees to sign you as a regular client. Sometimes the agent will be impressed enough to do so and everything works out wonderfully. Other times, an agent will say no. And other times, an agent might agree just to get the commission, but then do little to get you more work. Obviously, this last arrangement is not what you hoped for. But there are no guarantees that any agent will perform, and at the least, you can use the guy's name until you find a better agent.

You Get an Offer!

Finally, you get the call. A rep has read one sample, maybe two, and likes the work. He invites you in for an introductory meeting—*the* meeting. If all goes well, you will have an offer of representation before you leave his office.

Though the rep will try to make the meeting comfortable for everyone (you, him, and possibly another rep or two), treat it like a big job interview. You are out to make a sale, to get the offer. He is evaluating the way that you present yourself, to see if he thinks that you will impress producers and be pleasant to work with. What image should you present? Dress in casual clothes that look expensive, the type of things that you might wear to a nice brunch rather than an office job. (Think polo shirts and pricey loafers, maybe chinos or a hip skirt, rather than ties and formal jackets.) Be prompt. Be engaging. Be confident. And ask intelligent questions.

What type of questions?

- Who are his other clients, and which of them are currently working?

- Who else works at the firm, and will you be dealing with them?

- What are his firm's strengths?

- What strategy would he recommend for you?

- How often does he brief his clients regarding the status of submissions?

- What are the odds of you getting work quickly?

- What does he think you should be writing now?

And ask about his background, about how he got into the business. Show a personal interest in the man, to flatter him and to get a sense of how he really operates.

Take any promises of instant employment with a grain of salt. The key questions are: Does this person have a successful track record and the right connections, and will he aggressively circulate your material?

If the meeting goes well, he will offer to represent you. If you like what you see and don't have any other offers to consider, you can either shake hands on the deal or ask that he let you sleep on it overnight (so as not to seem desperate). If you have other offers on the table, tell him so; unless you rub his nose in them, they will only enhance your appeal. You might even name names and ask him why it would be better to go with his firm.

If you get an offer but are waiting to hear from a different rep who you think is a better choice, ask the first rep if you can sleep on the offer and immediately call the preferred rep. Without appearing pushy, explain your situation (without naming the agent making the first offer) and ask if the second rep has any interest in signing you. If and only if the preferred rep *pursues you aggressively*, sign with him and send your regrets to the first rep. But if you get a halfhearted response from the preferred rep, you would be wise to go with the person who has shown more interest.

Last thought: Remember that, when signing with an agent or manager, you are not hiring a new best friend. If a friendship does develop, terrific. But writing is a business, your business, and what you need most is a rep who can sell.

Signing the Contract

What do you actually sign when signing with an agent or manager?

An agent will offer you a brief contract, probably anywhere from one to ten pages long. If the agent is a signatory to the WGA, his contracts must include a number of standard provisions that protect you, the writer. These provisions include:

- **Term of the agreement.** An agent may only sign you for up to two years. If you are both happy after that, you can renew. If not, you are free to move on.

- **The ninety-day clause.** If you "do not receive a bona fide and appropriate offer of employment for an aggregate of at least [$43,000 (call the WGA for the current figure)], during any period of ninety consecutive days, you can terminate your contract with your agent." All you have to do is give him written notice and in ten days you're done. Of course, this clause works both ways—if your earnings fall short of the current cutoff figure, your agent can also terminate the contract.[1]

- **Rider W.** Every signatory agent's contract must include and be subject to a WGA-approved rider referred to as Rider W. This rider (it's often longer than the agent's contract) presents a long list of standard provisions that govern agreements between agents and writers. If an agent's contract includes a provision that contradicts a provision in this rider, the rider always prevails; that is good for you, since most of the rider's provisions are designed to protect the writer. If a copy of Rider W hasn't been attached to a contract offered you, find out why and rectify the situation.[2]

While it's always wise to run a contract by an attorney before signing it, agreements with agents who are WGA signatories are so closely regulated that they usually can't do much harm. Of course, you should study the documents and you might elect to ask for some changes. For example, some contracts state that the agent gets a commission from non-scriptwriting earnings such as lectures, recitals, concerts, novels, etc. Unless the agent is prepared to seek work for you in these areas, you might ask that they be deleted from the agreement. (If the agent wants to keep them in, put her on the spot—ask her to explain what efforts she plans to make to land you those types of work.)

Also, there are two secondary agreements that deserve mention, both of which might be included in the agent's primary contract or presented to you as separate documents (to sign). These documents grant the agent *power of attorney* to do the following: The first gives your agent the right to sign employment agreements on your behalf. The second allows your agent to collect your writing fees, deduct his commission, and then forward the remaining money to you. Should you sign these agreements? Personally, I don't care to sign the first; I feel uncomfortable giving someone else the right to commit me to a job before I have read the contract myself. As for the second agreement, which allows the agent to collect my fees and deduct his commission, I gladly sign that because I want my agent to know that I trust him and want him to get paid promptly. (Conversely, to not sign the second will irritate your agent by suggesting that you do not trust him—a bad start for the relationship.)

As for managers' contracts, those reps are not signatories to the WGA but must conform to labor laws regarding management agreements. Before signing one of these contracts, get an independent lawyer to review the document if you have any questions about its contents.

Once You've Signed with Someone

Congratulations, you landed an agent! Or a manager! Or both! But has anybody hired you yet? Ninety percent of nothing is still nothing. Your next step is to get potential employers to read your work.

16

STEP THREE: GETTING YOUR WORK OUT THERE

Any new writer who merely sits back and waits for her rep to generate work is likely to go hungry. Your success depends on getting your writing samples out to as many potential employers as possible. That means that you and your rep should both be trying to reach these people. Where can you find them?

Scouting the Market

Remember, you can forget about selling those wonderful spec scripts (for existing series) that you wrote. The only purpose in circulating those scripts is to land you an entry-level staff job or a freelance script assignment.

Staff jobs are likely to open up anytime that a new show gets picked up or an existing show receives an order for additional episodes. As for freelance script assignments, the WGA requires the producers of every show to assign a couple of episodes to outside writers every season; the exact number depends on how many episodes of that series have been ordered. Of course, most of these freelance assignments go to people who have an inside track: a deserving member of the production staff, a friend of a producer, the studio exec's nephew, a bored star who thinks he's a writer. (Once, I lost a promised assignment to a pair of attractive women whom the producer met in traffic school; they had never written a word before but thought it would be neat to write an episode, and the producer thought they were neat, so . . .) Certainly, it is irritating when favoritism robs you of an opportunity to work, but once you get going, personal connections might just as easily work in your favor.

How do you land a job? Your first priority is to get your spec scripts read by producers who currently have a show in production or who have just received a production order. Your second priority is to target programming executives at studios and networks; they don't hire staff writers directly, as producers do, but they do recommend writers to the producers of their shows. (Actually, executives will sometimes force a producer to hire a writer, but they usually do so only when the writer is already a hot commodity.) While it is best to catch these people when they have shows in production or heading into production, there is also a long-term benefit to making contact in their off season; two months later, that executive might recommend you to a producer, who three months later has an opening on a show. (This also illustrates why you should stay in touch with old contacts.)

Your third priority is to find people who can connect you with your first and second priorities, those producers and executives. Perhaps your friend, a gardener, mows a producer's lawn? Or your cousin, the CPA, does an executive's taxes?

Yes, your rep should already know many of these people and should have a good idea of what jobs are currently open; she and her partners are constantly trying to sniff out new opportunities. But two or more heads are better than one. And on some occasions, as is only reasonable, your rep will push other clients instead of you. So gather your own intelligence: Read the papers, read the trades, talk to neighbors, join your college alumni club, join industry organizations, etc.—take all of those steps we discussed in the last chapter. Develop an active social life that not only keeps you sane, it also continually expands your network. (And makes you a more well-rounded writer.)

But won't you risk irritating your rep by inadvertently contacting

Producer ELLEN SANDLER: Agents really don't get you work—you have to do the heavy lifting. They're only as strong as your reputation. They get you a meeting based on your credentials. You have to establish yourself, you have to have something that people are interested in.

someone whom he is already pursuing? The trick is to consult regularly with your rep so that that doesn't happen. And if it does, big deal. Now that producer has *two* copies of your script. Plus, your efforts will reap a side benefit—most reps will work harder for a client if they see that she is working hard.

While trying to get producers and execs to read your material, what if you trip over an actual job opening that your rep hasn't heard of? You have two options. First, many writers will ask their rep's assistant to send over a script after someone agrees to take a look; that way, the script looks more official since it bears the rep's script cover, and the writer doesn't have to play secretary. However, if you uncover an actual job opening and alert your rep to it, she will probably pitch a couple of other clients, in addition to you, for that job—you have just created competition for yourself! If you trust your rep, you can ask that she not submit other clients unless and until the producer passes on you. (Well, you can *ask*.) Or your second option is to just send the script over yourself. Include a brief cover note that thanks the producer for agreeing to read the script and identifies your rep (her name, firm's name, and direct dial number) for follow-up purposes. In fact, many reps, to save themselves delivery costs, are even willing to give their clients some of their agency's mailing labels and stationery, so that the writers' direct submissions look more official. (Ask for a bunch so that you have them when you need them.)

Hiring Windows

A few chapters back, I mentioned that the big broadcast networks tend to develop and air shows in a seasonal fashion. To reiterate, the traditional schedule runs roughly like this:

From fall to midwinter, pilot scripts for new series are commissioned and developed.

From January to April, a handful of the best scripts are produced as pilot episodes.

In May, the networks announce which shows, old and new, will be given production orders for the coming year.

From June on, the writing staffs work to get their episodes produced.

In August and September, new series premiere and old series return with new episodes.
In midwinter, failing series are replaced with midseason entries that have been held in reserve.

Nowadays, it seems that all networks, including the big broadcast networks, develop and premiere shows at all times of the year. However, many series are still produced per the traditional schedule outlined above. Since production dates dictate when most writers are likely to be hired, a smart writer and his rep try to capitalize on the resulting hiring windows in the following manner:

1. **Midfall to midwinter.** You and your rep should focus on getting writing samples to network and studio executives *months before* the networks decide which series pilots to order. That is the time when these people have the time to read the material. The hope is that the executives, if they are impressed, will later recommend you to those producers who are asked to produce pilots or given a pickup.

2. **January through April.** The second that a pilot production order is announced, your rep should try to get your material to that pilot's producers. (Actually, some producers will receive orders for multiple episodes at this point.) Reaching these people is a difficult task, since they are extremely busy with their make-it-or-break-it pilots. While they are usually not interested in hearing directly from an unknown writer right now, they will often accept a rep's submission. (Of course, if your rep won't make these calls, then you should try.)

3. **May through July.** The second that series orders for the coming television season are announced, you and your rep should pounce on the producers. After all, one of their first goals will be to lock up a strong writing staff.

4. **July through the fall.** Most staff assignments are filled by now, but many shows give out their freelance assignments during this period.

5. **Fall to midwinter.** As shows start to succeed or fail in the ratings, additional episode orders will be given out. Both staff and freelance assignments will open up.

Again, all networks produce shows at all times of the year and you never know when the next contact might result in a job. So, while these traditional hiring windows represent important opportunities, you should be applying maximum effort at all times.

Working with Your Rep

Your rep's time is valuable—to you. Call regularly, every couple of weeks, if you aren't hearing from her. When you call, be efficient. Have your updates and questions ready. Sure, a little pleasant chatter is healthy for your relationship, but try to follow her lead regarding the amount.

A great side benefit of being a buttoned-up client is that when the rep talks to you, she feels an added pressure to be buttoned up herself. At the same time, some reps don't like to "waste time" by keeping their clients updated on current submissions and news of job openings. That doesn't help you, because you need to know if your material is being sent out. If your rep tries to blow you off, persist, amicably. If she doesn't have the information handy, make an appointment to call back for a "quick chat regarding strategy." If your rep continues to blow you off and months go by without any indication that your material is going out, have a frank, friendly talk with her. If you still don't get any results, it's time to start looking for a new rep.

My first agent introduced me to a very productive practice: Prior to peak hiring windows, we would meet in her office for an hour or two to go over every opportunity that was currently available. She would interrupt the discussion to call producers as I sat there, tying up any loose ends that we uncovered. (And yes, she had to take a call or two while I sat there—a small price to pay.) I highly recommend that you try these sitdowns with your rep. If you both come prepared, they are a great way to get a lot done quickly. Plus, it's a chance for you and your rep to bond.

It is also helpful for you to act as your rep's *tickler file*. Every time that your rep names a new job opportunity or a place where he has submitted your material, write down the details. When you talk to the rep two weeks later, ask what came of that situation. If he has forgotten to follow up (it happens) or hasn't heard, nudge him gently to take action. Then check back on the matter again when next you speak.

Which Scripts to Send

Sometimes you or your rep might not be sure *which* of your samples will most impress a particular producer or executive. A *South Park* producer might like your *Two and a Half Men* script but feel that it is too "old-fashioned" to prove that you can write for his show. A *Two and a Half Men* producer might like your *South Park* script but feel that it is too "crude and sophomoric" to prove that you can write for her show. When possible, ask the contact which of your specs he would like to read. Otherwise, all you and your rep can do is submit whichever seems best in each case. Sometimes you win, sometimes you lose.

A related problem involves circulating spec scripts based on old or canceled shows. Usually, it is a mistake to submit scripts written for shows that no longer air. (They're ancient history, who wants to read them?) And even if an aging show is still getting good ratings, it might be better to send samples based on newer series. Why? Because producers and executives have to go through hundreds of scripts every season; after a while, they get tired of reading episodes from the same old shows.

Of course, everyone has his favorite shows and you can't always crystal-ball someone's reaction. I once got a job for an hour series by submitting a spec (the only one-hour spec I had at the time) written for the long-dead *Magnum, P.I.* series. Go figure.

Being Picky About Jobs

Unless you are independently wealthy and don't care if you antagonize your rep, you should probably take whichever legitimate writing jobs come your way. A producer wants to hire you, but you hate her show? So what. Just focus on your episode. Write thirty minutes of television that would make your mom proud. Get the credit and the money, and then move on to shows that you want to write for. Get picky later, when you have the leverage to call your own shots.

Cold-Calling Producers

I keep talking about cold-calling producers to get your material read. How do you do that? What should you say when you call?

Just ask to speak with the person whose name you dug up. When you get that person, or if you get blocked by that person's assistant, cheerfully plunge ahead with your pitch. If you have a rep, say that as you identify yourself, and ask if you can send a script over. If you don't have a rep, use some of the very same spin that went into your get-a-rep spiel and ask if you may submit a script.

The responses you will get will vary: Some people will cut you off with a no, some will invite you to submit, and some will insist that your rep (if you have one) call first. If they block you completely, make a note and try again later—who knows if the same person will answer? If they invite you to submit, do so promptly, remembering to include a brief cover letter that identifies your rep (if you have one) and thanks the contact person for authorizing you to send in your material.

If they say they'll read your script but only if a rep submits it, then, if you do have a rep, you're back to those two choices mentioned earlier. You can contact your rep to ask that he send a script over, or you can send it yourself with a brief note that thanks the producer for agreeing to read the script and gives your rep's contact information for further follow-up. Nine times out of ten, the producer will read the material because you mentioned a specific rep in the note. If the producer refuses, then on to Plan B: Have your rep send over the script.

NOTE: If an agent has agreed to a passive-representation arrangement, allowing you to use her name even though she hasn't actually signed you, use the same approach. Send the script yourself, with a cover letter that thanks the contact for agreeing to read the material and identifies "your agent" for follow-up purposes. If your passive agent will let you use some of her firm's mailing labels, even better.

The only downside to this arrangement? A few weeks after meeting you, a busy agent will probably forget your name. If someone calls to ask about you, he is likely to be greeted with "Who?" But no big deal. Just try to cover your bases by alerting the agent or her assistant if it seems likely that "an interested producer" will call about you. It's not a foolproof system, but it's better than having no agent at all.

Whenever you have a choice of people to call regarding a job opening, *try to get to the real decision-maker.* We have discussed how the producer hierarchy breaks down, but what about those programming executives? Generally, they are based at a network, studio, or large production company. Some are *development* executives, people who supervise the creation of new series, and some are *current programming* executives, people who supervise the ongoing production of existing series. Some executives handle both functions, depending on their company's needs. As for job titles, most executives work in departments that include a vice president, a director, a manager, and maybe a general programming executive.

How do these people spend their days? They take pitches (if they work in series development), read outlines and scripts, give notes, attend runthroughs, screen program footage, attend production meetings, work on program scheduling, supervise advertising and publicity efforts, evaluate ratings, and perform various administrative functions. Many executives have the authority to veto projects, but very few can actually authorize expenditures related to scripts and production—which is why you should aim as high up the ladder as possible.

Other Strategies for Reaching Producers

It's so difficult to get through to producers and execs, here are some out-of-the-box tactics you might try:

- **Pursue mid-level producers.** If you can't get through to a primary producer on a show, it might be possible to make contact with a secondary producer. Every week, executive producers are getting calls from all of the reps and half of the writers in town, hounding them about jobs. But a lower level producer (a co-producer? a supervising producer?) doesn't get those calls, yet is very well connected to the decision-makers on the show. If you can find a mutual personal connection or think one of the hooks in your spiel might interest her, or if you'd feel comfortable just saying that you liked the last episode she wrote (you better be able to say why!), try calling to ask for advice. (Production secretaries don't screen as rigorously when calls come in for these other producers.) See if the producer would be willing to meet with you to answer questions about the business, or—but only if he seems very receptive right up front—if he'd be willing to read a spec script. If he responds positively, you could end up with a well-placed champion on that show's writing staff or even a new writing mentor!

Most of these people will deflect this approach, but if you're charming and you don't sound like a stalker, some might invite you in for a chat. (If you don't live near enough for that, you can ask if the producer has time to give advice over the phone instead.) One warning though: Before calling, prepare a dozen excellent questions in case the producer tests you by saying, "Okay, I've got five minutes now, what are your questions?" If you have none, he'll shut you down and deflect your future calls.

- **Screenwriting competitions.** As mentioned in Chapter 15, there are a number of screenwriting competitions floating around that you might want to consider. It costs money to enter, but the good ones award winners with cash prizes, connections to industry pros, and bragging rights that can open doors down the road. Just proceed with caution—review our previous description of the pros and cons before writing a check.

- **Internet e-query services.** There are some web services that offer to, for a fee, "blast" a writer's query letter to a long list of reps, producers, and/or execs. It sounds like a great concept and I suppose that a few writers might have landed deals out of this direct-mail approach. However, I imagine that most of the pros who are flooded with these queries view them as bothersome spam. (Wouldn't you?) Plus, the notion of exposing your story ideas to the universe in such an anonymous fashion concerns me—how hard would it be for someone to steal your concepts? I recommend that you stay away from these services at least until you have tried the many approaches described in this book. If those don't work and you're really getting desperate, then maybe one of these e-query services is worth a shot.

- **Online script registries.** This is another type of Internet service which, for a fee, will post a writer's script (or a synopsis of it) in an Internet script bank that is accessible to Hollywood executives and producers. The better registries claim that real industry professionals subscribe to their service and regularly scan the postings, while low-brow versions post scripts so that they are available for *anyone* to read. Are these services worth the cost? Some, maybe—a few certainly boast that they've provided key connections that resulted in script sales. But most registries lack the connections and influence needed to attract industry professionals. And once you post a script or synopsis on the Internet, you run the risk that some anonymous reader might swipe your story. So, before going this route, see who the company's real industry subscribers are and check out its security provisions.

- **Pitchfests** Many modern screenwriting conferences now feature a component called a *pitchfest*. At these events, writers pay a fee in exchange for a chance to sit with an executive, producer, or rep for a few minutes, to pitch him one or several projects. (Sitcom writers might pitch a new series.) The professional gives feedback on the pitch and, if greatly impressed, might even offer to represent the writer or develop the project pitched. Are these sessions worth the cost? If you land a sincere hearing from a legit pro, sure. Unfortunately, most successful pros are too busy working to participate in such events, so there's a risk that you'll be stuck with some low-level schmo who's only there to grab a share of the session fees. My best advice is that before signing up, you check out the reputation of the particular conference and the credentials of the individuals fielding the pitches. If you proceed and nothing comes of the effort, at least you'll have gotten some practice pitching your ideas.

- **Shoot a homegrown pilot.** If you have a great pilot script and some video production know-how, you might want to consider producing an original series pilot or presentation tape, and putting it on the web and perhaps entering it into contests (like the New York Television Festival at www.nytvf.com). As mentioned earlier, today's producers and networks are now willing to consider fresh ideas from untested producers, and a sharp little pilot can be a terrific calling card for a new writer. Of course, there's one small obstacle—it's incredibly hard to write a good pilot and equally difficult to shoot one. But whatever the outcome, the experience would probably make you a better writer and you might just land work as a result.

■ **Perform stand-up.** Some comedy writers also like to perform in front of an audience. If you have any stand-up talent, use it! Get up on stage to not only strengthen your comedy ad-libbing skills, but also, if you live in L.A. or NYC, maybe catch the eye of someone looking for new talent. Sitcom producers, reps, and execs are always impressed by writers who have done stand-up or improv—they admire their spunk and assume that they must be at least somewhat funny. Plus, performing does enhance one's writing and you might make some useful connections with the industry pros backstage.

Keep Writing

Producer IAN GURVITZ: If someone's new and they haven't any credits and they have one great spec script, it really begs the question, did they shoot their wad on this? Did it take them ten years to write it? Did a bunch of friends help them punch it up? These are all stories you hear. So, often, you'll want to see a second sample. And more than that, you want to meet them to see whether they come off in a room like the person who wrote the script.

The best job-hunting strategy of all is to keep writing. Writing improves your writing. What's more, producing script after script gives you and your rep an excuse to keep calling producers. After a while, those producers will start to remember your name and the fact that you are very productive (a good thing). If your writing is strong, many will eventually become inclined to hire you—if only to keep from having to read more of your spec scripts.

On another level, being productive also keeps your rep interested in you. Even if work isn't coming your way, he sees that you are still making things happen. Which encourages him to follow suit.

If you start running out of steam and find it difficult to keep writing, do something proactive. Take a screenwriting class, change your work habits, join or form a writers group. Try to get one of the writers' internships occasionally sponsored by organizations like Warner Bros., Disney, and the Academy of Television Arts and Sciences; not only are these a great way to learn the craft, they frequently lead to personal connections that can launch a career.

Do whatever it takes to keep those scripts coming. You never know which script will be the one that lands you that next job.

Writing in Teams

Many sitcom writers embrace the "two heads are better than one" theory—they work in teams. There are definitely some advantages to the idea. Comedy writing is very demanding and subjective, and some days it is a huge relief to be able to share the load.

Some writers believe it's best if each partner complements the other. Maybe one is good with story structure and the other is a walking joke machine. Or one partner is the real writer of the pair but the other can sell anything to anybody. Whatever works.

Writing teams usually make producers happy because they can often get both bodies for the price of one. And the odds are good that, out of two people, one of them will be funny.

Of course, there are disadvantages too. Unless your partner and you are in great demand, you will have to split script fees and staff salaries. And there

---

Producer LAWRENCE KONNER: Print a sign that says, "Sit back down," and paste it over your computer. Keep writing. There's no substitute for writing. I think that young people have a tendency to focus too much on agents, deals, and whom you know. But I think that good writing wins. Good writing always wins.

Producer IRMA KALISH: Don't live or die with one script. Some people write a spec script and they keep sending it out, and sending it out, and sending it out, and they never write another script. Go on, do another one. Then another and another. And don't just think, "Well, I want to be a writer, so make me a writer." No one is going to make you a writer. You're not going to be a writer unless you actually write. That sounds simplistic, but a lot of would-be writers [have exactly that attitude].

Producer MICHAEL REISS: People always say, oh, find a partner who's very different from you, someone who complements your strengths. I think that's terrible advice. What made Al Jean and I a good team was we agreed on at least 80 percent of things—what should go into the script and what was funny, what movie was good, what we should eat for lunch. That's what made for a good partnership. . . . We just worked a line at a time. Here's what we've got, let's do this, what does the next guy say. It was slow, a little mechanical, but it was always friendly.

will be two names on the scripts that you write; if the team dissolves, most producers and execs will want to see writing samples and credits that bear only your name before they will hire you. (For all they know, the other guy was the talented half of the team.)

Still, half of a fee is better than none. If you know someone who shares your sense of humor, and you would feel more comfortable working with a partner, give it a shot. Allow yourselves a little time to develop a comfortable routine and see what you come up with.

Rejection

Rejection stinks, but all writers encounter it. If someone says that your material isn't funny, just remember that comedy is extremely subjective. That is why attracting a mere 10 percent share of the TV audience makes a sitcom a hit, and why blockbuster comedies produced in England and Canada (similar cultures, similar speech) usually don't play in middle America. It is also why many comedy writers opt to work in teams, depending on their partners to keep their humor on track. So the next time someone pans one of your sitcom scripts, chalk it up to different sensibilities. And remember that if it was easy to get work as a television writer, everyone would do it.

Producer LAWRENCE KONNER: The only true test of comedy is whether people laugh or not. There are a lot of situations where I and others say, "That's funny. Why aren't they laughing?" But they're not wrong. They're always right. If they're not laughing, it's not funny.

Of course, if everybody you approach thinks that your last ten scripts reek, then you have a problem. Time to seek some input on how to improve your writing, or reconsider med school.

Dealing with Writer's Block

Entire books have been written about how to deal with writer's block. Frankly, professional sitcom writers don't have the luxury of succumbing to this problem. The script is due in five days? Then you had better deliver. (A hard deadline does wonders for getting a writer unstuck.)

The little bit of advice that I can offer on this subject would be the following:

- **Set easy goals.** If you break the work up into manageable tasks, it won't seem so daunting. You don't have to write the whole script in one day. Tackle the opening scene first. Start that by outlining the beats of the scene. Decide who will be in the scene. Play with ways to open the scene. Pick one and just write a page. The next thing you know, you're three pages in and you know how the rest of the scene should go. Problem solved, you're on your way.

- **Check your story.** Sometimes you might have trouble getting into a script because a part of your brain knows that there is a problem with the story. If work grinds to a halt, step back to see if you have overlooked something that needs fixing. If so, fix it, and see if that loosens things enough so that you can get back to the script.

- **Fill some pages.** It is better to write badly than never to have written at all (according to some of my students). To get the creative juices flowing, force yourself to quickly write a hack version of the scene you're working on. As often as not, some of what you create will be useable. Or it might help you to trip over an alternative approach that does work.

If you still feel blocked, buy a book on the subject. Or save the money and *just do the work*.

> **Producer ELLEN SANDLER:** Deadlines are the best friend I have. If I'm writing on spec, I make my own deadlines. Or if I've got a writing buddy, I say I'm going to show him the pages by a certain time; I make a lunch date, we're going to exchange pages. . . .I tell myself to stay in my chair for one more minute. I stay in my chair and I write something, anything. I write something badly, the obvious thing. Or I write what the problem is—that will open some window usually.

Protecting Your Work

Probably all writers worry at one time or another that their work might be stolen. It does happen, rarely, but more times than not a perceived infringement is merely a coincidence—two writers living in the same universe, struck by similar thoughts at the same time. The only way to ensure that your material won't be stolen is to stop circulating it. Of course, then you won't be getting any work either. Can't you do anything to protect your ideas? Ideas, no. You cannot own, via copyright, a simple idea. However, you can take steps to protect "'original works of authorship' that are fixed in a tangible form of expression."[1] Meaning, a script or even a detailed treatment. How? You have several options.

First, you can register your script with the U.S. Copyright Office in Washington, DC. Interestingly, according to current copyright law, an original work of fiction is automatically copyrighted the moment you put the thing down on paper. However, who besides you even knows that it exists if all you do is print it out? To get some measure of copyright protection, you should register the script through the U.S. Copyright Office. Not only does this establish a public record of your claim to ownership, which can be presented as evidence in a court case, it also entitles you to sue for several types of compensation if someone does infringe on your copyright.

Sounds too complicated? Not at all. Just visit the Copyright Office website at www.copyright.gov and navigate to the online script registration form by clicking from "Publications" to "Forms." (You're going to use Form CO, which applies to screenplays.) There, you'll see two options: You can register online by uploading the script and using a credit card; or, you can fill out the form and print it out, and then mail the form in with a check and the script. If you use the first option the cost is $35, while the second costs $45. As long as the Copyright Office doesn't stumble over some conflict regarding the application, you will eventually receive a formal certificate of registration and you are done.

NOTE: It can take months for the Copyright Office to process your application and send you a certificate of registration. However, the registration is deemed effective on the date that the government "receives all of the required elements in acceptable form." If you want an idea of how long the wait might be, call and ask an operator for the current estimate.

ANOTHER NOTE: Some people believe that they can gain copyright protection by mailing a script to themselves in a sealed envelope and not open-

ing it. Sorry, but this process, called a "poor man's copyright," does not protect works in the United States. According to the Copyright Office, "There is no provision in the copyright law regarding any such type of protection, and it is not a substitute for registration."[2]

When preparing to circulate your script, you have the option of typing an official copyright notice at the bottom of your script's title page. A notice consists of three elements: the copyright owner's name, the year in which the copyright was registered, and either the word "copyright" or the symbol "©." Examples include "Copyright 2010 Joe Screenwriter" and "Sally Sitcom © 2015."[3]

Copyright registration is the best way to protect a script. However, for convenience' sake, and out of tradition, *most screenwriters prefer to register their work with the script registration department at the WGA.* This process is very similar to the copyright registration process. Simply visit www. WGAWRegistry.org and follow the steps for filing online or via regular mail. The cost is $20 for non–WGA members and $10 for members. Once your submission has been received by the WGA, you will be assigned a script registration notice that you can type at the bottom of your script's title page if you wish; the official notice will consist of "WGA Reg. #" followed by the number assigned to your script.[4]

Why did I say that copyright registration is better than WGA registration? Both services provide a public claim of ownership. However, WGA registration does not enable you to sue for full damages if you end up in court. And, though copyright registration costs more initially, the WGA registration lasts only five years, while government registration lasts for the life of the copyright (author's life plus 70 years). Though you can renew a WGA registration every five years, you must pay more each time you do.

And still, I'll repeat, most screenwriters prefer to register with the WGA. Go figure.

And just to hurt your head further . . .

If you're writing a pilot for a new sitcom, yes, you definitely should register the script before sending it out. But what if you're writing a spec episode for an existing show? You didn't create the premise or the characters, just a story for one episode. If someone rips off your idea—well, you can't copyright an idea, can you? So, while others might disagree, I don't see the value in paying to register a spec script for an existing show. Unless someone is stupid enough to copy sections of your script word for word, it would be hard to win the case, and even then the resulting compensation probably wouldn't be worth the legal expenses and lost sleep.

Should you register with both the Copyright Office and the WGA? No, pick one. And don't even think about putting two registration notices on your script—you'd seem distrustful and paranoid.

Even if you have registered a script and you come to believe that another party has injured you, pause to consider the pros and cons before charging off to file a suit. If you sue and win, what compensation might you actually receive (based on standard WGA writing fees)? Is it enough to warrant the effort and expense involved? Also, what impact might the negative publicity of a suit have on your other potential employers? Or on your relationship with your rep, who might have to keep dealing with the infringing party in the future? Bottom line, is a lawsuit worth all of the hassle? Many times, it is not. But if the answer seems to be yes, talk to a lawyer who specializes in copyright law.

Unfortunately, even registering a script with the U.S. Copyright Office does not, by itself, guarantee compensation or justice if someone else steals your work. Its primary purpose is to supply you with vital supporting evidence in case you decide to file a lawsuit.

NOTE: I am not a lawyer. The practical advice that I present in this book is intended to point you in the right directions rather than substitute for proper legal counsel. If you have an infringement problem or any other legal concern, talk to an attorney.

Ultimately, the best way to protect your work is to see that it only goes out to people who have legitimate connections to the sitcom world. But beyond that, limiting its circulation means that you are also lessening your chances of landing work.

Who Keeps the Copyright?

Since it is not likely that anyone will ever buy a spec sitcom script that you write, lucky you, you get to keep the copyright. However, if you are hired to write an episode of a television series, the producer who hires you gets to own the copyright. Why so, if she didn't write the script? Because it's written into your contract for the job. To protect the producer's investment in your episode, which might cost a million dollars or more to produce, it is important that she secure the underlying creative rights to the story. That way, if you suddenly object to her interpretation of the material, or you go insane and start insisting on bizarre changes, she doesn't have to worry. She owns and completely controls the property, and you no longer have a say in the matter.

A script written under this arrangement is called a "work for hire" or "work made for hire." (You will see this phrase in the contract provision that describes who retains the copyright.) While it might seem illogical or even unfair that an employer gets to, in effect, proclaim herself the author of something that she didn't write, do not fret about this issue. It is a standard provision in script deals and Writers Guild regulations ensure that it doesn't cause writers undue harm.

More to the point, if you don't agree to let the producer acquire the copyright, she will not hire you. Which leaves you with 100 percent ownership of a never-to-be-produced script.

The Writers Guild of America

Just what is the Writers Guild of America, this wonderful organization that protects hardworking film and television writers from the evils of Hollywood?

As explained earlier, the WGA, west and east branches, is the official screenwriters union. (It also serves interactive writers, animation writers, and some other media writing types.) Unfortunately, the WGA does not find jobs for its members. But it does provide many useful services, including the following:

- Negotiates the industry-wide agreements that protect writers' interests regarding compensation, working conditions, and creative rights

- Collects residual payments for its members

- Provides contact information to those who want to reach a writer or his agent

- Provides members with free legal advice regarding union- and contract-related problems

- Provides a home base for numerous writers' committees that explore everything from ageism to new technologies

- Provides health insurance for those who earn enough to be eligible for the plan

- Provides pension benefits for eligible members

- Governs writing credits and provides a process for arbitrating credit disputes

- Encourages networking by sponsoring seminars and business functions

- Publishes an informative monthly journal titled *Written By*

. . . And much more.

Sounds great! How do you join? Well, the bad news is that, as with many unions, you have to land some work before you are allowed to join the WGA. And that work must consist of legitimate writing assignments handed out by WGA-signatory producers, not your Uncle Leo.

But how can you get Guild-sanctioned work if you aren't even *in* the Guild? That's the good news. Producers don't care—and probably won't even ask—if you are a Guild member when they interview you for a job. If they love your writing samples and you, that's all that matters. Guild membership, once you qualify, comes later.

How much work must you get before you can join the Guild? Requirements are different for the WGA, west and the WGA, east. Since almost all sitcoms are produced in Los Angeles, geography dictates that most sitcom writers join the western branch. (As previously mentioned, membership is supposed to be determined by which side of the Mississippi you live on.) To become eligible for membership in the WGA, west, you must first obtain a minimum number of "employment units." The current requirement for *full* membership in the WGAW is twenty-four units, meaning that (Guild-signatory) producers have hired you to write at least two complete sitcom episodes or "the equivalent." If a writer gets some work but not enough to qualify for full membership, she may elect to become an associate member of the WGAW; this would entitle her to receive mailings and many benefits of Guild membership, but she could not vote on Guild matters or run for office.

And here is where I stop. The membership requirements for both branches are somewhat confusing. If you start to get work as a film or television writer, call the nearest Guild's Membership Department to get information on current requirements for full membership or details of how to become an associate member. The WGAW's department can be reached via (323) 782-4532 and the WGAE's at (212) 767-7802.

Or do nothing. Because—more good news—once you have landed enough Guild-sanctioned sitcom work to qualify for full membership, you are automatically admitted! You don't have to audition or know somebody or bribe somebody. In fact, the WGA will contact you without you having to do a thing. Based on hiring information that your producers must regularly supply to the Guild, it knows when you become eligible. At that point, the membership department will send you a delightful "Welcome to the WGA" letter—and a bill for $2,500 in initial dues. Then you will receive a continuing stream of useful Guild mailings, and you are on your way.

To sustain a full membership in the WGAW, you will be required to pay quarterly dues of $25 plus 1.5% of your gross earnings as a writer. The bookkeeping is easy; you receive regular invoices and just send back the payments.[5]

Is it worth the cost? What if you don't want to pay these fees? It is definitely worth it, considering the many benefits of WGA membership. And you don't really have a choice about paying if you want to keep working as a sitcom writer, because Guild-signatory producers are prohibited from hiring anyone who has qualified for membership but refuses to pay the required dues.

NOTE: *At this point, I should also mention that if you become a WGA member, you are prohibited from writing for producers who are not signatories to the WGA. If the Guild discovers that a member has written for a non-signatory producer, it has the option of subjecting that writer to disci-*

plinary actions, including a fine that can equal up to 100 percent of the amount that the writer earned on that job.

Moving On

You've got a rep and you are getting your work out to the people who count. Finally, the call comes in—a producer loved your spec script and wants to meet you. You're close, but how do you land the job?

17

STEP FOUR: PITCHING FOR ASSIGNMENTS

Years ago, sitcom writers usually started their careers by landing a couple of freelance script assignments. Then, if they proved themselves, they moved on to low-level staff jobs and began working their way up.

Today, thanks to the changing job market, many new writers land a staff job right out of the gate. And a few have even done so based on having submitted only one strong spec script. On one hand, that's great news for those seeking entry-level jobs. On the other, it means that some new writers aren't getting a chance to learn their craft before being thrown into a group writing environment.

Since either route, pitching for a freelance assignment or competing for a staff position, can lead to your first job, we will cover both. Let's start by taking a chapter to look at how freelance writing works.

Producer MATT WILLIAMS: Today, people are thrown into positions before they've had time to serve their apprenticeship. Somebody comes in and is really funny at the table, and in two years, all of a sudden they're a co-executive producer and they're asked to run a show. And they don't have the slightest idea of how to supervise an editing session, a sweetening session, a scoring session, or how to beat out three stories at once, or make sure that their stories are building properly. . . . You have to learn the basic building blocks of storytelling. There are certain dramaturgical elements that exist in one-act plays, full-length screenplays, Broadway musicals, and half-hour sitcoms. They're like molecules. The essence of storytelling.

The Call Comes In!

You and your rep have been circulating your samples like mad. Finally, the call comes in. Your rep informs you that a producer of SHOW X—your new favorite show—loves your work and wants you to pitch for a freelance script assignment. This means one of three things: either the producer is hoping you'll bring in the world's best idea for an episode; or he wants to hear what type of ideas you can come up with (to get a sense of your talent) but ultimately plans to assign you one of their ideas; or he might not even require that you bring in ideas because, if he likes you, he intends to assign you one of theirs.

Since the last two options don't happen as often as you might wish, let's proceed as if you are being asked to present a full pitch—getting the assignment depends on you selling one of your ideas.

Preparing for the Pitch

When your agent calls to schedule the pitch, try to get a date that gives you at least two to three days to prepare. And use that time, all of it, to get ready. Pitches are hard to come by and these people are already predisposed to hire you. (If the producers have named a specific meeting time that's convenient for them, say yes no matter what conflicts you have and make that time work; you don't want their first impression to be that you don't care enough to accommodate their schedule.)

Most of what you need to do was already covered in Part Two of this book. The first step in developing ideas for a show is to study that show. Get several scripts and episodes, and take a hard look.

Then create your springboards. How many? Some writers believe that half a dozen are plenty. I don't. Often, a show's producers will quickly eliminate one or two of your ideas because they think that they have already been done elsewhere. Then they might cross off one or two because they themselves have done or are about to do similar stories. That leaves you with only a couple of shots at making a sale. Why play those odds?

My philosophy is that, having worked so hard to get invited in for a pitch, it's worth my effort to generate *ten to fifteen solid ideas*. If the producers immediately dismiss four or five for assorted reasons, no problem—I've got plenty more. Not only do I increase my odds of hitting on a premise that the producers love, but I impress them by showing that I have tons of good ideas.

But is there enough time to fully describe ten to fifteen stories? (Since pitch meetings usually run only thirty to forty-five minutes?) Of course not. That's why you start out with those three- to five-sentence spring-boards. They don't like an idea? Fine, it's gone, next.

When an idea does spark the producers' interest, they will stop you to ask questions or let you fill in some blanks. Answer the questions. If it seems appropriate, quickly back up and tell a slightly longer version of the pitch (just a few paragraphs' worth), describing major plot points and funny highlights to build the producers' interest.

Preparing these concepts sounds like a lot of work. Do you have to be able to fully explain all of those story ideas? No, not all. Some stories, especially high-concept ideas, are instantly clear so that you don't really need to fill in any gaps. For other stories, yes, you should be prepared to lay out the key beats, quickly describing a beginning-middle-end. (Again, give just a couple of paragraphs' worth.) However the producers react, don't fight them; try to adapt to their vision *without complaint.* (Remember, the client is always right.)

If a producer asks for details that you haven't figured out yet, don't panic. If a workable answer pops into mind, toss it out. Or simply say, "Hm, I don't know. Could I get back to you on that this afternoon?" The producers will probably tell you not to bother, or promptly come up with an answer themselves. No problem; they know that all stories have elements that need to be worked out. What matters is that you aren't thrown by the question and that you have demonstrated an eagerness to solve problems.

Here are some other points to consider when preparing for a pitch:

- As you create your springboards and flesh out the story beats to back them up, remember that *your goal is to sell, not educate.*

- Since producers sometimes mull over a pitch before deciding on an assignment, some writers like to supply them with *leave-behinds.* These are written copies of the springboards (not lengthy story descriptions) that were pitched, each neatly typed on a separate page, with the writer's name and the date at the top. The thinking here is that a writer's carefully honed springboard can probably do a better job of selling the producers than their own vague recollections of the story will, so why not leave written copies of the ideas that the producers thought were worth considering? Of course, there are two caveats: Don't annoy the producers by leaving behind springboards that they passed on, and make sure that what you leave behind is very well written. (Let me stress this last point: It's harder to write compelling, intelligent, funny springboards than it is to pitch the same ideas verbally, so if you have any doubts about the quality of your leave-behinds, don't use them.)

- After you have developed your ideas, *practice your pitch*. Do it out loud, in front of a mirror or your roommate, bouncing off the sofa, throwing in sound effects, whatever. Find a style of presentation that works for you and rehearse until you are comfortable with the material. Yes, some people hardly prepare at all yet always manage to wow their listeners. And yes, it's a mistake to read at your listeners or memorize a pitch word for word. However, practicing until you have the story beats down pat, so that you can focus more on where the meeting is heading than on what happened in which story, is always a good idea.

- If desired, bring *index cards or notes to jog your memory*. As opposed to leave-behinds, these should be brief outlines of phrases or words that reflect major plot points, not a detailed description or some sort of pitching script. You're not handing these over or reading from these, they're there just in case you lose track of a story.

- *Try to pitch funny*—you're supposed to be a comedy writer.

- *Research the pitch-ees*. Find out what you can about the people to whom you will be pitching. At the least, you should know the names, titles, and perhaps some previous credits of any producers that might be in the room. With a little legwork, you might dig up a personal connection that tilts a hiring decision in your favor, and you might uncover information that clues you in to what types of stories the producers want to see.

The Pitch

On the day of the pitch, dress the part of a successful, easygoing comedy writer; as mentioned earlier, think expensive casual, hip but not in-your-face.

Take a notepad when you go, and maybe a tiny, handheld voice recorder with extra batteries and memory. If you sell an idea, the producers might end up dictating five pages of story outline to you, and there is no way you could remember the many details they'll want included. Also, the notebook's a place to tuck leave-behinds, if you bring any.

Give yourself plenty of time to get to the meeting. (Being late is not an option.) Sometimes it will take place in an office building, which means that your only concern is finding a parking space. Other times, it will take place at a studio lot, which means that you'll face a whole chain of time-consuming barriers. First, the guard at the studio gate will stop you while he searches for your *drive-on pass*, which is supposed to have been arranged for by one of the producers' assistants; half the time, he can't find the pass or your name on an admit list, and you have to wait while he calls someone to get clearance for you. Then, inevitably, you are instructed to park in a space located as far from your meeting's location as is geographically possible. After a brisk jog across the lot, you find that you have been directed to the wrong building and must now double back. Finally, you locate the correct structure and make your way to the office. (By now, you can forget about that relaxed bathroom check.)

You will probably be asked to wait in an outer office. Be pleasant to any assistants that you meet—a couple of nice words from one of them might greatly improve your chances of getting hired, just as a few pointed barbs could lessen those chances.

Eventually, you will be ushered into an office or conference room. You will probably meet with one to four people, usually a couple of producers and an assistant who will take notes. (No, your agent or manager will not attend.) Try to relax and enjoy the moment. You are the guest; these people want you to feel comfortable. After all, they loved your writing samples and they know what it's like to pitch to a bunch of strangers. If they are up for a little small talk before getting down to business, go with the flow. If they offer coffee, sure, have a cup, but *only* if they're having some too. Cigarettes? Chewing gum? No. Too many people find them offensive.

Bottom line, the whole key to a successful pitch is to *always follow their lead*. Most particularly, the lead of whoever seems to be in charge.

Okay, that's not the *whole* key to a successful pitch. There's one other maxim: *Never appear desperate or needy*. Hollywood is a billion-dollar business built on whimsical ideas. If you seem insecure, you won't get hired—how can an employer believe in you if you don't? So even if your knees are knocking and your car is being repossessed as you walk into the pitch meeting, put on your best "glad to be here but I won't die if I don't get this job" face when you arrive.

At some point after everyone in the room has gotten settled, someone will cue you to begin your pitch. Put on your happy face and crank your energy up a full notch. You worked hard on these ideas, they're good, and these people are lucky to be hearing them. Start going through your springboards, pausing after each to get a verdict. Sometimes a producer will cut you off because she can tell early on that an idea won't work; if you don't have the perfect solution for her problem, smile, toss the idea, and move on. Sometimes a producer will interrupt to ask a question. And sometimes an assistant or a phone call will interrupt. Just deal with those events and then get the pitch back on track.

Never begin a pitch by declaring that an idea is brilliant or saying it's flawed. The producers will be the judge of the first and need no help in recognizing the second. (And many a writer has sold the weakest, lamest idea tossed out in a pitch, much to his happy surprise.)

As you go through your ideas, remember that you are *selling*. Show some passion and excitement. Try to make the meeting fun for all involved.

At the same time, *listen and watch*. Look for cues—nodding heads and amused grunts that indicate interest, crossed arms and traveling eyes that indicate boredom. Make eye contact with everyone, particularly the person in charge. If someone seems unhappy with an idea, don't argue with that person. If someone suggests that a story should go a different route, and that someone is a senior person, try to go with her idea; she wouldn't waste time noodling with your story unless she was considering buying it.

At any point in the pitch, if someone seems very interested in a particular springboard, *stop pitching your other ideas and try to make the sale*.

Sometimes the producers will interrupt your pitch to get your reaction to a story concept that they have generated. Here's your response, whatever the idea—you love it! (Only, try to seem sincere when you say it.) They pitched the idea because they are sold on you and it. You are mere moments from landing an assignment. However, if you express reservations about the concept, no sale. It's not that you can't have questions about how to develop the idea—that's fine, it's part of the writing process. But if you make it clear that you don't *like* the idea, they would be foolish to assign it to you. (And, of course, once you have rejected their idea—and, in their thinking, *them*—you will probably find it much more difficult to sell them one of your own ideas.)

Advice from Our Producers

More thoughts on the subject of pitching:

MICHAEL REISS: Be very prepared. Many writers come in and have a good first act, and then the second act tapers off, and then they'll say "you can see how it ends," or "then a lot of crazy stuff happens." Don't do that. Come in with the whole story. And know the act breaks; people love you to come in with good, strong act breaks.

Also, when pitching, go in there and laugh. If you're dealing with producers and show people, they love to think they're funny. Even if you have to fake the laugh, fake the laugh. You'd be surprised how well disposed they will then be towards you.

IRMA KALISH: The main thing is enthusiasm. If you come in and you just say, "Well, I don't know. You may not like this, but . . ." [That's not good.] You've got to really sell it.

One person came in to me saying, "Have you done the one about . . . ?" Well, if anyone says, "Have you done the one about . . . ?" I'm not going to listen to whatever else he or she might have to say.

A producer, believe it or not, is not thrown off if a writer comes in with an idea that's already been done on the show. Because I, as a producer, would not believe that they would deliberately see that we had done a particular story and just come in with the same idea. What you would think is that, "Well, they've got the idea. They know what our characters would do or what we would like to do on the show." So, I would say, "Well, we've done that already. What else do you have?"

It's almost like the cliché saying, "I know what I like when I see it." You know? I know what I like when I *hear* it.

MATT WILLIAMS: When pitching, there's a saying—pitch the sizzle, not the steak. I think the biggest mistake with pitching is [that some writers] get too bogged down in details. You should have those answers in your head, but for instance, if [a producer asks], "Well, gosh, how did they get . . . ," [don't answer] "Well, they took the bus crosstown, then he got on the elevator. He went up to the fifty-fifth floor, he waited for a half an hour. . . ." We don't care. Just say, "He went across town and he's in the office." Get to the essence and pitch the two or three key moments in the story. If you embrace the major turning points or the two or three funniest moments in the script, then I'm hooked and I'll say, "But, I don't understand. How did he get to the office?" "Well, he took a bus, he went up to the fifty-fifth floor. . . ." Lay the details in *if* you're asked about them.

The big deciding factor [when hiring a freelancer] is the confidence of the writer. [He should] know exactly what this episode is about. It's not a collection of scenes where you're chasing jokes that have nothing to do with the story.

ELLEN SANDLER: Pitching is communication. You don't read it and you don't memorize it—it's talking to people. It's essential to be prepared, but don't memorize everything or there's no way for somebody else to get in on the conversation. And what you really want is to open a conversation about your idea. "This is what interests me about this idea, this is why I care about this idea, this is the crux of the idea." That's what you're pitching, not the entire plot.

The problem I find most often with pitches is that they're too long and too detailed and too involved. It's like when you ask somebody, "How'd you like the movie?" and they begin to tell you, "Well, it starts out . . ." and they give you every little detail, and you just want to shoot yourself before they're done.

IAN GURVITZ: The hardest thing about pitching from the outside is coming up with a fresh take on a show that the people on the inside have been thinking about every day for years. How are you going to think of something they haven't?

MAXINE LAPIDUSS: I think the best thing that you can do when you go in is to try to get as much information as possible from someone on staff before the meeting. Do sort of a pre-pitch, if you can. Call a low-level writer on the staff, a Story Editor or Co-producer, and say, "I'm sort of thinking . . ." That way, if you have five great ideas but they're the ones that they're already doing that season, you can avoid spinning your wheels by [perfecting a doomed pitch].

LAWRENCE KONNER: I always feel like I want to tell stories when I pitch and I want to hear stories when I'm listening to pitches. Stories that show that this person understands the series. Show the producers that you're smart enough and entertaining enough, and that you understand their show enough, and they will want to be in business with you. They need people to write this show more than they need ideas for new episodes.

Don't get so focused on trying to impress them with your story ideas that you fail to impress them with yourself. A smart producer would rather be in business with a talented writer who didn't pitch him the world's greatest idea, than with a less talented writer who did.

Remember that the person whom you're pitching to is controlling the room. If they want a lot of small talk, be ready for a lot of small talk. If they want little small talk and then straight to business, you're ready to go straight to business. . . . Remember that the guy sitting behind the desk has probably had ten writers in ahead of you and will have ten writers in behind you that day, and that he has fifty other problems, as well. If you come in with any kind of attitude like, "I'm here to bail you out. This is the greatest idea anybody's ever had," then you've already turned them off.

When you come to Hollywood, no matter how good you are, the industry doesn't need you. They will do just fine without you. They've done okay without you up to now, and if you never show up here and never get in, they'll keep going. And, I think you have to sort of suggest [to the producers] that you understand that. You understand that this is a big factory kind of operation and you want to be a cog. You're happy to be a cog and you want to be a cog.

SANDY FRANK: Let's say you're up for a new show. You'll generally be given a chance to watch the pilot [as part of your introductory meeting]. Sometimes, you'll be in a room down the hall, watching the pilot, and you've got to think of something good to say about it—which is not always easy. I've had the experience, when hiring, of showing a writer the pilot and coming in and just seeing by the expression on her face that she hated it. And, you know, she pretended that she didn't hate the pilot, but I didn't hire her because I knew her heart was not going to be in it. It's not that different from other jobs, where you have to pretend, "Oh, I love your toilets. I love the toilets that you manufacture, or the air freshener you distribute." You're expected to be reasonably enthusiastic. . . . You know, when you tell someone that their ugly baby is the most beautiful baby in the history of the world, they will smile and agree with you. They will not think, "What a ridiculous thing to say." So, in general, when you say, "Your pilot was really, really funny," they will think so too. So, it's hard to go too far in that direction with most people.

You may think that you know who the most important person in that room is, and you might figure that someone else must be a secretary or something. But that may not be the case. So, treat everyone nicely. Be courteous and don't interrupt people when they're talking. I once was sort of interrupting [Academy- and Emmy Award–winning writer-producer] Jim Brooks in a pitch meeting, and one of the people in the room motioned to me and made a sign. And he smiled when he did it, but I think he was serious.

You also have to realize that it's not really within your control. We all think, if we go to a job interview or whatever, that if we do and say exactly the right thing, things will work out. That may not be the case. It may work out no matter what you do, and it may not work out no matter what you do. So, just relax and try to be as much of a normal human being as possible under the circumstances.

What Might Happen

How does a pitch meeting usually end up? Generally, if you are up for a freelance script assignment, one of three things happens:

They Want Time to Decide

The producers might like a couple of your ideas but need time to confer with each other or—horrors—to take pitches from other writers competing for the same assignment. If they end the meeting with "We'll get back to you," offer up the leave-behinds for stories they liked (if you brought leave-behinds) and make a graceful exit. Then run to a phone and call your rep. Fill him in on the details so that he can call the producers to press for a sale. (If he doesn't volunteer to do so, suggest it yourself. Strongly.)

They Pass on All of Your Ideas

Not good. But it happens all of the time, for all sorts of reasons. Still, you have one chance to salvage the situation. Ask if you can come back for another pitch in a day or two. Explain that you now have a better idea of what they're looking for, and ask if there are story areas that they are thinking of exploring, and lobby for a return date. If they say no, you lose nothing. If they say yes, do your very best to come up with a better pitch. Because two strikes will leave a bad taste in their mouths.

If you do get a chance to pitch again, the producers might ask that you do so over the phone or via email. If you must, fine, but try for another face-to-face if you can get it—the more time you and they spend together, the better the chance that you'll win them over.

They Say "Go Write an Outline"

Congratulations! You made the sale! Now stop pitching before they change their minds.

At this point, the producers might just give you some notes on the story and tell you to go home and write the outline. Or they might sit with you for a while to sort out the big beats and then send you off to put the outline on paper. Or they or the entire writing staff might meet with you a couple of times, over a couple of days, to beat out the story together. In the last case, your job is to take very detailed notes (using your recorder and notepad) of the decisions the producers make about plot points, scenes, and jokes, and to pitch in your own ideas when you can. It's intimidating but, relax, they don't expect you to be the funniest person in the room. Writer-producer Sheldon Bull offers this advice:

> If producers pitch a joke, they will expect to find that joke in your outline. Write it down verbatim and put it in. . . . When you are a freelance writer in a story meeting with producers and staff writers, you are not an equal. You are a stenographer. Write down what they say and put it in your outline and in your script.[1]

And here's another tip: If you've sold an idea and are going in to beat out an outline with the show's writers, do your homework beforehand—come up with story ideas and jokes to take in with you, to impress the producers.

When you've been given your notes and it's time to go home to compose the official outline, be sure to ask the producers when they need it handed in. Also, ask a producer's assistant for copies of past outlines (written by the show's staff) so that you can format yours in the same manner.

As soon as you can get to a phone after making the sale, call your agent so that she can sew up the contract. Then all you have to do is write that outline. Do a good job and they'll assign you the script. Do a great job and they might put you on staff.

The Contract

Once a WGA-signatory producer tells you to write an outline, you've got a deal. And unless you are a very hot writer who can command overscale payments, there usually isn't much to negotiate. The production company will send your agent (or you, if you are agent-less) their standard contract for what is called a writer's *step deal*. Step deals are so-named because they allow a producer to terminate a writer's employment once a step has been completed, if the producer does not wish the writer to continue working on the script. In sitcoms, the main cutoff point occurs after the writer's delivery of a story outline. (Fortunately, few sitcom producers actually cut writers off.)

What sorts of provisions go into these standard contracts? A typical agreement is just a few pages long and includes elements such as the following:

- Introductory paragraphs that identify you, your agent, the production company, and the material that you are being hired to write.

- Clarification that you are being hired to write either a "story and teleplay" or a "story with option for teleplay." The latter pays a little more because that's the option that enables a producer to cut you off after the first step, if he chooses to.

- Details of how much you will be paid, at what points. Again, these figures are usually the standard minimum rates that must be paid to all Writers Guild members for this type of work. (These fees are dictated by an industry-wide collective bargaining agreement known as the writers' MBA, or Minimum Basic Agreement.) In sitcoms, your fee is usually paid in two or three installments, with separate payments following the delivery of the outline, the first draft, and the second (your final) draft.

- Language stating that you are required to deliver work on a schedule dictated by the producers.

- Language stating that the copyright in the story and script that you write will belong to the production company, since you are being hired to create a "work for hire." (As such, the production company is free to make any changes to the material that it wishes to.)

- Language stating that the production company is not obligated to produce the script that they are hiring you to write. (Though they still have to pay you for your work.)

- Warranties from you stating that the work you furnish will be your own original creation and that your employment will in no way infringe on a third party's rights.

- A description of the writing credit that you can expect to receive, barring a credit dispute.

While every company has its own standard contracts, the meat of these agreements doesn't change much from show to show. The primary reason is that all must conform to the provisions dictated by the above-mentioned writers' MBA.

That said, you should still read the agreement. And you should talk with your agent if you have any questions. If she is unable to satisfy your concerns, consult with an attorney who specializes in entertainment law. Or, if you belong to the WGA, seek the free advice of the lawyer that that organization makes available to its members.

The Money

Before you get paid, a producer's assistant will probably ask you to fill out a tax form and provide proof of U.S. citizenship. If you have granted your agent power of attorney to collect your fees, your checks will be funneled through him; his office will take 10 percent off the top and then send you the rest. (Yes, taxes are usually deducted up-front, even though you clearly are operating as a freelance employee.)

So how much will you make?

Below are a couple of the Writers Guild minimums (or *scale* payments) that have been negotiated to date. These fees are for a complete "story and teleplay" of a half-hour primetime sitcom episode being produced either for a major broadcast network (ABC, CBS, FBC, and NBC) or a pay-cable network (like HBO or Showtime):

FROM 5/2/09 to 5/1/10 $22,233
FROM 5/2/10 to 5/1/11 $22,900[2]

Script fees for a basic cable or syndicated show are usually less, a bit more than half of the standard network fees. To find the current minimum rates for other types of work or script fees for later years, check the WGA's Schedule of Minimums at its website (www.wga.org) or contact the Guild's Contracts Department at (323) 782-4501.

Again, if you eventually become a writer in great demand, your agent might be able to negotiate overscale fees for you. And, in addition to these up-front fees, you will receive more money (called *residuals*) if the show is re-run or distributed in other media. If the series is a big hit, those additional fees might even add up to more than your original payment.

Moving On

Today, fewer and fewer sitcom writers start their careers by pitching for freelance assignments. Let's examine the happy alternative—landing a lucrative staff job.

18

STEP FIVE: LANDING A STAFF JOB

There are so few freelance script assignments given out to new writers nowadays that building a sitcom career means trying to become a staff writer. Though the WGA still requires producers to dish out a few freelance jobs every season, a lot of those are handed out as favors to friends or are assigned to established writers. Also, as a freelancer, you have little say over what happens to your work; you hand in the second draft, get a check, and you're done—though you're welcome to attend the final taping. And you earn only basic script fees, not the big paychecks that come with being on staff.

Enough said; so how does one become a staff writer?

Becoming a Staff Writer

Sometimes, it's as easy as falling off a log. You write some great spec scripts and they generate a buzz. (Thanks in no small way to you and your rep pushing them like mad.) It comes around to staffing season, and suddenly, several different producers are asking if they can meet you. You go in, say some hellos, and the next thing you know, your agent has two job offers on the table. She uses the competing offers to negotiate a great deal with one of the producers and bingo—you've got a staff job!

No pitching, no writing freelance episodes. And not much chance to learn your craft either. You jump straight into a group writing environment and either swim or sink.

Other times, it's not quite so easy. You might have to land a couple of freelance assignments before anyone deems you a candidate for a staff job. Or you might be asked to pitch for a freelance assignment so that the producers can assess your abilities, even though they are inclined to offer you a staff job if the pitch goes well. Or you might end up writing one or more freelance episodes for a producer's show before he approaches you about working on staff.

You will probably receive one of two job titles when first hired. The lowest staff position is a Term Writer; this person (sometimes referred to as a staff writer), is hired on a week-to-week basis and is usually guaranteed a minimum number of weeks of employment. The next position up is a Story Editor; this position falls into a category of writers who are "also employed in additional capacities," which means that they receive a more favorable compensation package (as described below). If at all possible, try to obtain the second title—it brings in a lot more money and is a better professional credit to have on the résumé.

Whatever a new staff writer's title is, his responsibilities are pretty much the same from one show to the next. As we discussed in the "Writer's Workweek" section of Chapter 14, a staff writer participates in story sessions, read-throughs, run-throughs, shooting sessions, pitch meetings from outsiders, and many, many group writing sessions. Plus, he spends time alone or with his partner, dreaming up storylines and cranking out script drafts. His home base is usually a tiny writer's office located in a show's main production offices, on a studio lot. He also spends lots of time in rehearsal halls, the soundstage where his show is produced, and the studio commissary (a guy's gotta eat).

Some shows run so smoothly that they practically have a regular schedule for key production meetings, rehearsals, and even writing sessions. (Many experienced staffs designate one or two nights a week as a regular after-hours rewrite night.) These well-managed shows are usually a pleasure to work on because the producers are efficient and considerate. While you might still be working very long hours, little of that time is wasted and you are not being subjected to one crisis after another.

Then there are the other shows, frequently the newer shows, that have yet to work out the kinks. Working on these shows can be a nightmare of conflicting creative opinions, working long hours to solve problems that should never have occurred, and doing panicked rewrites at the last possible minute.

Still, a job is a job. Every show that you work for means another credit, money to pay the bills, a chance to make new contacts, and an education about the writing process. And to be honest, no matter how organized a show's producers are, problems will always surface when you are trying to create a half hour of quality television every week.

Office Politics

As in any business, a new employee should be particularly sensitive to office politics. Who has the power? How do they use that power? What do they expect of people lower on the food chain? Who is allied with whom? Who dislikes or is jealous of whom? And who might see bright-and-bushy-tailed you as a threat?

In a perfect world, you would only work on shows where the producers promote a collegial, supportive, sharing environment. In the real world, you might sometimes find yourself in a hostile, every-man-for-himself situation. What should you do? How should you act? Well, you should probably just try to act naturally or you'll give yourself a headache. Beyond that, you might want to consider the following:

- Do your homework. Get a copy of the draft that will be rewritten next and make notes before going into a roundtable session. That way, you're not just ad-libbing fixes as you go.

- Personal chemistry is very important. Show people that you are fun to have around and they will find ways to keep you around.

- Be open to other people's ideas. It's that whole karma thing—give, and you shall receive tenfold. (Wait, that's a pyramid scheme. Well, same difference.)

- Know that if you embarrass someone in front of his superiors, he is likely to come gunning for you. So try to couch criticism in a nonpersonal way. (See "karma/pyramid scheme" point above.)

- Take time to size up the group before you cut loose. Some established writer-producers are very into the staff hierarchy thing. If a new junior writer comes on too strong, they become annoyed. So unless you feel that it would stifle you intolerably, get to know your coworkers a bit before getting in their faces.

- Think twice before chiming in on someone else's in-joke. Some folks take great offense when an uninvited newcomer butts into a private conversation.

- Be a good sport. Writers kid and harass each other all of the time. Don't take offense, and feel free to respond if a good zinger comes to mind.

- Don't bash others behind their backs because it will always come back to you. If someone insists on bashing another person to you, be aware that, by listening, you are registering tacit agreement, which can also come back to you.

- Form alliances, preferably with those higher up the ladder. In a staff of fifteen, cliques will always form. Since you're going to be in a clique anyway, why not include a couple of big hitters?

- This is a big one: *Don't work at home!* Some producers will tell writers who have a draft to write that they can work anywhere that they want. But you need your producers to see your face on a regular basis, to become comfortable with you. Drop out of sight and suddenly you are no longer part of the family.

Gee, next I'll be telling you how to hold a salad fork.

Roundtable Writing

What does it feel like to work in "the room" for the first time? Sitting there with ten other writers, beating out stories and punching up scripts? Or even co-writing a first draft from page one? It's probably just what you imagine. Stimulating, yet exhausting. Rewarding, yet frustrating. Fun, frantic, and fattening.

You already know the basics of roundtable writing. A senior producer presides over the group, deciding what goes in and what doesn't. A writers' assistant or one of the writers records the changes; on some shows, the new words are fed to a big-screen monitor so that everyone can see them as they would appear "on paper." Some staffs also put corkboards or dry-erase boards up on the walls, to keep track of story beats, serialized story-lines, or a season's episodes.

Writing sessions can run late into the night, night after night. Some-times, producers will divide a large writing staff into two groups, one to break new stories and one to rewrite a script. Or one to group-write a new script from scratch. Sometimes, producers will send different writers off to write different scenes of a script, and then patch the resulting work together. And sometimes, a show will employ a punch-up person, a super-funny comedy writer who comes in just one or two days each week to help the regular staff punch up that week's episode.

How do you fit in? Some producers believe that junior writers should be seen and not heard. Of course, this doesn't do much to help you impress your new bosses. Your best bet is to watch the senior producers for clues. If they want their writers to keep pitching, pitching, pitching, then dive right in and don't worry overmuch about censoring your ideas. If they seem to frown on poorly formed suggestions, then pick and choose which ideas to toss out.

In short, listen, watch, and learn. What do the other writers do, with what results?

Advice from Our Producers

Some other thoughts on landing your first staff job:

MAXINE LAPIDUSS: I want somebody who wants that job. I want some-body who's going to be there and not bitch and moan at eleven o'clock at night if we're having a bad week, rather than someone who's looking at his watch every half hour. I want somebody who's enthusiastic and wants to be there as long as it takes.

At a staff-writer level or a story-editor level, if you're new and haven't worked in the system, it's almost better to kind of not speak up too much. Because generally, nine times out of ten, the show that gets on the air is a reflection of the executive producers and the producers. It's all funneled through their sensibilities. So if you're new and you're always pitching ideas, sometimes it gets a little invasive because this is the executive producers' chance to put their ideas out there.

LAWRENCE KONNER: The ideal candidate, I think, is the person who can have fun throwing Chinese food at three in the morning when you're all getting a little silly, but who also is prepared, has done his homework, when it comes time to get the work done.

You're in a room full of eight or ten people who like to insult people and often do it very well. So you can expect to hear about everything from your choice of shirts that day to your haircut, but don't take it personally. Try to blend in and show things that demonstrate professionalism. Be on time. Don't take long lunches. Don't make a hundred personal phone calls. You know, all the kinds of things that you would do at any new job apply here.

One of the things that's most difficult to understand is that—because the nature of what we're doing for a living is not corporate—the senior people are sometimes going to flout, to be disrespectful of, the rules. But that doesn't mean that *you* have the right to follow suit. You haven't yet earned the right to show disrespect.

IAN GURVITZ: Every room has its own personality. If it's more autocratic and the executive producer says, "It's this way because I want it this way," then that's that. If you think your idea is better—the only thing you can do is, it's a long week, so you just wait to see who's been proven right.

Not everyone can be big and loud in the room, and you don't want that. Otherwise, nobody gets a word in. If [someone is quiet in the room but a terrific writer], then great. Occasional contribution is fine if the writer's scripts are good.

Some people [tend to always say], "Oh, we need a better joke here," or "No, no, this won't work. That won't work," which pisses everybody off. Because your job is not to just identify the problems, your job is to pitch a better joke or story fix.

Know the show inside and out. Have all of the characters' names in your head. Know what the backstories are. Know where the show has been for the last year or two so you can talk about it intelligently. One time, I think it was on *Wings*, we were hiring a new writer-producer and he came in and just could talk the show very well, so that we were going, "This guy obviously did his homework." [Which helps, because] there's going to be a very short learning curve [when you join a staff].

IRMA KALISH: Don't be afraid to speak up just because you're new. A lot of times, you will be thinking, "Gee, I'll bet we could solve that problem if we did such and such," but you don't say anything and then someone speaks up two minutes later with the same idea and gets all the credit. So don't be afraid; it's okay to be wrong. People throw things out on the table, and even if you only have a half-formulated idea, someone might pick up on the other half of it. [Emmy-winning producer] Norman Lear always impressed me by saying, "Don't be afraid to put your finger on something that's wrong, even if you don't know how to fix it." Other people will say, "Well, if you don't know how to fix it, shut up." But that's not true. It's good to know that something is wrong and then everybody can work on how to fix it.

SANDY FRANK: I always think of a TV season as if it's a race with a boulder. You have a head start on the boulder and your job as a producer is to stay ahead. You have to constantly have people out breaking stories, writing new scripts, and tabling scripts. You always have to be two, three, hopefully more scripts ahead. If the boulder catches up with you, you are in big trouble. If you are shooting a show on Tuesday and you don't have a script for the next morning's table reading, you are in trouble. But it happens, it happens a lot. Especially if a show is troubled. And so, when you're under that kind of time pressure and you're starting to lose the race with the boulder, the first scripts might not all be great, you know? You have to either write the show as a group or just write it during the production week, and hope that by Friday or Tuesday or whatever day you shoot that it's working. It's not ideal by any means, but it's the nature of trying to write twenty-two episodes in nine months.

When you're writing in a room, your job is to pitch jokes. And some of your jokes will be funny and some won't. You shouldn't be too inhibited about pitching jokes. That's what you're there for. If people make a face at you or whatever, well, some rooms are more vicious than others. Everyone gets that. Just keep pitching and hopefully things will work out.

When someone says, "I think we should do this," and you or whoever is in charge says, "No. Thanks, but no," or whatever, you try to say it politely the first time. Then, when that person says, "No, no, but I really think we should do this. Here's why . . . ," you think about it and say, "Well, I understand what you're saying, but we're not going to do it that way. We're going to do it this way." "But, but really . . ."—All right, by that third time, you just want that person to go away, because you're under a huge amount of pressure—time pressure. You want to finish. You want to go home, maybe see your family every once in a while. And at some point, that person just will be resented for doing that.

I've seen a person pitch to the executive producer; he didn't like the pitch. Then she pitched to the co-executive producer, he didn't like the pitch. Then she pitched to the supervising producer; same thing, he didn't like the pitch. Eventually she's pitching to one of the other story editors, and they're agreeing that it's really funny, and that's not helping anyone.

MATT WILLIAMS: I want to see how a new writer is going to contribute to the room. Is this a punch mind? Is this a joke mind? Is this a story mind? Is this somebody who's really good at character?

Usually what happens is, you're focusing on a single problem. It could be a plot problem, or how do we get this character from here to here. . . . Focus on that. Don't worry about the blow of the second act right now. Help the room solve *this* problem. Later, when you're finally at the end of act two and you need the big blow, shift gears and focus on that.

Young writers will try to chase everything in the script at once. Watch the room, see what it's landing on at that moment, what problem. . . . I guarantee you, if a young writer comes into the room and helps me solve two, three, four key problems in a script, I want that person in the room all the time.

I can sit at a table, with ten writers around a table, and the second a writer leaves the room or his mind drifts, I feel it. I know it. And a good room runner knows the second someone's checked out and their head isn't in the script. . . . Again, it goes back to, help the head writer solve problems. That's your job.

Staff Job Contracts and Compensation

When a signatory producer hires you as a staff writer, your agent will negotiate your job title, rate of pay, the minimum number of weeks that you will be employed, a guaranteed number of scripts that you will write (for which you might be paid separately), and perhaps a schedule for future promotions. In addition, your contract will incorporate many of the same provisions that are included in a step deal for a freelance script. As with those contracts, a staff writer's deal is a pretty standard agreement and it must conform to the protective rules established by the screenwriters' MBA. (Again, if you have any questions or concerns, consult with your agent or a lawyer.)

As mentioned earlier, a new writer's job title can have a big effect on her compensation. Term Writers are hired on a week-to-week basis, usually with a guarantee that they will be employed for a certain minimum number of weeks, at the least. The more weeks a producer is willing to guarantee a Term Writer, the lower the weekly rate that he must pay that writer. (The sliding scale of weekly fees can be found in the WGA's Schedule of Minimums.) Term Writers can be let go at any time, but if they are fired before their guaranteed term of employment has ended, they must still be paid the money that was promised. The fees that a Term Writer makes for writing episodes of her show are applied against her week-to-week salary, and she must be paid the greater of the two; meaning, if the writer's accumulated script fees represent more money than her staff salary, she must be paid the difference, in addition to her salary.

As noted earlier, writers who are employed as Story Editors or above are referred to as writers "also employed in additional capacities." A Story Editor's rate of pay might be based on a weekly rate or it might consist of a set fee for each series episode produced. However, in the latter case, if his cumulative per-episode fees equal less than the cumulative weekly fee minimums that would normally be paid for that period of employment, he must be paid the higher (weekly minimums) figure. Plus—and this is the best part—Story Editors are paid separate script fees for each episode that they write, *in addition* to their per-episode compensation. (Rewriting other people's scripts does not count.) And, if the show is produced for

ABC, CBS, FBC, or NBC, they are also paid small *program fees* (currently $857) for each episode they write that is produced.

Exactly how much money are we talking about? Here are a few representative pay rates for Term Writers and Story Editors employed on a primetime sitcom aired by a major network:

Term Writer (if guaranteed up to six weeks)
From 5/2/09 to 5/1/10 $3,951 per week
From 5/2/10 to 5/1/11 $4,089 per week

Story Editor (if guaranteed up to nine weeks; does not include script and program fees)
From 5/2/09 to 5/1/10 $7,369 per week
From 5/2/10 to 5/1/11 $7,627 per week[1]

Again, the more weeks of employment that are guaranteed, the lower the pay rate. At the same time, a successful show could mean about forty-five weeks of high-paid employment in a year. (Shows usually get a month or two of hiatus each year.) And agents can negotiate higher fees than these, the WGA minimums, as their clients are promoted up the ladder.

Of course, staff writing fees for basic cable and syndication shows are proportionately less, typically slightly more than half of the broadcast network rates. If you would like more information regarding compensation for staff writers, check the WGA's Schedule of Minimums at its website (www.wga.org) or contact the Guild's Contracts Department at (323) 782-4501.

Moving On

You've studied the craft of comedy writing, written your specs, secured representation, and landed your first job. What comes next? Let's look at how one turns a job into a career.

19

STEP SIX: CLIMBING THE LADDER

It seems that very few people work on one series for any length of time. A typical writer might start out on one show as a Term Writer and then jump to another show as a Story Editor. When that show is canceled after only two episodes, the writer might land a Story Editor job on yet another show. A few seasons on that show and the writer is now a Co-producer. She is recruited to serve as a Co-executive Producer on another show and eventually becomes a show runner. Or a studio lures her into taking a lucrative development deal in the hope that she will create a new hit sitcom for them.

Along the way, the writer's fees are going up, usually, and she gradually gains new responsibilities to go along with her new job titles. She becomes involved in postproduction, casting, promotion, and meetings with executives. She supervises writing sessions and makes decisions regarding budget expenditures. Perhaps she even directs a few episodes.

Of course, this is just one example of a career path. A writer might ascend the ladder more quickly and find himself running his own show at age twenty-six (as Matt Stone of *South Park* did). Or he might stop halfway up the ladder to pursue some other career. Or he might stumble out of work at any point and find that he is unable to get rehired (as a writer).

What should a sitcom writer do to build a healthy career? Good question. Some people bounce happily from one job to another whether they are talented or not, largely because they happened to work on a hot show early in their careers. The spin from that early job gets them other jobs, until their extensive credit list has enough of its own momentum to keep them employed.

Some people get occasional boosts up the ladder because they have strong social skills. They develop a network of fans among the industry's heavy hitters and can usually count on landing a new gig through those contacts. (Network and studio executives can be very aggressive about forcing their favorite writers on producers when it comes time to assemble a staff.)

But most writers succeed the old-fashioned way—they just work damn hard. They keep turning out good material, which provides ongoing proof of their talent. They bring a positive attitude to the job and they try to develop their own network of professional contacts. When caught between jobs, they sit down and write something new: a sitcom spec for their agent to peddle, a pilot script, or perhaps a feature script that they hope to sell.

Do all of these things:

- Keep turning out your best work.

- Be a pleasure to have around.

- Take the initiative when it comes to getting work done.

- Keep writing when between jobs.

- And NETWORK, NETWORK, NETWORK! That young Term Writer or studio executive that you befriended last year might call to share a job lead next year. (And you can return the favor the year after.)

What part does your agent or manager play in building your career?

The Care and Feeding of Reps

The higher up the ladder you climb, the more demands you can make of your agent or manager. And the more your rep will want to please you, because you now earn bigger commissions for her.

Ideally, your rep would constantly be looking for better opportunities for you—a new job on a more successful show, ammunition to negotiate a promotion for you, better terms or fees for your current position, or freelance script deals on the side when work is slow. In reality, if you already have a steady job on a show, sometimes your rep will tend to focus on other clients. (Which is understandable.) So if you feel restless, you might have to nudge her if you want more attention.

As time passes, you are likely to become friends with your rep. Great, what could be better? As long as she doesn't take your professional goals for granted, that is the best working relationship to have. Whenever you have a concern, make it known and both of you can strive toward a solution.

Of course, sometimes a rep will gradually lose interest in a client. Perhaps you have realized that you are being stereotyped as a particular kind of writer and you fear that your career will suffer if you don't move to a different type of show. (Smart, long-term thinking if you want to keep building your "business.") But maybe your rep pooh-poohs your concern because "at least you have a job," or she expresses concern but then makes no effort to pull your career out of its rut.

Or, even worse, perhaps you are out of work and your rep isn't taking aggressive action on your behalf. Or any action.

What should you do?

First, call the rep regularly, every week or two, to share your job-search updates. Hopefully, she will respond to your aggressive actions by doing her part. To help the joint search, keep cranking out brilliant new writing samples so that both of you have fresh material to circulate.

If your calls make it clear that she is not doing her part, ask for a meeting to discuss strategy. If she bothers to prepare and has something to contribute, great, you're on track again. If not, let her know that you are disappointed. Hopefully, she will get the message and start taking action.

Of course, at this juncture, you are running a slight risk. A rep who isn't "working you" is almost certainly considering dropping you as a client. If you pressure her, she might do so on the spot.

What would you lose? Not much, if she isn't making any efforts on your behalf. But, since one of your options is to seek new representation, you might want to tread lightly. It is easier to land a new rep if you already have one in hand, because the latter lends you a degree of credibility.

NOTE: If interviewing reps, never disparage your former or current rep. It reflects poorly on you and is likely to get back to that person. In fact, it's best to always assume that any conversation that you have with a potential new rep will get back to your current rep.

What if the rep that you need to replace is a friend? That's a tough one. But if that rep isn't able to find work for you, a true friend would understand that you need to find someone who can. As long as you have communicated your concerns and given your rep-friend a chance to make something happen, you have done all that should be expected. And there is nothing to keep you from maintaining the friendship just because you have accepted representation elsewhere. (Many writers even end up resigning with a former rep later in their careers.)

What if you are happy with your rep but someone from a bigger, hotter agency offers to represent you? If your career is progressing nicely, other reps are likely to seek you out. They might introduce themselves at a taping, or call you out of the blue, or meet you through another client. Next thing you know, you're being invited to lunch or a basketball game, or to the rep's office for a formal hello meeting. The new rep hits you with a lot of flattery and promises of great career moves, all of which is very tempting. Should you switch? Especially when your current rep worked so hard to get you this job, the very thing that made you so marketable? Another tough question. I once turned down such an opportunity out of loyalty and lived to regret it. Others have made the jump, only to be unceremoniously dumped a year later when their career hit a rough patch. This type of decision involves more than just business considerations; it's also about the relationship that you share with your current rep and your own set of personal values. So for once, I won't even try to suggest an answer.

Is it hard to fire a rep? Aren't you bound by your contract? If the rep is a WGA-signatory agent, the ninety-day clause described in Chapter 15 enables a writer (or an agent) to end the relationship if the writer hasn't been offered at least a minimum amount of work within a three-month span. All either party has to do is send the other written notice of the decision.

If the rep is a manager, a writer's ability to disengage is determined by the contract he signed—the WGA is not involved in these deals. Consult a lawyer if you need assistance in this area.

Contract obligations aside, most reps do not want to keep a client who is unhappy with them. If they discover that you are planning to move elsewhere, they might press you for a second chance, especially if you are a big moneymaker. If you believe that their renewed interest will make the difference, perhaps you should stay with them. But if you or they don't see a future together, they will probably let you terminate the relationship, contract or no, on one condition: They get to keep all commissions generated by the jobs that they have landed for you to date. This demand is entirely fair. But it might put a crimp in your efforts to secure new representation, since the new reps won't see a dime until you change jobs, which could conceivably take years (e.g., if you're on the staff of a hit show). Still, the new reps would make the same demand if the situation was reversed.

Sometimes there is a disagreement over who deserves which commissions when a writer changes representation. Rather than taint your relationship with either rep, it is probably best that you step back and ask them to resolve the matter. After all, your job is to write comedy, not negotiate commission splits.

Taking a Development Deal

Every sitcom writer dreams of creating and producing his own series. Usually, only proven writer-producers get the chance to do so, but nowadays the networks are actually willing to consider pilot scripts and produced pilots created by new writers. (A result of skyrocketing development costs and the huge buzz caused by homegrown videos posted on the web.) Let's talk about the proven professionals first.

You don't get to be a successful writer-producer unless you are proactive when it comes to your career. Most established writers find time between gigs to develop new show ideas and write pilot scripts. Then they might approach a studio or successful production company before pitching to a network, hoping to add a heavyweight partner to the project, or they might just go straight in to pitch a network. Ultimately, only a very few of these projects result in a script deal, a pilot order, or a series, because so few new shows are produced every year. But the pros and their ideas are at least taken seriously because of the pros' credentials.

Sometimes, a studio or production company will offer a *development deal* to an established writer, and other times a writer's agent might pitch her for such a deal. The writer is usually someone who has worked on a hit show in a mid- to upper-level producing capacity, but not necessarily as a show runner. A typical development deal provides the writer with a salary, an office, an assistant, and perhaps a fund for acquiring story rights (to properties, like novels, that could be developed into TV series). The term of the agreement is usually one or two years, with options to extend the deal.

In exchange for receiving this package, the writer is required to give her partners first—or sometimes, exclusive—crack at producing any concepts that she creates. If a TV series results from the deal, the writer will assume some already-negotiated role as one of the main producers.

It sounds like a great opportunity and often is. But it can also turn into one of the many paths through what is called *development hell*. The writer might dream up a brilliant concept or write an inspired pilot script, only to get a quick "Pass, no thanks" from the studio. If her deal is exclusive, that's it; the writer can't take her baby elsewhere and she must move on to the next project. Sometimes, not only can't the writer get her own projects off the ground, but the studio pressures her to consult on other people's projects or to accept a producing job on one of its other shows. Still doesn't sound so horrible? When you have finally reached a position from which you might actually be able to launch your own show, such obstacles can seem intolerable.

Producer ELLEN SANDLER: I've done twenty pilots for networks. Major networks, minor networks, all kinds of networks. And I've got all their little graves in my backyard, I visit them regularly. It's frustrating—the networks pay very well but at the end of the year, you have nothing, they own everything. You can't even re-purpose the material.

How much effort should *new* writers put into developing a new series? My advice is that your first priority should be to crank out several really strong spec scripts based on current shows. You know why, we've gone over this before.

Then, okay, if you have a terrific idea for an original series, go ahead and write a pilot script, while you are circulating those spec scripts. Notice that I didn't say to start lining up story pitch meetings—if you don't yet have some serious credentials, there is little (no?) chance that someone is going to buy one of your clever concepts and pay you to write the pilot script. You need to just sit down and write the whole thing, but good news, you can get a lot more use out of a completed pilot script than from some ideas you'd like to pitch. Even if you don't snag the brass ring and sell the pilot, you've now got another polished sample to throw at agents, managers, producers, and execs, and this script is completely original.

All right, so just what goes into a pilot script? How does one sell a new series?

20

CREATING A NEW SERIES

There are a number of ways to develop a new TV series, but here is one path that many shows follow: A writer pitches her pilot script to an established producer, to add credibility to the project and because that producer has connections with the town's buyers. The writer hopes that the producer will want to option or buy the property, but it's just as likely that an interested producer will offer to pitch the project but refuse to pay any money up-front, in which case the writer must decide whether this is an acceptable deal or not. (If the writer agrees to this arrangement, it should be understood that the writer retains all rights to the project and that this casual deal will last for a finite period of time; consult an attorney if you're asked to sign something.)

The producer might then take the project to a studio's TV division in the hope that it will agree to back the series (by supervising its production and covering a share of future costs), and then both parties would pitch the networks that seem best suited for the project. (The networks are the ultimate buyers.) Or the producer might pitch the networks without first acquiring a studio production partner, assuming that one can be found if a network wants to develop the project.

If a network decides to move forward with the project, it (or the studio partner) will option or buy the rights to the series and hire the writer to perform more rewrites on the pilot script. (Every script, no matter how brilliant, is subjected to rewrites.) At some point, the network might also ask that the producer approach certain actors to see if they're interested in the project, and it might bring a new writer on board if that's deemed necessary. (If a network or studio buys the rights to a series, it can replace the original writer if it chooses to; you'll still receive money and a credit, but you might not continue working on the series.)

Eventually, if the rewrites go well and the show seems an excellent fit for the network's schedule, the network might do one of four things: order several scripts for future episodes (to further evaluate the show), order the production of a pilot episode, order the production of a *presentation pilot* (one of those less expensive partial pilots), or even order several episodes of the series. Unfortunately, very few projects make it this far. Only a few percent of those that are pitched to the networks are picked up for script development, only a few of those result in a produced pilot, and only a few of those result in a successful series. But this is the dream, and a strong pilot script can still be used to seek work on other shows, so why not take a shot?

Though writing a pilot script is probably the best way for a new writer to peddle a series, you should know that established writers sometimes use a *series format* to pitch a show. This is a brief selling document that describes the series premise and hints at how future episodes would develop. Other times, writers might opt to use both a pilot script and a series format when pitching, to cover all bases.

Let's talk about this second document for a moment....

Creating a Series Format

A typical format will start with a *title page* that identifies the series title, the creator's name, and contact information for the creator's rep (or the creator if he has no rep). See Appendix A for a description of how these elements should be positioned on the page.

On the first inside page, one might see a brief chunk of *clever sell copy*—perhaps a logline for the series, the lead character's personal credo, a thoughtful statement or question that expresses the theme of the show, a famous quote, or some other such snippet designed to make the reader want to hear more. Many formats omit this element, and they do present a risk of seeming cutesy if poorly written, so writer beware.

Next, you will probably see an amusing one- to three-page *description of the series premise*, which describes the characters, relationships, setting, time frame, types of stories, and ongoing sources of conflict that will drive this series. This is a tough section to write because it must introduce the show's universe—which means presenting lots of information—in an amusing and compelling fashion. And it must convince the reader that the show has *legs*, a premise rich enough to generate a hundred or more episodes down the road. Some writers opt to cover this ground by describing what would be the pilot episode of the show, using the comedy and drama of that first story to help convey—in other words disguise—the information. (One note about introducing characters in this section of the format: Keep the descriptions short and sweet. Use just a phrase to describe each new person; let her actions and dialogue define her for the reader.)

Next, if the writer did not use the pilot story to introduce the series premise in the previous segment, he might now include a page or two that describes the *pilot episode*. This helps to sell the show by illustrating the premise with an actual story, and it's the best way to prove that the series will actually be funny. (And that you are talented enough to write this show.)

Next, the writer might present a list of eight or ten *loglines or springboards for possible future episodes*, to help prove that this series has legs and to entice the reader with funny story concepts. Or, if the show is a serial, the writer might *briefly* describe several of the primary story arcs that would develop during the first season. Or the writer might combine both approaches, lacing story arcs through a list of springboards for future episodes.

Then the writer might include a *list of continuing characters*, using a separate paragraph to describe each in as interesting a manner as possible. (Better to have these detailed descriptions here than jammed into the earlier segment that describes the series premise, where they would surely bog down that material.) Obviously, main characters should receive more attention, supporting characters less, and it's important to point out key relationships (the character mix) that will generate much of the show's conflict and humor.

Some series formats include a *market analysis*, a review of how similar shows have performed in the recent past (ratings wise) and a rundown of current shows that are competing for the same audience. (At networks and studios, it is common practice to do comparative research when deciding whether or not to buy a new show.) It's best to keep this section very short and objective, and it only helps if the numbers strongly suggest that the proposed series will be a hit. Even then, some writers would advise against including a marketing section; its dry nature can dilute the excitement generated by the creative sections of the document.

If an experienced producer is involved with the project, he might be able to contribute a brief *budget summary* to the format (one or two pages), or at least cost estimates for a pilot and/or a first order of episodes. If the producer has ways of producing the series on the cheap via some special production or co-financing arrangement, that could be mentioned here.

A format might also include information or sections that describe *unique aspects of the series*. Perhaps a sought-after star is attached to the project, the show is based on a published work (that the writer has optioned), or impressive producing or financial partners are already involved. Any of these might help to make a sale.

Though a word of caution here. Be aware that many people in the business are always eager to attach themselves to new projects in the hope of landing work. Do not assume that this (used-to-be-a-star) actor or that (working-his-way-up) producer will help you to make a sale. That person might be wonderfully flattering, sincere, and talented, but if the networks and studios aren't dying to work with her, her involvement could sink your project! Unless you *know without doubt* that that person is currently considered a hot property around town, avoid making a commitment.

At some point in a format, there might be a brief section that lists the creator's *credits* and those of any producers or talent attached to the project. Of course, if you have no industry credits and no notable people are attached, it's best to just omit this section.

Lastly, the document might end with a brief *closing bit of sell copy*, much like the opening bit that you'd put on the first page. Again, clever and enticing are the key words here—a corny closer can kill a sale.

Otherwise, a few final notes to consider:

- This is only one blueprint for a series format. The order and mix of elements can change per the project's unique nature and your creative instincts.

- Like everything else you submit, a series format is a sample of your writing ability. Make it sharp and compelling, keep those adjectives and adverbs at bay, and look for opportunities to show that the series will be timely, unique, and *funny*. (Stress that last word—you can't sell a sitcom with a document that reads like an annual report.)

- How long should a format be? Unless you're adding supplemental material like an article that inspired the show (and that you optioned), ratings data sheets, or letters of interest from business partners or sought-after talent, these documents usually run ten to fifteen pages, with lots of white space.

Though a well-written format can answer many important questions about a proposed series, it still can't beat a pilot script when it comes to generating excitement about a new concept. Let's talk about . . .

Writing a Pilot Script

You already know how to write a sitcom episode—what's so different about writing a pilot episode?

Well, in the same time that you're given to tell a typical episode's story, you also have to introduce all new characters in a new setting; establish the show's time frame, style of humor, themes, and episode structure; tell a fantastic and funny story; and show proof that the series has those legs I keep mentioning. Though you're throwing tons of information at the reader, you need to so hook him with a concept and characters he's never seen before that he finishes the script and wants more. And you need to accomplish all of this without drawing attention to your efforts or over-writing the story!

Where can you find great ideas for a new show? The best place to start is you. Your interests, your unique experiences and knowledge, a theme or issue that's important to you, characters that have sprung up in your head and just won't fade away.

Or you might spot a new trend or arena that seems ripe for exploration—though, while those things can serve as a great catalyst, it's always the execution of the concept that counts. (Others will probably spot the same trend, but if your take on it is the most interesting, you win.)

Here are some other ideas that might help:

■ **Look at other pilots.** Find copies of pilots and pilot scripts from successful series and analyze them just as you analyze scripts when preparing to spec an existing series. Pay special attention to how much exposition was presented and how it was delivered, and identify the elements that suggested that the series had legs.

■ **Study the market.** Successful writer-producers make it their business to learn what shows are already being developed around town and which types of series appeal to which networks. Sometimes, you might even hear that a buyer is trying to fill a particular time slot on a particular night, with a particular type of series. Remember, especially now that niche-audience cable networks are producing so many series, new shows are picked up because they're likely to appeal to a specific audience demographic. Each network is interested in reaching certain segments of the population, as defined by characteristics like age, sex, race, education, etc., because those are the viewers that that network's advertisers want to reach. You might have the best new space-western concept ever conceived, but it's not likely that Lifetime is going to buy that pitch.

■ **Decide whether you should write a *premise pilot* or a *typical-episode pilot*.** The first type launches a series by showing the event or circumstances that create the show's overall premise. Example: A Martian/caveman/mermaid lands in a guy's backyard and creates havoc, but the pilot story ends with the guy letting it/him/her move in; we can guess that the rest of the series will feature this guy trying to keep his new pal from doing crazy things and being discovered. Premise pilots can be fun to write because they feature the primary hook of the series, so you have plenty to work with when sorting out the story. Unfortunately, they do a poor job of actually showing what typical episodes would be like, because that Martian won't crash-land in someone's yard every week. Also, premise pilots don't always repeat well because they are so different from the average episode.

Therefore, most network executives prefer to see a typical-episode pilot, a half hour that plays just like episodes 17, 52, and 89 of the series would. When we meet the new characters and see the setting for the show, there is very little exposition provided to establish who or what is on the screen—less is more as the pilot artfully reveals the minimum amount that we need to know. We just dive right into the story, and either start relating to the characters or not. If all goes well, we connect with the premise and want to see what happens next week, and the network's executives see enough story possibilities to order more episodes.

- **Focus on character appeal.** Your pilot script's plot structure might have a weak spot or maybe some of the jokes fall flat, but if you create main characters that are fresh, relatable, and appealing, an audience will want to know what happens in future episodes. The characters don't have to be likeable or nice, cheerful or honest, but they must have drive, purpose, a soft spot, unique skills, or at least some small spark of passion. Michael Scott is a pompous, often cruel idiot, but he also is a top paper salesman at Dunder Mifflin and he usually tries to do the right thing (but then doesn't). Earl was a lazy, shiftless thief who hurt so many people that he couldn't remember all of his victims without a list, but then he doggedly tried to right all of those wrongs because he feared that karma demanded it. *South Park*'s Cartman is a nasty, conniving little boy who seems happiest when trashing others, but he is incredibly clever and persistent when pursuing one of his crazy schemes. Characters don't have to be thoughtful and caring to be appealing—in comedy, it's usually the troublemakers that we like best.

- **Make it funny from page one.** Yes, it's incredibly hard to smoothly weave all of that information into one story, but a pilot script still needs to be as funny as any other episode. No, the reader will not cut you slack because this is the pilot, and she will not wait until page six "when the comedy really kicks in!" Your script must be funny from page one, so, to be sure, I advise that you literally count the laughs in the first scenes to make certain that you're not just imagining jokes where they don't exist.

- **Proximity counts.** Most sitcoms are set in someone's home or workplace for a reason—you need your characters to keep bumping into each other so they can keep generating conflict and comedy in episode after episode. This doesn't mean that you have to create yet another office- or living room–based series, especially when single-camera production offers such freedom of travel, but your premise should include some setting or dramatic device that regularly forces your characters into close proximity.

■ **Keep things simple.** Avoid the urge to overwrite your pilot story. Your goal is to come up with a dynamic but straightforward plot that presents a few unexpected turns, fresh humor, a satisfying ending, and perhaps a bit of a cliff-hanger that makes us want to see Episode 2. Introduce the lead characters and primary conflict quickly, and limit and delay exposition as much as possible. (We can learn about Cousin Billy and those nuts at the office another time.) Your reader has enough to do just figuring out the show's premise—don't confuse (and lose) him by adding a convoluted plot to the mix.

■ **Know your rights.** You can't sell what you don't own. If you wish to create a series based on someone else's original story—a book, movie, comic book, article, life story, etc.—you should option or purchase the rights to that material before writing or pitching your project. Otherwise, you're likely to spend a lot of time developing a series that will soon be stopped dead in its tracks, because one of the first questions producers and execs always ask about adaptations is, "Do you own the rights?" When you say no, you'll look like an amateur and that contact will probably lose your number. The good news is that if you don't have the funds to option stories and the property is not a huge commercial success, sometimes you can persuade a rights owner to give you a *free option* on a property. This approach goes beyond the scope of this book, so for details on the strategy, search the Internet and bookstores for further information or contact a capable attorney.

■ **Get some feedback.** Either once you've fully developed a concept or after you've finished a first draft, ask a few people for their opinions, paying particular attention when they identify logic gaps and confusing sections. Perhaps you already have the answers in your head but neglected to weave them into the story—anything you can do to avoid confusing future readers is well worth the effort.

■ **Remember to register the script with the Copyright Office or the WGA** before circulating it. Unlike an ordinary spec, this is an entirely original work and you should protect it. (See Chapter 16.)

Selling a Pilot

Once your pilot script is written, rewritten, polished, and all shiny, you can include it with the spec scripts that you are using to land a rep and writing gigs, and also begin peddling it as a new project for sale. In the latter case, you're trying to land pitch meetings with established sitcom producers, execs at production companies, execs in the TV divisions of the studios, and execs at networks. (Obviously, you are focusing on people and companies that have a track record of developing shows like the one you've created.)

Why would you approach a producer when this is your baby and *you* want to retain control? Unless a writer actually has the resources and talent to produce a professional-looking pilot, proving that she might be able to produce an ongoing series, it is highly unlikely that a network is going to let her supervise a series given the enormous costs involved. (Some new writers have met this challenge, such as the guys who created *It's Always Sunny in Philadelphia*.) More likely, if the series goes, the creator will be included as one of the writer-producers on the show's staff and will receive handsome royalties for creating the show, and she can use that first big achievement to launch her career with a bang.

Of course, first you have to sell the show. It's a lot easier to get meetings with a studio or network if you're already partnered with an established sitcom producer, and a lot more likely that you'll sell the project. So, as a first step, I advise that you work with your rep and use the tactics presented earlier in this book to get your pilot script to those established producers. This process will take some effort because many producers are not interested in taking another writer's project on, since they have plenty of their own projects to develop. But others are always looking for new projects, and a good rep will know who some of those people are.

Speaking of reps and pilot scripts . . .

If you don't yet have representation, good news: Many of the reps who are unwilling to add new writers to their roster are happy to represent a new series project through one of those hip-pocket deals mentioned earlier. This arrangement means that they won't take you on as a client, at least not yet, but they will peddle your pilot script if they're really impressed by it. If a producer, studio, or network wants to buy the project, the rep will represent you during negotiations and take a fee. Usually, the rep is the one who suggests a hip-pocket deal, but if a desirable rep refuses to represent you yet seems to like your pilot, you can make the suggestion.

These hip-pocket agreements aren't always the best deal for the writer because you have little control over where the rep will send the material or how she will present it. Often, the rep will just deliver copies of the script to a handful of producers or execs after barely pitching it over the phone. However, if you have yet to secure representation and the rep has a successful track record, this deal is probably better than nothing.

Going in to Pitch

You already know how to handle a standard pitch meeting, but there are some differences to consider when selling a series pilot:

While you would take a long list of springboards in if pitching for an episode of an existing show, when meeting to pitch a pilot, you should *take in just that one big idea* and maybe a couple of backup ideas for other new shows. Chances are that your rep or you have already given the people hosting the pitch a vague idea of what type of show you're bringing in, and they are probably willing to give you a full hearing. If they like your big idea, do not pitch the backup ideas under any circumstances—you'll confuse matters and kill the sale. However, if they pass on the big idea in the meeting, throw out your backup ideas one at a time and see if one gets a bite. Lastly, if they pass on everything, ask them what type of show they're looking for, then go home and see if you can develop a premise that better fits their needs.

When you're attempting to set up a pitch with someone you've contacted, the other person might try to get you to describe the idea over the phone to save time. If you must provide a very brief description to avoid seeming rude, do so, but then still *try to get that face-to-face meeting* for a full pitch. You'll greatly increase the odds of making a sale, and that face time will help you to establish a relationship with this person.

If you have a producing partner involved in your project, do not be alarmed if there are times when he wants to pitch the pilot while meeting with someone regarding a different project, when you won't be present. While it would be ideal if you were at every pitch meeting, *there are times when squeezing you into a meeting might seem awkward.* That said, if your partner is trying to do *all* of the pitching without bringing you along, you should talk about the matter—remember, you want that face time with the buyers too.

Producers and execs sometimes feel more inclined to buy a project if it's based on some other profitable or well-known work, or on someone's amazing-but-true story. If your project happens to be based on such material, and you have secured the underlying rights as previously discussed, feel free to *bring copies* of the book, article, video, etc., to the pitch meeting. (Don't confuse this with trying some silly gimmick during the pitch, like planting a ten-dollar bill in the pilot script; this is just about adding relevant visual aids to help make the sale.)

Lastly, in today's everything-digital world, when producers pitch a new show, they're sometimes expected to include ideas for making interactive connections with the show's target audience. See if you can spice up your pitch by including a quick description of some *new-media links for your show*—innovative website ideas, links to a social network, a promotional campaign aimed at mobile devices, etc. Don't go overboard or you'll confuse the pitch—just a hint of the possibilities will make your project (and you) seem cutting edge.

How do you come up with this new-media razzle-dazzle? Look for inspiration by visiting the official network websites devoted to your favorite shows. There, you'll see the latest innovations in new-media series promotion, including features like:

- Recaps of past episodes or even past seasons

- Entire episodes or clips that you can download for free

- Fan blogs or blogs hosted by cast members

- Subplots for the series that can only be viewed on the website

- Video and audio podcasts, or downloads for your phone or other handheld device

- Online games based on the series

- Voting features that decide a plot turn or simply express the fans' opinions

- Shopping links to series merchandise or episode compilations

- Banner ads or short commercials attached to the higher-value features of the site (e.g., episode downloads)

And these are just the basics, features that you'll find on many sites for successful shows. If it seems that some digital buzz might spice up your pitch, see if you can toss in one or two new and exciting ideas specifically designed to promote your series. Don't worry about having to actually execute these ideas—that work is handled by marketing and promotion experts that the network pays to support a series.

Just to be clear, this optional step of pitching a couple of new-media ideas to promote your show is all about adding a quick bit of sizzle (perhaps thirty seconds' worth) to help get the buyer excited. Do not dwell on the subject unless the buyer clearly wants to.

Producing a Homegrown Pilot

So far, we've focused on how a writer might use traditional methods to market a new series project, but how about shooting your own pilot? Practically everybody has access to a high-quality video camera and editing software nowadays, and anybody can post just about anything on the Internet.

If you have the resources and production expertise, shooting a series pilot can definitely help to get your material and you noticed. You can post the show on web video-clip sites like YouTube, feature it on its own dedicated website, and enter it into festivals and contests (see Appendix B). When pitching reps, producers, and execs, you can hand them a copy of the pilot on a disc, or email them a link to its website.

While the dream is that you'll be one of the few to sell a series based on a homegrown pilot, you might still see secondary benefits even if that doesn't happen—if the show's production values are strong, it will increase your credibility in the eyes of the professionals you pitch. You're not just another new writer now; you've made a show happen and that takes some doing.

Of course, there's one little proviso here: That pilot better look good! While a few (very few) people will cut you some slack because it's a non-pro effort, and nobody expects to see big stars in the cast, most people will judge your show by comparing it to the quality of shows seen on network television every night. If you offer up a poorly acted, shaky-cam production, you'll only hurt your chances of selling the pilot and landing other work.

To get a sense of the production quality needed and the competition already out there, visit sites like YouTube and the New York Television Festival (www.nytvf.com) to look at pilots others have produced. You'll see all lengths of shows, from five-minute presentations to full-length pilots. (The former, less-is-more approach is something to consider; it's far easier to produce five to ten minutes of professional-looking sample scenes than it is to produce a full-length pilot episode.)

Lastly, if you want to shoot a pilot but do not have the expertise, you might be able to find partners who would be happy to handle the production chores for you. Try contacting local video production companies and television/film professors at local colleges. Sometimes those folks are interested in expanding into entertainment work but don't have the written material to do so. If they ask that you pay for their services, you probably should decline, and suggest instead that they and you share any future revenues that might come from the effort. You're offering to supply the content, they would supply the means—both parties are bringing something valuable to the table, so neither should have to pay the other.

Similarly, when it comes time to recruit actors and a director, many local theater people are happy to participate in such projects in exchange for copies of the show and perhaps a promise of compensation if the show sells. (Obviously, if production is proceeding, you and your partners probably should hire an attorney to help sort out business terms and legal agreements.)

The Money

Finally, you did it! You wrote, pitched, and actually sold a new sitcom—so how much does a writer get paid for creating a TV series?

Based on the WGA Schedule of Minimums, the minimum (or scale) fee for a complete "story & teleplay" half-hour, primetime sitcom pilot script produced either for a major broadcast network (ABC, CBS, FBC, and NBC) or a pay-cable network (like HBO or ShowTime) must equal at least 150 percent of the minimum episode fee. Currently, sitcom pilot minimums are:

FROM 5/2/09 to 5/1/10 $33,349.50
FROM 5/2/10 to 5/1/11 $34,350.00[1]

And that's the minimum—an established writer might be able to negotiate a higher script fee.

In addition, the writer might negotiate additional rewrites into the deal, which could bump the pilot script fee up by $5,000 to $10,000.

Also, the writer is likely to be hired as one of the producers on the pilot, which would earn her a non-WGA-regulated fee of anywhere from $10,000 to $50,000, or more, depending on the writer's professional credits and leverage with this project. If the show goes to series and her employment in this capacity continues, she'll earn much more over time.

Plus, the writer might receive a bonus if the pilot goes to series, and she should receive a commitment to write a certain number of future episodes of the series (for which she'll be paid extra). Plus, she will receive a "Created By" credit and royalty payment for each episode produced, and perhaps a percentage of net profits (though few series ever see profits). And if the series is sold in other markets or goes into reruns, she will eventually receive residuals too.

Of course, these are fees that a WGA writer might receive on a high-budget series. If the show is bought by a basic cable network, the minimums will be much lower, a bit more than half of the broadcast network fees. Also, the separate producing fees, series bonus, and royalties would be much less.

If the writer is not a WGA member and the network is not a WGA signatory, then everything's up for grabs. The writer will get whatever her rep and she can negotiate, and that won't be nearly as much as is described above. (Hey, something's better than nothing; you might not get rich but at least you're able to see your show produced and collect an impressive credit for your résumé.)

Lastly, if the writer is a WGA member but ends up having to share the "Created By" credit with another writer, which often happens, her compensation will be reduced accordingly.

No question—sell a pilot and there's a lot of money at stake. If you land a pilot deal and don't have a competent agent to negotiate on your behalf, you should hire an entertainment attorney to do so. For more information about WGA regulated fees, check the Guild's Schedule of Minimums at its website (www.wga.org) or contact the Guild's Contracts Department at (323) 782-4501.

TIME TO WRAP UP!

And, believe it or not, I think that's it.

Thank you for reading the book. We've covered just about everything—humor theory and creating premise-driven comedy . . . writing a professional script . . . how the business works . . . launching your career, pitching a new show, embracing new media . . . jokes, reps, dollars, and deals.

If I have one last piece of advice, it's "be bold." Write, pitch, take your shot—whatever the result, you'll always be glad you did.

Best of luck and I wish you great success!

Evan Smith
writingsitcoms.com

APPENDIX A
SCRIPT FORMAT GUIDELINES

Sitcoms are produced in three formats: live-action film (single-camera), live-action tape (multi-camera), and animation. (Though, out of tradition, the first label says "film" and the second "tape," the real distinction is single- vs. multi-camera; either form might actually be shot using film, analog tape, or digital media cameras.) Below are script format guidelines for each type of show.

Please note that these are generic guidelines. While they reflect current professional standards, every show is different. If you are writing a spec script for an existing television series, try to obtain copies of scripts produced for that show so that you can precisely duplicate their format. (The more that your script resembles the real thing, the better.) At the very least, if writing for a live-action series, find out whether the show is shot on film or tape so that you can choose the correct generic model below.

Also, note that the following models are appropriate for *spec scripts*. They deliberately omit some elements that are usually added only if a script is heading into production. These items include scene numbers, page headers that identify the script draft, cast lists under each scene heading, and separate slugs for sound effects and special effects. While it isn't a crime to include these elements in a spec script, they slow down "the read" and imply that the script is a production draft (that might have been punched up by the show's writing staff).

Lastly, as noted earlier, there are several excellent software programs that provide automatic script formatting. If you become serious about screenwriting, these time-savers are well worth the investment. The best even have templates for specific shows, though you might have to turn off some functions (like scene numbers and special-effects slugs) that belong only in a production draft and not in a spec script. I recommend both of the leading programs, Final Draft (available at stores and www.finaldraft. com) and Movie Magic's Screenwriter (at stores and www.screenplay. com). Each goes for about $200 to $250.

Topics Covered in This Appendix

I.   THE TITLE PAGE

II. WRITING IN FILM FORMAT
Page Numbers
Script Headings
Scene Headings
Scene Descriptions
Dialogue Blocks
Transition Cues
Vertical Spacing
Margin Settings
Act Breaks
Tags
Ending a script

III. WRITING IN TAPE FORMAT
Page Numbers
Script Headings
The First Scene
Scene Headings
Scene Descriptions
Dialogue Blocks
Transition Cues
Vertical Spacing

Margin Settings
Act Breaks, Tags, and Endings

IV. WRITING IN ANIMATION FORMAT

V. GENERAL GUIDELINES (Listed By Key Words)

I. The Title Page (See Figure 1)

Every spec script starts with a title page that identifies the work, its author, and a contact person. Regardless of whether the show is taped, digitized, filmed, or animated, the layout of this page is the same. As for typeface, always use the industry standard, pica-sized (12-point) Courier New font throughout the script; this uniformly sized typeface produces ten letters per horizontal inch.

1. The **series title** is typed one-third of the way down the page. It should be centered, written in all caps, and either underlined or printed in bold type. (When "centering" any part of the script, add six extra character spaces to the left margin to compensate for room taken up by the script binding. See "Margin Settings" below.)

2. The **title of the episode** appears two lines below the series title, centered, typed in upper- and lowercase letters, and enclosed by quotation marks.

3. The word [by] appears four lines below the episode title, centered, in lowercase.

4. The **writer's name** appears two lines farther down, centered, in upper- and lowercase.

5. **Contact information** (i.e., the address, phone number, and email address of the writer or, preferably, the writer's rep) is typed in a single-spaced block in the lower right corner of the page, in upper- and lowercase, typed flush left within the block. You might wish to start the block with the heading [CONTACT:].

6. If the script has been registered with the Copyright Office or the WGA, you have the option of placing a **registration notice** in the lower

left corner of the page, across from the lowest line in the block of contact information. If writing a spec script, I suggest you skip this. If writing an original pilot, it would be smart to include a notice. (See "Protecting Your Work" in Chapter 16.)

7. Suggestion: DO NOT label a spec script as a "First," "Second," or other draft. "First Draft" implies that the script still needs work, while "Second" or later draft designations suggest that the script might have been punched up based on other people's input. Similarly, DO NOT write the date that you completed the script on the title page. Doing so will only serve to age your script, since anything over six months old might be perceived as yesterday's news. (Draft numbers and dates are not needed until a script goes into production, when they are used to help producers keep track of rewrites.)

II. Writing in Film Format

The elements of a script written in "film format" are described below. See the sections on "Vertical Spacing" and "Margin Settings" for details on proper positioning.

Page Numbers
Starting with the first page of dialogue, type each page number, followed by a period, in the top right corner of the paper, just half an inch in from the top and side edges.

Script Headings (See Figure 2)
Drop five or ten lines below the first page number and type the series title in all caps, centered, underlined or in bold type. (Again, when centering any part of the script, add six extra character spaces to the left margin to compensate for room taken up by the script binding.)

Then, skip a line and type the episode title in upper- and lowercase, centered, in quotes.

Then, skip two lines and type, centered, underlined, in all caps, whichever of the following is used in that television series:

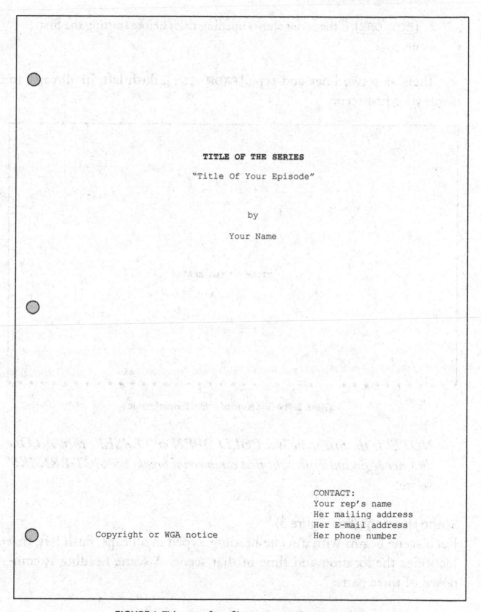

TITLE OF THE SERIES

"Title Of Your Episode"

by

Your Name

CONTACT:
Your rep's name
Her mailing address
Her E-mail address
Her phone number

Copyright or WGA notice

FIGURE 1. Title page for a film, tape, or animation script.

1. [COLD OPEN], if the series starts with a brief teaser before going to an opening title sequence; or

2. [ACT ONE], if the series shows opening titles before starting the first scene.

Then, skip two lines and type [FADE IN:], flush left, in all caps, to begin your first scene.

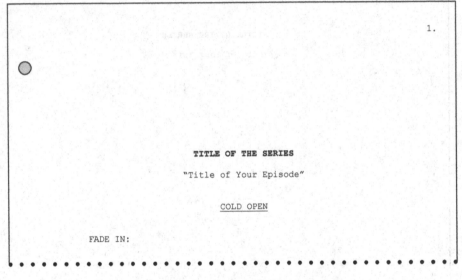

1.

TITLE OF THE SERIES

"Title of Your Episode"

COLD OPEN

FADE IN:

FIGURE 2. The first page of a "film format" script.

NOTE: If the first scene is a COLD OPEN or TEASER, then Act One does not begin until after the first commercial break. See "ACT BREAKS" below.

Scene Headings (See Figure 3)

Each scene begins with a scene heading, typed in all caps, flush left, that identifies the location and time of that scene. A scene heading is composed of three parts:

1. The first part is an abbreviation, either [INT.] or [EXT.], which tells us whether we are viewing the interior or exterior of the scene's location.

2. The second part identifies the scene's **location**, be it [JOEY'S CAR], [THE COURTHOUSE], or [SUE'S BEDROOM]. If writing about a new location within a larger location, try to combine both in one phrase, as in [HOSPITAL WAITING ROOM]. If that seems awkward or confusing, name the larger location, add a dash, and then name the more specific location, as in [HOSPITAL — WAITING ROOM].

3. The third part, typed following a dash, identifies the **time** during which the scene occurs. This can be designated as either a daypart (e.g., [DAY], [NIGHT], [DAWN], or [DUSK]), or as an indication that time has passed since the last scene (e.g., [30 MINUTES LATER], [MOMENTS LATER], or [LATER]), or as a specific clock time (e.g., [NOON] or [6PM]). If no time has passed since the previous scene ended, that is indicated by typing the word [CONTINUOUS] or, better yet, by simply leaving the third part of the scene heading blank.

Every time that the story's location or time frame changes, even if your characters are just walking from one room to the next, you are starting a new scene and should type a new scene heading.

Keep your scene headings simple; unless it is mandatory that we know that it is exactly [2:37 PM] in the story, just write [DAY].

Some sitcom producers prefer to underline scene headings in film format—either way works if you're not sure.

Scene Descriptions (Fig. 3)

Scenes often begin with a scene description, typed in upper- and lowercase letters, flush left, starting on the second line beneath the scene heading. A scene description is a dynamic but *very brief* description of the location, characters, and/or actions in a scene. Functional in nature, it can range from one word, such as [Beat.], to several sentences of description. (Some argue that anything over four lines of description is too much.) A scene might include a number of separate scene descriptions, depending on the actions within the scene.

The first, and only the first, time that a *new* character is identified in a script, her name should be typed in all caps. The names of series regulars do not need to be called out in this manner except in a pilot script.

Some writers capitalize descriptions of sound effects and/or special effects when they occur within a scene description, while others (this writer included) believe that this only serves to clutter up a spec script.

Scene descriptions are written in the present tense. Some writers use proper grammar when writing them, while others use clipped phrases or a loose conversational style.

When writing scene descriptions and dialogue, leave two blank letter spaces between sentences.

Dialogue Blocks (Fig. 3)

In film format, dialogue is typed in a single-spaced block and consists of three parts (see "Margin Settings" for correct positioning):

1. The first part is the **character's name**, typed in all caps.

2. Then, immediately beneath that, or between segments of speech that follow, come **dialogue cues** (or *parentheticals*). Typed in lowercase and bracketed by parentheses, these brief phrases either indicate how a line should be read or cue a specific movement (e.g., [(claps his hands)]).

3. The third part of the dialogue block is the **dialogue** itself, typed in upper- and lowercase.

If a character's dialogue is interrupted by a scene description, type his name again when he resumes speaking and continue his dialogue.

If a character's dialogue is running too long to fit on a page, move the entire speech to the following page. Or interrupt the speech with a line containing the single word [(MORE)] typed forty-five spaces in from the left side of the page. Then, at the top of the next page, type the character's name and [(cont'd)], and continue the interrupted speech.

NOTE: Go light on dialogue cues! Professional writers hardly use any. Trust that the director and actors know what they're doing.

Transition Cues

Transition cues describe how the episode will segue from one scene to the next. Typed in all caps, they include the following: [FADE IN:],

[CUT TO:], [DISSOLVE TO:], [FADE OUT.], [CUT TO BLACK], [FREEZE FRAME], etc.

The one opening cue, [FADE IN:], is typed flush left, while all other cues are typed sixty spaces in from the left side of the page.

In the old days, writers placed a transition cue—usually [CUT TO:]—at the end of every scene. Today, most writers deem ending cues superfluous in film format and skip them, unless a cue is needed to indicate a specific effect (e.g., dissolving to a dream sequence) or to help a script's pacing by "putting a period" at the end of a scene or sequence.

Vertical Spacing (Fig. 3)

In film format, all elements within a scene (including scene headings, scene descriptions, dialogue blocks, and transition cues) are separated from each other by a *single* blank line. However, for ease of reading, some writers insert *two* blank lines between scenes (i.e., before the next scene heading).

Margin Settings (Fig. 3)

TOP AND BOTTOM: There should be one inch of margin space at the top and bottom of the page, regardless of the page number squeezed into the top right corner. Obviously, due to irregular breaks between dialogue blocks, you will often have more than one inch of blank space at the bottom of a page. (Do not crowd margins to accommodate an overlong script; professional readers will notice.)

SIDES: To accommodate the script's binding, the body of a script is shifted six spaces to the right (see "Script Binding" in the "General Guidelines" section of this appendix). Accordingly, using the standard screenwriting typeface (pica-sized Courier New font), set the margins in from the left side of the page as follows:

FROM SPACE 16 TO SPACE 75—Body of the script (includes the cue [FADE IN:], scene headings, and scene descriptions)
FROM SPACE 28 TO SPACE 63—Dialogue
FROM SPACE 34 TO SPACE 57—Dialogue cues
FROM SPACE 40—Character names (Character names are NOT centered—they all start at Space 40.)
FROM SPACE 60—Transition cues (except for [FADE IN:])

NOTE: Margin and space settings presented in this document are general guidelines; a few spaces left or right will not mar your script.

Act Breaks

Unless it airs on a commercial-free cable network, a half-hour sitcom episode is usually interrupted by two or more commercial breaks. Indicate planned act breaks in your script by doing the following:

1. End the last scene of each act by typing the transition cue [FADE OUT.].

2. Skip two lines, then type [END OF ACT ONE]—or [. . . ACT TWO] or [. . . ACT THREE], as the case may be—centered, underlined, in all caps.

3. Start the first scene of the next act on a *new page*. Drop five to ten lines below the page number and type [ACT TWO]—or [ACT THREE] or whichever—centered, underlined, in all caps.

4. Then, skip two lines and type the transition cue [FADE IN:].

5. Then, skip one line and begin the first scene of the new act.

NOTE: If the script's first scene is a COLD OPEN, then the scene that immediately follows the first commercial break will begin ACT ONE. To indicate that the cold open has ended, follow the steps above, substituting [END OF COLD OPEN] for [END OF ACT . . .] in step two. Then, start Act One on a new page.

Tags

Just as some series start with a cold open before (or while) showing opening titles, many also close with a *tag*—a brief, amusing scene placed at the end of the episode, after the episode's storylines have already been resolved. Tags, formatted like the first scene of a new act, are indicated as follows:

1. After indicating that the last act of the episode has ended, start the tag scene on a new page. Type [TAG] five to ten lines below the page number, centered, underlined, in all caps.

8.

INT. OFFICE - ACCOUNTING - DAY

Michael approaches, waving flyers.

                    MICHAEL
          My number crunchers! I know you
          want to hear about how much cash
          you'll save under the Packer tax
          plan. What do you say? Debate
          flyer? Kevin?

                    KEVIN
          Debates are lame.

                    MICHAEL
          Oh yeah? Well, you're lame.

                    KEVIN
          But I am planning to vote for
          Packer.

                    MICHAEL
          And when I say lame, I mean it as
          an acronym for Largest...Amazing...
          Man...Ever. Not large. You're not
          large. Your Amazingness is large.

Michael sticks out his hand for a high five.

                    MICHAEL
          Packer Backer!

Kevin looks confused but slaps Michael's hand.

                    OSCAR
               (to Kevin)
          I can't believe you.

FIGURE 3. Dialogue written in "film format."[1]

2. Then, skip two lines and type the transition cue [FADE IN:].

3. Then, skip one line and begin the tag scene.

Ending a Script

End the final scene of the script by doing the following: type the transition cue [FADE OUT.], and then skip two lines and type [END OF EPISODE], centered, underlined, in all caps.

III: Writing in Tape Format

The elements of a script written in tape format are described below. See the sections on "Vertical Spacing" and "Margin Settings" for details on proper positioning.

Page Numbers

Starting with the first page of dialogue, type each page number, followed by a period, in the top right corner of the paper, just half an inch in from the top and side edges.

Script Headings

Some tape shows include series and episode titles on the first page of dialogue and others don't. If you wish to do so, follow the same guidelines used when writing in film format.

The First Scene (See Figure 4)

Drop five or ten lines below the first page number and type, centered, underlined, in all caps, whichever of the following is used in that series. (Again, when centering any part of the script, add six extra character spaces to the left margin to compensate for room taken up by the script binding.)

1. [COLD OPEN], if the series starts with a brief teaser before going to an opening title sequence; or,

2. [ACT ONE], followed by a blank line and then [SCENE A], if the series is a sitcom that does not start off with a cold open. (In tape format, sequential letters or numbers are usually assigned to all scenes except for Cold Opens and Tags.)

Then, skip three more lines and type [FADE IN:], flush left, underlined, in all caps, to begin the first scene.

ACT ONE

SCENE A

FADE IN:

FIGURE 4. An act heading in a "tape format" script.

Scene Headings (See Figure 5)

As just mentioned, scenes written in tape format are usually assigned letters or numbers (in sequence), and **many producers prefer that each new
scene starts on a new page.** To do so, type the scene designation (e.g.,
[SCENE A]) in all caps, centered, and underlined, five to ten lines below
the page number. Then, skip two lines and start the scene.

Each scene begins with a scene heading (or "slug line"), typed in all
caps, underlined, flush left, that identifies the location and time of that
scene. A scene heading is composed of three parts:

1. The first part is an abbreviation, either [INT.] or [EXT.] that tells us
whether we are viewing the interior or exterior of the scene's location.

2. The second part identifies the scene's **location**, be it [JOEY'S CAR],
[THE COURTHOUSE], or [SUE'S BEDROOM]. If writing about a new
location within a larger location, try to combine in one phrase, as in
[HOSPITAL WAITING ROOM]. If that seems awkward or confusing,
name the larger location, add a dash, and then name the more specific
location, as in [HOSPITAL — WAITING ROOM].

8.

SCENE D

INT. OFFICE - ACCOUNTING - DAY

MICHAEL APPROACHES, WAVING FLYERS.

                    MICHAEL

          My number crunchers! I know you

          want to hear about how much cash

          you'll save under the Packer tax

          plan. What do you say? Debate

          flyer? Kevin?

                    KEVIN

          Debates are lame.

                    MICHAEL

          Oh yeah? Well, you're lame.

                    KEVIN

          But I am planning to vote for

          Packer.

                    MICHAEL

          And when I say lame, I mean it

          as an acronym for Largest...

                    (MORE)

FIGURE 5. Same dialogue written in "tape format."[2]

3. The third part, typed following a dash, identifies the **time** during which the scene occurs. This can be designated as either a daypart (e.g., [DAY], [NIGHT], [DAWN], or [DUSK]), or as an indication that time has passed since the last scene (e.g., [30 MINUTES LATER], [MOMENTS LATER], or [LATER]), or as a specific clock time (e.g., [NOON] or [6PM]). If no time has passed since the previous scene ended, that is indicated by typing the word [CONTINUOUS].

Every time that the story's location or time frame changes, even if your characters are just walking from one room to the next, you are starting a new scene and should type a new scene heading.

Keep your scene headings simple; unless it is mandatory that we know that it is exactly [2:37 PM] in the story, just write [DAY].

Scene Descriptions (Fig. 5)

Scenes often begin with a scene description, *typed in all caps,* flush left, starting on the second line beneath the scene heading. A scene description is a dynamic but *very brief* description of the location, characters, and/or actions in a scene. Functional in nature, it can range from one word, such as [BEAT.], to several sentences of description. (Some argue that anything over four lines of description is too much.) A scene might include a number of separate scene descriptions, depending on the actions within the scene.

The first, and only the first, time that a *new* character is identified in a script, her name should be underlined. The names of series regulars do not need to be called out in this manner except for in a pilot script.

Every time that a character enters or exits a scene, her name and the accompanying verb should be underlined (e.g., [JAKE ENTERS], [LIZ EXITS], or [CHARLIE RUNS OUT]).

Some writers underline descriptions of sound effects and/or special effects when they occur within a scene description, while others (this writer included) believe that this only serves to clutter up a spec script.

Scene descriptions are written in the present tense. Some writers use proper grammar when writing them, while others use clipped phrases or a loose conversational style.

When writing scene descriptions and dialogue, leave two blank letter spaces between sentences.

Dialogue Blocks (Fig. 5)

Dialogue in tape format is *typed in a double-spaced block*, and consists of three parts (see "Margin Settings" below for correct positioning):

1. The first part is the **character's name**, typed in all caps.

2. Beneath that is the **dialogue**, typed in upper- and lowercase.

3. Within the dialogue, you might include **dialogue cues** (or *parentheticals*). These are brief phrases that either indicate how a line should be read or cue a specific action (e.g., [(CLAPS HIS HANDS)]). Dialogue cues are typed in all caps, bracketed by parentheses, and positioned as if they were just another sentence in the character's speech.

If a character's dialogue is interrupted by a scene description, type his name again when he resumes speaking and continue his dialogue.

If a character's dialogue is running too long to fit on a page, move the entire speech to the following page. Or interrupt the speech with a line containing the single word [(MORE)] typed forty-five spaces in from the left side of the page. Then, at the top of the next page, type the character's name and [(CONT'D)], and continue the interrupted speech.

NOTE: Go light on dialogue cues! Professional writers hardly use any.

Transition Cues

Transition cues describe how the episode will segue from one scene to the next. Typed in all caps and underlined, they include the following: [FADE IN:], [CUT TO:], [DISSOLVE TO:], [FADE OUT.], [CUT TO BLACK], [FREEZE FRAME], etc.

The one opening cue, [FADE IN:], is typed flush left, while all other cues are typed sixty spaces in from the left side of the page.

Unlike film format, scenes written in tape format usually end with a transition cue, like [CUT TO:] or [DISSOLVE TO:], because the next scene usually starts on a new page.

Vertical Spacing (Fig. 5)

In tape format, all elements within a scene (including scene headings, scene descriptions, dialogue blocks, and transition cues) are separated from each other by a single blank line. Likewise, lines within the dialogue blocks themselves (including character names and lines of dialogue) are double-spaced.

Margin Settings (Fig. 5)

TOP AND BOTTOM: There should be one inch of margin space at the top and bottom of the page, regardless of the page number squeezed into the top right corner. Obviously, due to irregular breaks between dialogue blocks, you will often have more than one inch of blank space at the bottom of the page. (Do not crowd margins to accommodate an overlong script; professional readers will notice.)

SIDES: To accommodate the script's binding, the body of a script is shifted six spaces to the right (see "Script Binding" in the "General Guidelines" section of this appendix). Accordingly, using the standard screen-writing typeface (pica-sized Courier New font), set the margins in from the left side of the page as follows:

FROM SPACE 16 TO SPACE 70—Body of the script (includes the cue [FADE IN:], scene headings, and scene descriptions)

FROM SPACE 26 TO SPACE 60—Dialogue (includes dialogue cues)

FROM SPACE 40—Character names (Character names are NOT centered—they all start at Space 40.)

FROM SPACE 60—Transition cues (except for [FADE IN:])

NOTE: Margin and space settings presented in this document are general guidelines; a few spaces left or right will not mar your script.

Act Breaks, Tags, and Endings

Follow the guidelines presented in the film format section above.

IV. Writing in Animation Format (See Figure 6)

The script formats used for animated sitcoms vary widely from show to show. If you are unable to obtain a copy of a produced script from a series to use as a template, I suggest that you do the following: Format your

8.

```
        INT. OFFICE - ACCOUNTING - DAY
        Michael approaches, waving flyers.

                    MICHAEL
            My number crunchers!  I know you

            want to hear about how much cash

            you'll save under the Packer tax

            plan. What do you say?  Debate

            flyer?  Kevin?

                    KEVIN
            Debates are lame.

                    MICHAEL
            Oh yeah?  Well, you're lame.

                    KEVIN
            But I am planning to vote for

            Packer.

                    MICHAEL
            And when I say lame, I mean it as

            an acronym for Largest...Amazing...

            Man...Ever.  Not large.  You're not

            large.  Your Amazingness is large.

        Michael sticks out his hand for a high five.

                    MICHAEL
            Packer Backer!
```

FIGURE 6. Same dialogue written in "animation format."[3]

script as if you were writing for a *live-action film format* show, but make these changes . . .

Headings and Transition Cues
All script headings and transition cues should be in bold type.

Scene Descriptions
Scene descriptions should stop seventy spaces in from the left side of the paper, leaving an inch and a half of right-hand margin, and should be single-spaced. Since animated shows are not bound by the limitations of live-action production, it is acceptable to include some camera directions in an animation script.

Dialogue Blocks
Dialogue blocks in animation format should be double-spaced.

Dialogue Cues
Dialogue cues should be typed in all caps and bracketed by parentheses, and positioned as if they were just another sentence in the character's speech.

Script Length
Script length should be forty to fifty pages. (It's impossible to be more specific because some animation shows use very different script formats.)

V. General Guidelines (Listed by Key Words)

Hey, don't skip over this section, it's important! The following apply to all three script formats.

Camera Directions
DO NOT include camera directions like [PAN LEFT], [WIDE SHOT], or [ZOOM OUT] in your script. Or, if you must include a very few, try to limit your directions to suggestions regarding dramatic focus (e.g., [ANGLE ON TOYOTA]), rather than specific camera commands (e.g., [CAMERA ZOOMS IN FOR ECU OF THE TOYOTA]). Script-format-wise, camera angles are

written in one of two ways: typed in all caps on a separate line, flush left, like a scene heading; or typed in all caps within the body of a scene description.

Intercutting Between Locations

If you need to cut back and forth between characters at different locations (say, during a phone call), establish the first scene location and first speech, and then type the transition cue [INTERCUT:], flush right. Then, establish the second scene and continue the dialogue as if both/all characters are at the same location. Or, establish the first scene and then, as if you were starting a new scene, type [INTERCUT BETWEEN *name* AND *name*] as if it were a scene heading, and continue the dialogue as if both/all characters are at the same location.

Interruptions by Another Character

If one character is interrupting another, indicate this by cutting off the first character's speech with a dash. Then, begin the second character's dialogue block. There is *no need* to type [(interrupts)] as a dialogue cue when the second character begins speaking.

Length of Script

On average, one page of a script written in film format equals about a minute of screen time. Accordingly, a sitcom script written in *film format* usually runs twenty-seven to thirty pages in length. A script written in *tape format*, which features double-spaced dialogue, usually runs forty-five to fifty pages in length. And a script written in *animation format* usually runs forty to fifty pages in length. Of course, every show is different, so read scripts produced for the show to determine the correct average length for your spec.

> *NOTE: Longer is not better when it comes to spec scripts; only your mother wants to see that three-hundred-page* Entourage *script you wrote.*

Montage (See Series of Shots)

A montage is a quick succession of related scenes, often sans dialogue, that offers a compressed view of some development—a dream sequence, a blossoming relationship, a training sequence, etc. To start a montage, simply

[DISSOLVE TO:] a scene heading that reads [MONTAGE], or to one that describes the coming sequence (e.g., [TRAINING MONTAGE], [MONTAGE: PETER PREPS FOR BATTLE], [CARTMAN GOES UNDERCOVER]). Then list three, five, or more scenes, describing each in just a sentence or two, in separate paragraphs, typed as regular scene descriptions. To end the montage, simply [DISSOLVE TO:] the next regular scene heading and continue with your story.

Paper
Use a standard quality white bond—no fancy, flimsy, erasable, or perforated paper.

Pauses
To indicate a pause in action or between lines of dialogue, type [beat], [a beat], or [pause] as a line of scene description or as a dialogue cue, capitalized per the appropriate script format. Or, to indicate pauses *within* a line of dialogue, or that a sentence fades off before its last words are spoken, use an ellipsis (typed [. . .]).

Script Binding
The script should be three-hole-punched on the left side, with sturdy brass brads placed in the TOP AND BOTTOM HOLES ONLY. Fancy binders suggest that the writer is an amateur, as does a third, superfluous brad. Avoid the flimsy tin/aluminum brads found in most stores; they give out easily and the reader is left with a bunch of loose papers—not good.

If you wish to add a script cover, place a sheet of simple, blank card stock on the front and back of the script. Pick a solid, plain color (white is fine) and avoid any patterns or designs.

Series of Shots (See Montage)
While a montage is a quick succession of related *scenes*, a series of shots is a sequence of images that all take place at the same location over one continuous span of time (e.g., shots from a chase sequence or soldiers colliding in battle). Format-wise, write [SERIES OF SHOTS] as a scene heading and then list the three, five, or more shots in the series, typed as regular scene descriptions. To end the series, simply type the next regular scene heading and continue with your story.

Sound/SFX Cues

When a script is being prepped for production, cues for sound effects and special effects are usually typed as separate, underlined slugs. However, in a spec script, it is best to simply describe these effects in the scene descriptions to avoid distracting the reader. As usual, less is more.

Typeface

Use the industry standard typeface, pica-sized (12-point) Courier New font; it produces ten characters per horizontal inch.

> *NOTE: Presentation counts; if you get creative with type fonts, type size, spacing, etc., or if your spelling and grammar are sloppy, that script that you slaved over will just end up on the recycling pile.*

Voice-Over Narration

One can indicate voice-over narration by typing [(v.o.)] after a narrator/character's name, on the same line. If we hear the voice of a character in a scene but cannot see her (e.g., she's yelling from another room), type [(o.c.)] after her name, on the same line, to indicate that she is off camera.

White Space

Do not cram your script pages full of ink. Producers and executives, who usually have dozens of other scripts to read, love "white space" because it makes the read go faster and the script feel lighter. Feel free to break longish scene descriptions into paragraphs and leave big bottom margins when dialogue will not fit on a page.

APPENDIX B

ADDITIONAL RESOURCES

Below is a list of resources for sitcom writers. For ease of reference, some information that has already been presented in the text is repeated here.

Script Consulting

Producers and screenwriters frequently contact me to ask if I provide script consulting services. I do—please see my website (www.writingsitcoms. com) for details.

In addition, I recommend the services of two people: Blair Richwood, head of Richwood Script + Media (www.scriptnotes.com) and William Akers (www.yourscreenplaysucks.com). Blair is a former development executive turned full-time consultant, and Will is a screenwriter and author of the popular guide *Your Screenplay Sucks! 100 Ways to Make It Great*. I've seen both in action and am impressed.

Otherwise, while there are some excellent, experienced writers out there who also work as script consultants, be warned: Many of the people who sell script consulting services ("coverage") are ill equipped to perform the work. Check the credentials of the specific individual who'd be reading your material; most have never sold a script, some are kids fresh out of film school, and others are just guys who created the consulting service to collect fees from you. If the reader you'd be hiring has no writing credits, or if a consulting service doesn't even identify its readers, I strongly recommend that you look elsewhere.

Recommended Books

I recommend that every sitcom writer add the following craft-oriented books, all of which are available through local bookstores and the web, to his or her library:

Akers, William. *Your Screenplay Sucks!: 100 Ways to Make it Great*. Los Angeles: Wiese Productions, 2008.

Campbell, Joseph. *The Hero with a Thousand Faces*. Princeton: Princeton University Press, 1973.

Egri, Lajos. *The Art of Dramatic Writing*. New York: Touchstone/Simon & Schuster, 1960.

Helitzer, Melvin. *Comedy Writing Secrets*, 2d ed. Cincinnati: Writer's Digest, 2005.

Jowett, Benjamin, and Thomas Twining, trans. *Aristotle's Politics and Poetics*. New York: Viking Press, 1974.

Saks, Sol. *The Craft of Comedy Writing*. Cincinnati: Writer's Digest, 1985.

Sandler, Ellen. *The TV Writer's Workbook*. New York: Delta, 2007.

Seger, Linda. *Making a Good Script Great*, 2d ed. Hollywood: Samuel French, 1994.

Snyder, Blake. *Save the Cat*. Studio City: Michael Wiese Productions, 2005.

Truby, John. *The Anatomy of Story*. New York: Faber, 2007.

Free Sitcom Scripts

Here are some websites that allow free downloading of a variety of scripts (for personal, educational use only). Note that many are transcriptions or copies of production drafts, so don't follow their page formats unless you're sure they're correct.

The Daily Script: www.dailyscript.com/tv.html

Drew's Script-o-Rama: www.script-o-rama.com/oldindex.shtml

Screenplays for You: www.sfy.ru

Simply Scripts: www.simplyscripts.com/tv.html

Twiz TV: www.twiztv.com

Sitcom Scripts for Sale

In addition to the resources described in Chapter 7, you can buy some scripts over the web or by phone (for personal, educational use only) for about $10 per episode, plus shipping, by contacting the following companies. Note that some are transcriptions and many are copies of production drafts, so don't follow their page formats unless you're sure they're correct.

Book City Script Shop
8913 Lankershim Blvd.
Sun Valley, CA 91352
818-767-5194
www.bookcity.net/TVScripts

Larry Edmunds Books
6644 Hollywood Blvd.
Hollywood, CA 90028
323-463-3273
www.larryedmunds.com

Planet MegaMall
P.O. Box 4773
Chatsworth, CA 91313
(No phone orders accepted)
www.planetmegamall.com/screenplays/TV_scripts.html

Script City
8033 Sunset Blvd.
Los Angeles, CA 90046
800-676-2522
www.scriptcity.com

Recommended Periodicals

The following periodicals explore topics ranging from recent industry developments to the craft of screenwriting:

Creative Screenwriting
6404 Hollywood Blvd., Suite 415
Los Angeles, CA 90028
800-727-6978 or 323-957-1405
www.creativescreenwriting.com
Annual subscriptions cost $29.95; features critical and historical essays about screenwriting.

Written By (The Official Journal of the Writers Guild of America, West)
7000 W. Third Street
Los Angeles, CA 90048
Toll-free subscription line: 888-WRITNBY / 888-974-8629
www.writtenby@wga.org
Published monthly; single issues for $5 (minimum order of $10), annual subscriptions for $40, free subscription for WGAW members; features interviews with screenwriters, essays about the craft, industry news, and a regularly updated TV production contact list.

Mediabistro.com
www.mediabistro.com
A free website that provides industry news and job listings.

Variety and *The Hollywood Reporter*
The daily edition of either *Variety* ($299.99 a year) or the *Hollywood Reporter* ($229) if you live *in* Los Angeles, or the weekly edition of *Variety* ($329.99) if you live *outside* of Los Angeles. Similar in style and content, these publications provide news about the business of Hollywood, and you can subscribe to print or online editions. (An

online subscription costs less and gives you twenty-four-hour access to the publication.) News coverage includes announcements of production deals, the hiring of personnel, network scheduling moves, and weekly ratings charts. Subscriptions for *Variety* (either format) can be ordered by calling 866-MY-VARIETY or going online to www.variety.com, and those for the *Hollywood Reporter* can be ordered by calling 866-525-2150 or going to www.hollywood reporter.com.

Recommended Websites

The Futon Critic: www.thefutoncritic.com
Hollywood Creative Directory: www.hcdonline.com
Internet Movie Database: www.imdb.com (and subscription service IMDbPRO)
Nickki Finke's Deadline Hollywood Daily: www.deadlinehollywooddaily .com
Scriptwriters Network: www.Scriptwritersnetwork.org
Showbizjobs.com: www.showbizjobs.com
Sitcoms Online: www.sitcomsonline.com
TV.com: www.tv.com
TVland: www.tvland.com
WGA, East: www.wgaeast.org
WGA, West: www.wga.org
Zap2it.com: www.zap2it.com (includes TV ratings)

Writers Guild Offices

Most sitcom writers end up joining the WGA, *West*, but here is contact information for both branches of the Writers Guild.

WGA, West
7000 West Third St.
Los Angeles, CA 90048

General Information: 323-951-4000
www.wga.org

Agency: 323-782-4502
Contracts: 323-782-4501
Credits: 323-782-4528
Library: 323-782-4692
Membership: 323-782-4532
Publications: 323-782-4522
Script Registration: 323-782-4500
Signatories: 323-782-4514
Written By: 323-782-4522

WGA, East
555 West 57th St.
New York, NY 10019
General Information: 212-767-7800
www.wgaeast.org
Call the main number above to ask for a particular department or visit
the website to forward an email directly to the department as listed
under "Resources."

U.S. Copyright Office

For answers to all of your questions regarding copyright issues or to
request a copyright application form (Form CO), visit the website or
contact:

Copyright Office
Library of Congress
101 Independence Ave., SE
Washington, DC 20559-6000
202-707-3000
www.copyright.gov

Internships and Workshops

Below are several programs designed for promising screenwriters. Admittance is competitive, some programs are only open to college students/grads, some exist to promote diversity, some pay a stipend, and all involve a workshop experience with industry professionals. Contact each organization for a description of its program and application process.

Academy of Television Arts & Sciences Foundation
Student Internship Program
5220 Lankershim Blvd.
N. Hollywood, CA 91601
818-754-2800
www.emmys.tv/foundation/internships.php

CBS Writers Mentoring Program
www.cbscorporation.com/diversity/cbs_network/institute/writers_
    program.php

FOX Diversity Writers Initiative
www.fox.com/diversity/creative/writer_submission.htm

Maine Media Workshops
70 Camden St.
Rockport, ME 04856
207-236-8581
www.theworkshops.com/filmworkshops

NBC Diversity Initiative for Writers
www.nbcunicareers.com/earlycareerprograms/diversityinitiative.shtml

Nickelodeon Writing Fellowship
www.nickwriting.com

UCLA Extension Program
Dept. of Entertainment Studies

10995 Le Conte Ave.
Los Angeles, CA 90024
310-825-9971
www.uclaextension.edu

Walt Disney Studios and ABC Entertainment Writing Fellowship
    Program
500 S. Buena Vista St.
Burbank, CA 91521
818-560-6894
www.abctalentdevelopment.com

Warner Bros. Comedy Writers Workshop
4000 Warner Blvd.
Bldg. 36, Room 155
Burbank, CA 91522
818-954-7906
www.writersworkshop.warnerbros.com

Industry Directories

A number of industry directories are published in book form, but that
means they're partially out of date by the time you buy them. Frankly, I
only recommend two directories, the HCD and IMDbPRO, because they
provide specific information and are updated regularly. (Sadly, I don't get
paid for these plugs.)

Hollywood Creative Directory (includes *Hollywood Representation
    Directory*)
3000 W. Olympic Blvd., Suite 2525
Santa Monica, CA 90404
800-815-0503 (outside California) or 310-315-4815
www.hcdonline.com
In addition to providing general contact information for companies,
HCD gives names and titles of individual staff members. Updated sev-

eral times a year; single issues (of any directory) available for $64.95, yearly subscription to *Representation Directory* (two editions) is $109.95. Also available online with full access to *all* of the company's directories and frequent updating: $24.95 for a one-week trial and $249.95 for a year's subscription.

Internet Movie Database PRO (IMDbPRO)
To find similar business information regarding who's representing whom or who works where, check out www.pro.imdb.com. It's another excellent web service that offers its own "free trial subscription period."

Screenplay Competitions

If you win or place highly in a screenwriting contest, you might receive cash prizes, script consulting services, and, most importantly, professional contacts and a credit that opens some doors. However, many screenplay competitions are bogus because the organizations running them carry no clout and the point of their competitions is to make money by collecting entry fees. So take the time to evaluate the people running a contest, the credentials of its judges, and the track records of its past winners before sending in your check. Lists of contests are available at websites like www.moviebytes.com/directory.cfm, www.screenwritersutopia, and other sites you can easily find in a web search. Last I heard, the following competitions, not all of which currently accept TV scripts, were legit, but check them out via their websites:

Academy of Motion Picture Arts and Sciences "Nicholl Fellowships in Screenwriting": www.oscars.org/nicholl/index.html

Austin Film Festival (Teleplay Competition): www.austinfilmfestival.com/new/submission

New York Television Festival/FOX Comedy Script Contest: www.nytvf.com

Screenwriting Expo: www.screenwritingexpo.com

Scriptapalooza: www.scriptapalooza.com

Script Marketing Sites
(aka Script Registries)

In addition to online script competitions, there are script marketing sites that charge a fee to post your work so that industry professionals (who subscribe to the service) can find it and contact you if interested. These services are mostly for film writers and they are a bit scary—anyone could steal your best idea and you'd have no recourse. However, the better sites do claim that some of their writing clients have actually gotten work via their service. I've heard positive things about inktip.com but, as usual, proceed at your own risk.

ENDNOTES

INTRODUCTION

1 Rankings based on Amazon.com and bn.com "comedy writing," "sitcom writing," and "television writing/authorship" trade-book category rankings, including Amazon.com, Book Search: *Writing Television Sitcoms* (September 18, 1999) and bn.com, Book Search: "Television Authorship" (September 10, 1999).

CHAPTER ONE

1 Movieweb, "2009 Movie Releases," www.movieweb.com/movies/releases/year.php.

CHAPTER TWO

1 Sigmund Freud, *Jokes and Their Relation to the Unconscious: The Standard Edition*, ed. James Strachey (New York: W. W. Norton, 1989), 171–93.

2 Dana Sutton, *The Catharsis of Comedy* (Lanham, Maryland: Rowman & Littlefield, 1994), 19–31.

3 Herbert Spencer, "The Physiology of Laughter," *Macmillan's Magazine* (March 1860), 395.

4 Freud, *Jokes*, 9.

5 Hunter Covington, *My Name Is Earl*: "The Bounty Hunter," production draft (Twentieth Century Fox, March 13, 2006), 5.

6 Freud, *Jokes*, 107–39.

7 Theodor Lipps, *Komik und Humor* (Hamburg and Leipzig, 1898), 90, quoted in Freud, *Jokes*, 11.

CHAPTER FOUR

1 Freud, *Jokes*, 248-53.

CHAPTER FIVE

1 Sheldon Bull, *Elephant Bucks* (Studio City: Wiese Productions, 2007), 142.

CHAPTER SIX

1 Greg Garcia, *My Name Is Earl*: "Joy's Wedding" (Twentieth Century Fox, airdate November 15, 2005), 1, transcribed on TwizTV.com, www.twiztv.com/scripts/mynameisearl/season1/mnie-108.htm.

2 Tina Fey, *30 Rock*: "Untitled Tina Fey Project," pilot script (Broadway Video Television, January 24, 2005), 16–17.

3 Jeff Abugov and Mark Roberts, *Two and a Half Men*: "A Bag Full of Jawa," table draft (Warner Bros., August 9, 2004), 5–6.

4 David Cohen, *The Simpsons*: "Lisa the Vegetarian," production draft (Gracie Films, March 1995), 24–25.

5 Bill Masters, *Seinfeld*: "The Alternate Side," table draft (Castle Rock, November 1, 1991), 15–16.

6 Alex Taft, *The Office*: "The Debate," spec script (April 28, 2008), 17.

7 Mindy Kaling, *The Office*: "Hot Girl" (Reveille Productions/NBC Universal, airdate April 26, 2005), 2, transcribed on Fanpop/TwixTV.com, www.fanpop.com/external/968750.

8 Abugov and Roberts, *Two and a Half Men*, 10.

9 Ibid., 17–18.

10 Ibid., 26–27.

11 Ibid., 29.

12 Melvin Helitzer, *Comedy Writing Secrets* (Cincinnati: Writer's Digest, 1987), 57.

13 Alan Kirschenbaum, *My Name Is Earl*: "Bad Earl," writer's draft (NBC Universal, September 5, 2007), 34.

14 Philip Vaughn, *King of the Hill*: "Pulp Arlen," draft status unknown (Twentieth Century Fox, March 23, 1998), 3.

15 Freud, *Jokes*, 157.

16 Sol Saks, *The Craft of Comedy Writing* (Cincinnati: Writer's Digest, 1985), 31–32.

17 Anders Holm, *The Office*: "The Beastmaster," draft status unknown (Reveille Productions/NBC Universal, March 1, 2006), 15.

18 Larry Gelbart, "One Question . . . ," *Written By* (May 1998).

CHAPTER SEVEN

1 Jurgen Wolff, *Successful Sitcom Writing* (New York: St. Martin's Press, 1988), 64.

CHAPTER EIGHT

1 Ellen Sandler, *The TV Writer's Workbook* (New York: Delta, 2007), 38.

CHAPTER NINE

1 Linda Seger, *Making a Good Script Great*, 2d ed. (Hollywood: Samuel French, 1994), 62.

2 Sandler, *Writer's Workbook*, 88.
3 Benjamin Jowett and Thomas Twining, trans., *Aristotle's Politics and Poetics* (New York: Viking Press, 1974), 230–57.
4 Bull, *Elephant Bucks*, 88–89.
5 William Goldman, "Rocking the Boat," *Premiere* (April 1998), 85.

CHAPTER TEN

1 Lajos Egri, *The Art of Dramatic Writing* (New York: Touchstone, 1960), 33–59.
2 Robert Storey, "Comedy, Its Theorists, and the Evolutionary Perspective," *Criticism* 38 (summer 1996), 424–37.

CHAPTER ELEVEN

1 Maggie Fremont, *Family Guy*: "Predator" outline (March, 2009), 3.

CHAPTER TWELVE

1 Segel, *Making a Good Script*, 74.
2 Classic TV Quotes, "Ari Gold Quotes (Page 4)," www.classictvquotes.com/quotes/characters/ari-gold/page_4.html.
3 List After List, "Entourage: Johnny Drama Quotes," www.listafterlist.com/tabid/57/listid/7109/TV/Entourage+Johnny+Drama+Quotes.aspx.
4 Cuzoogle, "The Best of Hank Moody: Quotes and Clips," http://cuzoogle.com/2008/10/02/the-best-of-hank-moody-quotes-clips/.
5 Classic TV Quotes, www.classictvquotes.com/quotes/characters/ari-gold/.
6 Evan Smith, *Seinfeld*: "Someone Killed Bambi" (May, 1992), 1.

CHAPTER FIFTEEN

1 Writers Guild of America, "1976 Rider W," www.wga.org/uploadedFiles/writers_resources/contracts/agency.pdf.
2 Ibid., 8.

CHAPTER SIXTEEN

1 U.S. Copyright Office, "Copyright Basics: Circular 1," www.copyright.gov/circs/circ1.pdf.
2 U.S. Copyright Office, "Copyright in General (FAQ)," www.copyright.gov/help/faq/faq-general.html.
3 U.S. Copyright Office, "... Circular 1," www.copyright.gov/circs/circ1.pdf.
4 Writers Guild, "WGA West Registry," www.wgawregistry.org/webrss/.
5 Writers Guild, "How to Become a Member," http://wga.org/content/default.aspx?id=84.

CHAPTER SEVENTEEN

1 Sheldon Bull, *Elephant Bucks*, 180.

2 Writers Guild, "2008 Schedule of Minimums," www.wga.org/uploadedFiles/writers_resources/contracts/min2008.pdf, 6.

CHAPTER EIGHTEEN

1 Ibid., 16.

CHAPTER TWENTY

1 Ibid., 6.

APPENDIX A

1 Taft, *The Office*, 8–9.
2 Ibid.
3 Ibid.

INDEX

P.O. 0004907473 20200504